MANAGEMENT
INFORMATION
SYSTEMS:
Planning and Decision Making

MANAGEMENT
INFORMATION
SYSTEMS:
Planning and Decision Making

Jerry L. Koory

Head, Computer Services Department
The RAND Corporation
Santa Monica, California

Don B. Medley

Professor
Computer Information Systems
California State Polytechnic University
Pomona, California

Published by

J17 **SOUTH-WESTERN PUBLISHING CO.**

CINCINNATI   WEST CHICAGO, IL   DALLAS   LIVERMORE, CA

ISBN: 0-538-10170-9

Library of Congress Catalog Card Number: 85-61783

1 2 3 4 5 6 D 2 1 0 9 8 7

Printed in the United States of America

Cover illustration:
Fractal Perspective
© 1986 Mr. Screens

CONTENTS

PREFACE

THE WIDENING RANGE OF CIS CHOICES

The world of computer information systems (CIS) has taken on many new dimensions over the years. In one dimension, there has been a change from exclusivity to participation. At the outset, computer operations and systems development functions were a domain dominated by technicians and specialists who communicated with operational and top managers with great pain. Eventually, however, users and line executives acquired understanding and a degree of sophistication in computer-related areas. In this dimension, CIS professionals acquired partners in the planning process. The CIS or management information systems (MIS) function became part of the overall corporate and organizational world.

Technological and market conditions also changed. At one time, CIS planning involved getting on the right waiting lists for equipment that might be needed somewhere downstream. Then came plug-compatibles, minicomputers, and, finally, microcomputers to usher in an era of computing for everyone. Both the scope and magnitude of hardware and software impacts multiplied rapidly. CIS professionals, in the process, acquired responsibilities for supporting a range of services that encompassed office automation, telephone and computer communication, reproduction services, and others. CIS or MIS planning became financially and operationally critical.

Recognition of real-world need, in due course, led to educational recognition. The Data Processing Management Association (DPMA) Model Curriculum for Undergraduate Computer Information Systems, released in

1981, specified an elective course in CIS planning. This book was developed under DPMA cognizance specifically to meet the requirements of the CIS-14 course entitled *Information Systems Planning.*

VALUE OF THIS BOOK

This book can be of value both for students majoring in CIS or other computer-related disciplines, MIS, and for business majors, particularly those following a sequence in management. With these target audiences in mind, the book has been structured to encompass both the general principles of organizational planning at multiple levels (strategic, tactical, and operational) and the special needs of planning for computer systems and operations.

A theme carried throughout this book stresses that CIS planning is part of the managerial planning process. That is, it is essential both for line and top-level managers to participate in planning for information systems needs and for CIS professionals to dovetail their planning and functions closely with those of the organization at large. The content structure of this book, described below, has been designed to meet the needs of these identified audiences and to deal with the realities of CIS or MIS planning in the modern business or governmental organization.

The relationship to reality is promoted by the fact that a practical, believeable case scenario is woven throughout the book, beginning with the final portion of the first chapter and carrying forward into succeeding chapters. The challenges of CIS planning are dramatized in the case through consideration of the CIS planning implications of a corporate merger between two organizations with noncompatible computer systems and methods. As a special feature of this text, one of the RFP documents generated by an actual organization addressing problems similar to those in the merger case is provided for further student study and for actual practice. Appendix B provides a series of problems that the student can undertake, while Appendix C is an extensive RFP for a complex, computerized telephone switching system.

CONTENT ORGANIZATION

This book is about planning as a discipline within the field of management science and as a specific, vital need for the growing group of CIS professionals with managerial capabilities and credentials.

Chapter 1.   Given the book's emphasis, the first chapter begins with an overview of the planning process. It is established that planning is results oriented and is necessary to implement growth and goal attainment for any organization. A planning process is reviewed that is based upon a proven decision-making model involving the sighting of targets, the identification of alternatives for meeting needs or solving problems, and the selection and implementation of the most favorable alternative.

The planning function is categorized to conform to basic levels of management responsibility—strategic, tactical, and operational. A distinction is made between strategic plans and strategy, a set of policies and/or guidelines that establishes what a company will be, what markets it will serve, and what organizational structure will be maintained.

The chapter ends by establishing a study case to be pursued throughout the book. This situation involves a merger of two major consulting ("think tank") organizations with divergent business bases and vastly different approaches to CIS management and services.

Chapter 2.   In the text presentation, CIS planning is positioned within a framework that includes corporate planning, planning by user departments, and coordinated planning for the CIS function. Elements considered include the set of beliefs, policies, and traditions that establish a corporate culture. CIS planning, it is stressed, must take place within a framework of corporate needs and projections. The impact of the state-of-the-art in the computer industry is covered as a factor in the setting and implementing of CIS plans. CIS planning factors reviewed include methods for budgeting and/or charging user functions for CIS services. The planning factors associated with the study case are used to reinforce the review of principles within the main portion of the chapter.

Chapter 3.   This chapter deals with planning strategies and methods. At the outset, planning is defined as an organized method for supporting the achievement of corporate goals and objectives. Planning is achieved through a process of information exchange at multiple organizational levels, both top-down and bottom-up. Tentative plans are formulated and exchanged for review in several iterations until planners at all levels are satisfied with the targets and their responsibilities for achieving defined results.

Advantages that can accrue from an organized planning process are enumerated. These include the value of plans in directing the efforts of employees, in setting measurable goals to encourage achievement, in resource allocation, in providing a basis for control, and others. Potential pitfalls of the planning process also are discussed, including use of budgets to constrain plans, difficulties in dealing with unexpected developments that do not fit plans, and the possibility that ineffective plans will constrain progress.

Additional discussions deal with the nature of the planning function, the role of the budget within the planning process, and some specifics about planning at strategic, tactical, and operational levels. In the case, a framework is evolved for the CIS plans of the merged company.

Chapter 4. The planning process is reviewed in terms of the sequence of events—the planning cycle—followed in the development and release of formal plans for implementation. Cycles occur in the timing of the work done and in the organizational level at which activities take place. Typically, preliminary plans are initiated at the top, or strategic level. These first drafts are cycled down the organization for responses and inputs about projected achievements. These reviews, then funnel upward for responses and evaluations at succeedingly higher levels. At the top level, revisions are made and the cycle is repeated until sufficient consensus is achieved so that the plan provides a basis for managing the company during the future period covered by the plans. The chapter becomes highly specific about the process for developing budgets that implement plans. Emphasis and in-depth reviews are conducted on the specific requirements and methods used in developing CIS budgets.

Chapter 5. The area of systems planning is identified as the point at which a CIS function interfaces with its environment. Emphasis in this chapter is on identification of opportunities and the selection of systems to be developed. This presents a conscious separation between evaluation of needs and actual project planning involving the development of selected systems. User requirements for development of information systems are seen as a driving force that motivates and guides the management of a CIS function. Activities associated with selection of systems for development are reviewed from a managerial perspective. Topics range from allocation of CIS costs among users, to motivations that lead users to request computer systems, to procedures appropriate for selection of projects to be developed from among a portfolio of candidate systems.

Chapter 6. Planning for systems development projects is presented as a major CIS management responsibility. A major, early planning requirement is a decision on whether to buy and possibly adapt an application package or to do custom programming. Criteria are provided for justification of either alternative, depending upon situations. Planning steps for review and acquisition of software packages are covered, as are the needs associated with custom development. This chapter is worth citing for its objective, complete set of guidelines comparing the alternatives of application packages and custom software development.

Chapter 7. Planning for CIS staffing is presented as an activity that requires coordination with corporate personnel practices and operations if plans are to be respected and implemented. Options covered include the hiring of temporary personnel, consultants, and contract workers. In-depth discussions deal with employee evaluation and career consultation with people who can make a significant contribution.

Chapter 8. Hardware planning requires a special set of structure activities, which are reviewed in this chapter. The first requirement is identified as recognition that there are major differences between plans that establish new facilities and those that upgrade or modify existing computer centers. Another special requirement lies in determining the lead times involved in implementing any hardware plan. Lead times can be long. Further, on complex systems, lead times can vary dramatically among multiple vendors. Another highlighted requirement is consideration of the state of technology. Decisions frequently involve trade-offs between ordering available equipment for early delivery and decisions to wait in the belief that current equipment will be superseded within the time frame of the plans being formulated.

Chapter 9. This chapter presents and provides guidance in the use of a systematic approach to decision making. A procedure for considering, reaching, and implementing major decisions is provided. This includes a series of steps, or phases, for stating objectives, identifying alternatives, evaluating and choosing the best alternative, and implementing the choice. Also described are requirements and mechanisms that provide and capitalize upon feedback dealing with decision-making effectiveness.

Chapter 10.   A major trend in the management of computing resources— known as information resource management (IRM)—is reviewed in this chapter. IRM is a management style based upon recognition that databases or other sets of information are major resources of the owning organization. Accordingly, it is felt, information resources should be managed with the same caliber of care and at the same corporate level as financial, manufacturing, or natural resources. Effectively managed, information resources are shown to represent a potential for a competitive edge, or even for increased profitability, for the organization as a whole. One effect of the acceptance of IRM approaches is increasing stature and professional recognition for computer professionals.

Chapter 11.   Conversion planning, the topic of this chapter, involves preparation for implementation and activation of new computer information systems. Conversion plans, in turn, center around the setting up of the files that will support new applications. Detailed coordination is needed for installation of hardware, acquisition of software, and validation and capture of data. Conversion methods, including parallel, phased, or abrupt, are covered.

Chapter 12.   In this chapter, emphasis is on the role oversight management plays in relation to the CIS function and its effect upon communication between CIS management and top management. CIS planning is related directly to an organization's capital budgeting processes. The point is stressed that the level of expenditures involved in CIS programs requires continual policy review and evaluation. Charts, reports, diagrams, and other tools appropriate for overseeing the information resources function and its operations are reviewed.

ACKNOWLEDGMENTS

Thanks and recognition should be accorded to the developers of the DPMA CIS curriculum, who showed pioneering leadership in recognizing CIS planning as a worthy topic for academic study. The working committee that developed the original course outline on this topic was chaired by Vince E. Heiker, of Boise Cascade.

The manuscript for this book benefited markedly from modifications recommended by Allen N. Smith, Manager, Corporate Information Services, of Atlantic Richfield Company.

A final review to establish compliance of the content of this book with the DPMA CIS Curriculum was performed by Donald E. Price, of the Ventura County College District, Ventura, CA.

Vital contributions to the quality of the finished book were made by David Strybel and Bettijune Kruse of i/e, inc., who provided valuable editing and production supervision assistance.

The cover for this book was designed by Gary Palmatier of i/e, inc.

Content for Chapter 12 is adapted in part from Willis H. Ware and Robert L. Patrick, *Perspectives on Oversight Management of Software Development Projects*, The RAND Corporation, Note N-2027-AF, July 1983. Used with permission. Thanks are also expressed to Robert L. Patrick for contributing the content of Figures 6-7 and 12-3.

1

THE PLANNING JOB

Abstract

Strictly defined, planning refers to the organizing of activities to accomplish specific results. The purpose of planning is to guide a business into the future. Secondary purposes include the anticipation and management of change. A top-down view of planning involves strategic, tactical, and operational levels. From long-range goals generated at the strategic level, planning proceeds to the tactical level at which short-range plans are produced, then to the operational level at which specific schedules and assignments are determined. Budgets are produced at all levels and provide a mechanism for evaluating results. In addition, deviations from plans can occur at any time for innumerable reasons. Thus, planners must be ready to initiate alternative courses of action in a decisive fashion. Alternatives also are generated in the initial stages of planning—and are evaluated according to specific criteria. This overview of planning by organizations can provide a framework for the specific planning requirements of information systems.

CIS PLANNING: THE NEED

Planning is one of *the* major responsibilities of top-level managers. Management, by nature, is a future-oriented profession. Past and present experiences are valuable guides. But planning cannot impact or change events that already have occurred. Therefore, it is logical to state that planning is a major management concern and responsibility.

Further, planning must be applied across the spectrum of an entire organization. It does little good, for example, for top-level managers to enunciate plans without involvement of all major units within an organization. Plans must be integrated from the very top of an organization through each group, department, or section that contributes to meeting the organization's goals and objectives.

The CIS function is involved in and plays a vital role in enabling any organization to achieve a future success. If a company is to grow or move in new directions, the information resources must be there to support projected achievements. The role of the CIS function is particularly critical because the CIS group must provide information that supports the planning of all elements of the organization. In turn, CIS also must gather and integrate information from throughout the organization as a basis for meeting its own planning responsibilities.

Within a planning context, then, it can be said that:

- A CIS plan must be assimilated with and must reflect the overall organizational plan.
- The overall organizational plan and the processes used to derive overall plans provide a framework within which CIS managers must do their own planning.

Therefore, this opening chapter begins by establishing a context for CIS planning by reviewing the basics of corporate, or organizational, planning. CIS planning principles then are presented within this overall framework.

PLANNING: DEFINITION AND NEEDS

This book is about planning requirements associated with information systems. An information system represents a support service to the organization that owns and/or uses the data resources maintained by the system. Planning for an information system, therefore, is affected and controlled to a degree by the objectives and requirements of its host organization. That is, information systems planning takes place within an environment of organization planning. This chapter presents an overview of organization planning as a basis for identifying specific concerns related to planning for information systems.

Organizations implement plans for many reasons, but primarily to anticipate and/or manage change. Changes can be predetermined or may be the result of forces external to the organization. Planning for the computing disciplines may be impacted by many forces of change. These include technological developments in hardware and software, shifts in the perceptions of the market or society, regulations by government, creation of new marketing opportunities, and fluctuations of costs of resources.

Webster's New World Dictionary defines the word *plan* in an appropriate light for this text: "A scheme for making, doing, or arranging something." Plans, then, are organized sets of statements, or blueprints, aimed at guiding future actions toward achievement of desired results. In business, managers increasingly are stressing the importance of plans as critical to the success of an organization. In turn, the success of an organization may depend upon the shrewdness of its plans and its ability to implement the plans.

Developing and implementing effective plans requires a team effort within an organization. The point is made earlier that planning for information systems takes place as a component of the larger, organizational picture. This is true within any function or department of a business. Without a grasp of the overall goals of the organization, it is difficult for operational managers to direct the activities of their respective departments. Thus, planning touches all levels of the organization; and effective planning involves a range of personnel, from operational employees, through first-line supervisors, to top-level executives.

The planning function provides a basis for managers at all levels of the organization to set and to achieve objectives and goals. Through planning, management determines a course of action for the future. The planning function also determines the activities, personnel, and controls that are needed to implement a particular course of action. In effect, planning is the basis of sound management at all levels. Without planning, there are no criteria by which to measure individual, departmental, or organizational performance.

STRATEGY: FRAMEWORK FOR PLANNING

A *strategy* is a collection of principles, policies, and beliefs that enunciates what a company is or is to become. Every company has a strategy, though an organization's strategy may be informal, unspoken, or even unrecognized.

As a management guide, strategy establishes the products or services a company offers, the markets served or targeted, and the posture to be adopted in providing identified products or services to targeted markets. Given these ingredients, a strategy also can be said to give an organization its unique identity and/or *driving force.*

Management establishes a strategy through the policies and priorities it sets in the deployment of people and the allocation of other resources. Typically, a strategy will gravitate toward one of a few driving force alternatives:

- *Financial results* are often the driving force for a conglomerate or multi-division organization. Top corporate managers are apt to behave much like bankers. That is, they invite the separate divisions to make presentations that are not unlike loan applications. Investment of allocated funds is monitored periodically, generally with the view that the highest return represents the greatest success.

- Productivity, with emphasis on cost-effectiveness or economy of scale, often is the driving force for organizations described as *product driven.* A classic example of this type of strategy is the major automotive manufacturer. Heavy investments are made in product design and tooling. Long production runs are committed to minimize unit costs. Marketing supports the existing products and options. Once a model is in production, the company's policies and positions are fixed for as long as it takes to amortize the tooling and/or to rework massive production planning and manufacturing facilities.

- A *market driven* company is apt to organize itself and conduct its business specifically for responsiveness to market conditions. If products are involved, production commitments are minimized and kept as flexible as possible. Inventories also tend to be minimized. Apparel, cosmetics, soap, health-care, food, and other consumer products companies typically adopt a market-oriented strategy.

The elements of strategy tend to establish the uniqueness, or differentiation, among companies. This applies even to companies in the same field that sell apparently interchangeable products. For example, consider the market-oriented strategies that guide the way in which fast-food organizations present themselves to the public. One leader in this field stresses service ("We do it all for you"), cleanliness of facilities, playgrounds and coloring books for children, and other family amenities. This organization pre-cooks its menu items in the interest of much-advertised, fast service. A major competitor, on the other hand, stresses that each hamburger is cooked to order. Another entry in this field stresses the juiciness of its hamburgers. The point is that each company has identified an appeal to a single market segment and has structured its business accordingly. For as long as this posture is maintained management policies, plans, and actions are shaped by the in-place strategy.

Strategies exist and guide management planning even if they are not stated formally. Strategies, for example, can exist as a result of custom, accidental events, or tacit understanding. Putting it another way, strategies may be formal or informal. Formal strategies result from conscious study of management aspirations for the organization. Formal activities generally result in written statements distributed to employees and to all levels of management. Informal strategies are imbedded in the consciousness of the people who run a company. Although informal strategies are undocumented, there tends to be considerable uniformity in interpretation and presentation of ideas about what a company is and where it is headed. The difference is that planners in a company with an informal strategy often must conduct interviews and document assumptions to be sure that they are operating within the strategic framework that defines their responsibilities and constraints.

Strategies tend to be considered as permanent, or fixed. In reality, however, they are subject to change or to being overwhelmed by new opportunities or new economic and market conditions. As an example, consider a prominent operator of convenience stores that added gas pumps to many of its locations in response to the addition of convenience markets by chains of gasoline retailers. Changes of this type clearly require plans. In turn, the plans require development of implementation programs.

This specific example suggests a basic factor in the relationships among strategies and plans: Strategies always exist, through default or intent. Strategies are part of the nature of and operational background for an organization, but are not necessarily time related. For example, consider the situation of an international oil conglomerate in which management decides over a weekend to complete a multi-billion-dollar purchase of another petroleum company. Such a decision, reached in days, alters the strategy of the acquiring organization profoundly. Financial situations, production considerations, and marketing approaches all have to be changed drastically, and quickly.

To implement these changes, plans and workable implementation schedules must be developed. These plans cannot be put in place over a weekend. Rather, plans have to be tiered into a series of levels and integrated for workability. Plans, then, are time oriented, while strategies establish the position, or framework, within which planning takes place. To illustrate, a strategic plan may envision programs or conditions within a time frame of three to five years. These plans are based on the known (or assumed) strategy that is in place. When and if strategy changes, plans must be adapted accordingly.

LEVELS OF PLANNING

Just as planning takes place at all levels of an organization, there are many levels of planning. These levels are not necessarily determined by organizational hierarchies, but there are connections. The levels at which planning is applied are:

- Strategic
- Tactical
- Operational.

Strategic Planning

All plans begin with ideas. In business, owners or top-level managers determine the general course or direction for an organization. That is, the ideas and consequent decisions of these managers focus upon what a company should be, how it should be run, and where the company is going. These ideas are expanded into broad-based statements that become the organization's long-range objectives and goals. This is the nature of *strategic* planning. Strategic plans are general and far reaching, and are determined at the top levels of the organization. Figure 1-1 lists parameters that are used to describe strategic plans and their general characteristics.

Tactical Planning

Working in a top-down pattern, the next planning level is *tactical.* See Figure 1-1. The tactical level of planning moves to a more concrete level of specification. Whereas strategic plans target overall achievements, tactical plans address specific implementation actions. At this level, planning assumes a more procedural perspective. Long-range objectives and goals are broken down into a series of workable, discrete steps that are directly achievable and manageable. Implementation of these steps should lead to specific results. That is, tactical planning provides guidance for producing *short-range plans.*

STRATEGIC	TACTICAL	OPERATIONAL
Conceptual	Developmental	Execution
Corporate Level	Divisional Level	Departmental Level
General Direction	Specific Products	Task Oriented
Long Term	Intermediate	Short Term
2 to 5 Years	18 Months or less	Immediate

Figure 1-1. *This table identifies the parameters that delineate levels of corporate planning: strategic, tactical, and operational. As shown, strategic planning is conducted at the top level and sets general, long-term directions for the entire organization. Tactical planning encompasses division-level responsibilities and involves intermediate-range time frames. Operational planning covers short-range objectives and is done at the departmental level.*

Operational Planning

The third level of planning is *operational*. As shown in Figure 1-1, this level is concerned with the physical implementation of plans. Thus, operational planning activities include the establishment of production schedules, major activity milestones, and costs of labor and materials. By comparison, strategic plans would target markets and revenues. Tactical plans might deal with staffing levels, tooling, and procurement of materials.

BUDGETS: PLANNING AND CONTROL

To repeat, a plan is a description of the resources, activities, and events necessary to achieve a desired result. In business, no plan is complete without a *budget*. In the simplest terms, a budget is a plan for collecting and spending money. Businesses produce budgets to project income and expenditures for a given time period. Figure 1-2 shows a portion of a sample Expense Budget Summary.

EXPENSE BUDGET SUMMARY

LABOR

Operations	$93,750
Systems	27,915
Information Center	16,665
Engineering Services	17,445
Applications Support	24,435
Business Office	15,625
Department Headquarters	12,500
Total Labor	$208,335
Fringe @ 27%	56,250
Overhead @ 95%	197,918
Total Labor Cost	$462,503

NONLABOR

Travel	$4,085
Equipment Rent/Lease	103,085
Maintenance	13,350
Depreciation	102,456
Software Rent/Lease	8,900
Supplies	29,675
Total Nonlabor Cost	$261,551
TOTAL EXPENSE	$724,054

Figure 1-2.   *This illustration contains a portion of an Expense Budget Summary of the type included in plans at all organizational levels.*

Though financial content is paramount, budget reports also contain other types of planning information. Budgets may include entries that reflect the personnel required to complete a project, products to be bought and/or used to complete the project, a breakdown of the distribution of staff time within the project, and so on. Of course, most budget reports relate all these entries to their potential cost to the organization. But information from budgets also can be used to measure many kinds of performance within the organization, as discussed in the section that follows.

PLANS AND PERFORMANCE

Planning provides a basis for the objective evaluation of performance. A plan represents a goal, or a desired outcome. Actual performance surpasses, meets, or falls short of the goal. The comparison of actual performance to plan provides a management tool for *accountability.* Accountability refers to the responsibility for achieving results. Accountability follows lines of authority from superiors to subordinates. A well-stated plan, therefore, provides a yardstick by which accountability can be measured. This section presents organizational planning in light of this concept.

A plan often is used as a measuring tool for evaluating employee performance. Such an evaluation may result in a "pat on the back" for a job done adequately or a salary increase for an outstanding performance. This measurement also may provide the basis for a reprimand if the employee has not performed well enough to meet the planned outcomes.

Consider this example of a plan used as the basis of measuring performance. A stated, strategic plan of a banking organization is to improve the delivery of services to customers. At the tactical level, the decision is made to improve services by installing a network of interactive automated teller machines (ATM). The operational specification calls for a total elapsed response time of less than five seconds at the ATMs and an internal execution time of two seconds or less for all inquiries. Operational specifications typically include quantitative objectives such as specific response times—especially when equipment purchases are involved.

After the system is installed, data items representing the response times for a selected sample of inquiries are gathered. Figure 1-3 shows a sample of a timing worksheet that can be used for this application. Response times are derived by performing typical customer transactions and measuring system performance with a stopwatch. Results are recorded on the timing worksheet. Internal execution times for inquiries can be recorded automatically through use of the internal clock of the computer or computers that support the ATMs.

At this point, the operational objectives of this project can be evaluated objectively and definitively. In other words, it would be difficult to argue that the system has succeeded if the recorded response times are slower than the stated objectives. However, if the response times have been achieved at the expense of major cost or labor overruns, the project may be deemed only a partial success. The point is that a realistic and specific plan builds a foundation upon which a project can be managed.

RESPONSE TIME FOR INQUIRY TRANSACTIONS

TIME	Mon	Tues	Wed	Thur	Fri	Sat	Sun	AVERAGE
8:00								
Average								
10:00								
Average								
12:00								
Average								
2:00								
Average								
4:00								
Average								
6:00								
Average								
SYSTEM AVERAGE								

Figure 1-3. *This is an example of a worksheet used to monitor performance of operational computer information systems. Response times represent processing performance for typical user transactions.*

This simplified example illustrates the importance of preparing effective plans. Included within the top-level policies of most organizations are guidelines for preparing plans to be followed by managers. These guidelines include factors for making decisions about employee assignments and the distribution of administrative hours. Other considerations include employee sick time, vacations, holiday pay, and overhead factors.

Performance evaluation of all these factors is accomplished in several ways. Generally, data that represent *actuals* are collected, reported, and compared with plan or budget reports. Consider the sample labor-distribution report shown in Figure 1-4. This type of report is used to present actual performance in light of budget projections. Typical budget reports contain a breakdown of the hours allocated to each project the department supports. At the end of each fiscal period, the accumulated actual hours reported in the labor-distribution reports are compared with the budget.

Notice that each line item in this report includes a department number, along with actual hours, budget hours, variance between actual and budget, actual to date, and budget to date. The department number indicates the exact organizational location of serious variances. Thus, appropriate managers or supervisors can be held accountable for successes or failures. In addition, because these reports present only numbers of hours (instead of financial information), they can be shown to and discussed with lower-level personnel.

To summarize, plans and budgets provide tools for measuring performance. Plans and budgets also indicate who is accountable functionally for specific performance areas. Look again at the labor-distribution report in Figure 1-4. The authors recommend that any line item that has a ±2 percent or greater variance should require a written explanation to the next higher level of management. Thus, the 6 percent overall variance presented in Figure 1-4 is a cause for investigation. The next section discusses courses of action when such actionable variances are encountered.

EXCEPTIONS, PROBLEMS, AND ADJUSTMENTS

Perhaps the most important concern for a manager is the recognition of a condition that is a *deviation* from the plan. A deviation is a variance between planned and actual performance that is deemed serious enough to warrant corrective action. Once a deviation, or exception, is identified, the appropriate manager is responsible for adjusting activities to correct the situation.

COMPUTER INFORMATION SYSTEMS DEPARTMENT
LABOR DISTRIBUTION
FISCAL PERIOD 2: 28 OCTOBER XX — 24 NOVEMBER XX

	NAME	DEPT	CURRENT PERIOD HOURS	BUDGET HOURS	HOURS VARIANCE	ACTUAL TO DATE	BUDGET TO DATE
2025-MICRO, ENG SUPPORT	N B ARNOLD	101	13.0			17.0	
2025-MICRO, ENG SUPPORT	D R BUDY	101	19.0			51.0	
2025-MICRO, ENG SUPPORT	K A CANE	101	12.5			65.0	
2025-MICRO, ENG SUPPORT	D L FRY	101	32.0			53.0	
2025-MICRO, ENG SUPPORT	N S JAMES	101	22.5			57.5	
2025-MICRO, ENG SUPPORT	K M MOTT	101	17.0			28.0	
2025-MICRO, ENG SUPPORT	L J RICE	420*	32.0			44.0	
2025-MICRO, ENG SUPPORT	I R SMART	101	9.0			15.0	
Sub-Total			157.0	180.0	-23.0	330.5	360.0
2027-TERMINAL REPAIR	N B ARNOLD	101	17.0			57.0	
2027-TERMINAL REPAIR	D R BUDY	101	63.5			142.5	
2027-TERMINAL REPAIR	K A CANE	101	21.5			23.5	
2027-TERMINAL REPAIR	D L FRY	101	8.5			38.0	
2027-TERMINAL REPAIR	N S JAMES	101	15.0			23.0	
2027-TERMINAL REPAIR	L J RICE	420*	65.0			127.0	
2027-TERMINAL REPAIR	J R ROGERS	101	64.0			64.0	
2027-TERMINAL REPAIR	I R SMART	101	0.0			27.0	
Sub-Total			254.5	259.2	-4.7	502.0	518.4
2083-ENGR SERVICES	C A ABBOTT	515*	1.5			1.5	
2083-ENGR SERVICES	N B ARNOLD	101	133.0			234.0	
2083-ENGR SERVICES	D R BUDY	101	37.5			58.5	
2083-ENGR SERVICES	L P CABLE	515*	1.5			1.5	
2083-ENGR SERVICES	K A CANE	101	38.5			61.0	
2083-ENGR SERVICES	D L FRY	101	112.5			217.5	
2083-ENGR SERVICES	N S JAMES	101	61.0			106.5	
2083-ENGR SERVICES	K M MOTT	101	42.0			97.0	
2083-ENGR SERVICES	L J RICE	420*	59.0			59.0	
2083-ENGR SERVICES	T R THOMAS	101	105.0			211.0	
Sub-Total			591.5	508.8	82.7	1047.5	1017.6
TOTALS			1003.0	948.0	55.0	1880.0	1896.0

*Cross charged from another department

Figure 1-4. *This computer-generated labor distribution report compares actual performance figures with corresponding budget projections.*

Such exceptions and problems may be identified either internally or externally. For an example of deviations caused by external sources consider the scenario that follows.

A large organization has identified a need for a new accounting system and has initiated a systems development project to design and build the new system. Project specifications call for the installation of a Brand ABC computer. Delivery of the computer is scheduled for 18 months after the development project has started. After 10 months of effort, Brand ABC quits business because of corruption at the corporate level and has underpriced its equipment so severely that no one is willing to take over the operation of the company. A quick study reveals that an order can still be placed for equipment rated second in the evaluation process, Brand X. However, this action requires a six-month extension of the project and adds significantly to project costs.

This type of problem also involves many secondary considerations. A large number of programs already may be written in a language not supported by the Brand X equipment. Any training manuals already written may have to be revised. User training classes must be revised and, perhaps, held again. This may cause users to lose confidence in the project, in the project manager, and in the decision-making process in general. Conversion of data files that already has taken place or conversion programs that have been written must now be redone. These are serious concerns for management personnel.

Other deviations can be caused by internal forces. In the above example, suppose the company solves its equipment problem by purchasing a Brand X computer. Then the company experiences a sudden change in management personnel. The controller who ordered the new system and approved the funds for the modifications necessitated by the original problem has left. The new controller is not convinced that the new system has value. The new controller is considering canceling the project and selling the Brand X machine as part of an austerity program.

Problem situations like this one require a mechanism for dealing with change on an ongoing basis. In the above example, one solution involves modifying the plan with an eye toward saving as much of the completed work as possible. Assume the programs written for the Brand X machine can run on existing computers within the company. Then, even though the Brand X purchase is canceled, at least a large part of the new system can be implemented by rescheduling use of existing equipment. No matter what course of action is chosen, the important consideration is that a built-in mechanism is provided within planning functions to deal with such situations.

Many exceptions that come about from expected sources can be dealt with early in the planning process. For example, the government frequently passes laws that impact business plans. These exceptions may take the form of a new tax or the approval of a rate increase request by a utility company. Federal and state income tax tables tend to change each year and changes in local property tax and sales taxes occur often. All these situations can be foreseen and prepared for effectively by monitoring legislation processes.

One method for recognizing exceptions and/or problems in advance involves the establishment of *checkpoints*. Checkpoints in planning processes may be time or event related. For example, managers may decide that after 100 labor hours, a project should be 50 percent complete. That is, a checkpoint is established at 100 hours. Then, an evaluation takes place and corrective action is taken if necessary. An event-related checkpoint might involve a formal *walkthrough* at a specific point during system or program development. A common outcome of walkthrough checkpoints is a decision on whether to continue the project.

Thus, exception or deviation situations may occur at any time and from many sources. This is a given, and must be considered in any type of planning. One method for dealing with these situations is to provide for alternative courses of action, as are discussed in the section that follows.

ALTERNATIVE COURSES

The availability of alternative courses of action is vital to thorough and effective planning. For example, consider a plan to change from a *disk operating system* (DOS) to a relational database operating system in the form of a commercial software package. A review of available information about the requirements for such a change reveals that:

- The changeover requires five man-months of effort.

- Considering the present workload and the preparation required, the changeover effort can begin in six months.

- The present systems programming staff is qualified to implement the change without any additional training. In fact, the lead systems programmer has installed this particular software package on a similar computer for a previous employer.

The plan appears solid; management authorizes the project; and expenditures and development begin. Three months of the six-month lead time have passed and the project is proceeding according to plan. In fact, documentation changes, preparations for file conversions, and employee training all are ahead of schedule. THEN THE KEY SYSTEMS PROGRAMMER RESIGNS!

This situation calls for decisive implementation of an alternative course of action. One alternative is to offer the key individual an incentive to stay for the duration of the project. This may be the most desirable alternative to managers, but it may be unfair to other project personnel whose compensation may suffer by comparison. Another alternative is to select the most qualified person from the existing project staff and to provide him or her with a concentrated training opportunity. This may extend the project slightly but could achieve the desired results on an equitable basis for all concerned staff members.

Thus, alternative courses of action are necessary when unexpected or deviation situations occur. Alternative courses of action also are considered at the time planning decisions are made. That is, a plan establishes a course of action designed to achieve a desired result. However, there may be more than one course that leads to the same result. It is, in fact, standard planning procedure within most businesses to generate and evaluate several alternatives before developing a specific plan. The next section examines the criteria by which such decisions are made.

SELECTIONS AND DECISIONS

The selection of a plan for implementation from among several alternatives may be based on several factors. As a basis of discussion, these factors may be categorized as:

- Selection criteria

- Weighted criteria for decisions

- Decision-making hierarchies.

Selection Criteria

Generally, multiple criteria are used to evaluate alternative plans. These criteria apply at all levels of planning, but especially for strategic planning because of the extensiveness and long-range nature of such plans. Some of the considerations among selection criteria include:

- The financial budget
- Personnel requirements
- Facilities
- Software and hardware
- Calendar (When must the project be done?)
- Impact on users.

The financial budget.   A complete plan should include a budget. Guidelines under which budgets are prepared should provide exacting standards for generating estimates of future needs, such as policies setting targets for return on investments. Then, budget requests should be justified before approvals are granted. Often, a written statement of explanation is required for requests that exceed budgeted figures by a specific variance. This provides a means for exercising control over project expenditures. After an approved budget is in place, it becomes a standard against which performance can be evaluated.

The information contained in budget reports is not limited solely to financial considerations. A budget report may provide labor-hour figures or specifications for physical facilities, such as square-feet area requirements. Thus, the control capabilities provided by budgets can be applied in many areas. For example, it may be more important to know that an administrator will devote 10 hours per week to a project than to know that a certain amount of money has been set aside for administrative tasks. It may be necessary also to schedule labor hours for systems analysis and programming in terms of man-years instead of dollar amounts. A budget also provides control capabilities that extend across organizational levels.

Budget reporting requirements vary with the organizational level for which the reports are prepared. At the project level, managers may work only with figures concerning allocation of labor hours, facilities, equipment, services, and overhead. Within this context, overhead consists of operating costs that cannot be applied to specific projects or operations. In accounting terms, overhead encompasses indirect costs of doing business, differentiating these expenses from direct costs of projects or operations. At operational levels, reports may be derived from budgets, such as the labor-distribution comparison shown in Figure 1-4. This type of report is used to compare actual hours with budgeted hours—and may even be presented to individual employees to support evaluation discussions. Inclusion of detailed financial data in reports used by operational-level employees would be undesirable because attention could focus upon earnings figures for fellow workers rather than upon the performance criteria to be evaluated.

A general rule of thumb is that the higher the organizational level, the more financially oriented are the reporting needs. Numeric figures representing labor hours, facilities usage, equipment usage, and overhead are converted to dollar values for top-level managers. Figure 1-5 presents a sample of an executive-level report. At this level, the figures can be evaluated against income data and strategic forecasts as part of control activities.

Personnel requirements.   Among the important considerations for most plans are personnel requirements. The personnel needed to develop and implement a planned activity must be presented in terms of the effort required. For example, a project that requires two man-years actually may be completed in six months. That is, four employees working six man-months each probably can finish the job. The required employees often are available "in house" and merely need to have their schedules altered to include project activities. If additional staff is needed, the expenses of advertising, interviewing, new-hire training and *start-up time* must be included in the budget. Start-up time refers to the time it takes new employees to become familiar with company policies and procedures.

Facilities.   Facilities planning encompasses many factors. An initial requirement lies in determining whether existing facilities are sufficient. Efficient and comfortable work areas must be set up. Furniture purchases may be required. Related factors may include the availability of parking and the proximity of public transportation.

In addition, environmental controls must be implemented to meet the requirements of people and, if necessary, machinery—particularly computers. For example, computers may need environmentally controlled areas with raised floors to accommodate cables, moisture detectors, and air conditioning ducts. Often, a lowered, false ceiling is constructed for efficient distribution of air conditioning, effective smoke detection, and sound control. The introduction of computers in an environment also creates new storage requirements. Existing file cabinets may not accommodate the wide paper used for many types of computer reports. Magnetic media may require special storage racks and/or heavy bank-type safes that must have a reinforced floor.

**CIS BUDGET VS. ACTUAL
CURRENT FISCAL YEAR-TO-DATE
AS OF PERIOD 2**

	ACTUAL DOLLARS	BUDGET DOLLARS	DOLLAR VARIANCE	PERCENT VARIANCE
Equip Rent/Maintenance	103,088	123,637	20,549	17
Supplies	86,539	64,232	<22,307>	<35>
Depreciation	226,549	205,942	<20,607>	<10>
Property Tax	9,646	17,076	7,430	44
TOTAL NON-LABOR	425,822	410,887	<14,935>	<4>
Salary	244,672	262,890	18,218	7
Fringe Benefits	102,762	113,046	10,284	9
Consultant(s)	8,949	0	<8,949>	.
Overhead	182,468	184,204	1,736	1
Overtime	1,420	0	<1,420>	.
Publications	230	0	<230>	.
Travel	4,081	5,425	1,344	25
TOTAL LABOR	544,582	565,565	20,983	4
TOTAL EXPENSE	970,404	976,452	6,048	1
REVENUE	1,053,172	938,040	115,132	12
Gain/<Loss>	82,768	<38,412>	109,084	284

Figure 1-5. This is a sample of an executive-level summary of budget vs. actual performance for a CIS department.

Software and hardware.   Because of the variety of ways in which information systems can be implemented, planning decisions involving these systems also involve several factors. These factors center around software and hardware.

Software can be developed in several ways. Commercial software packages may be purchased; an outside vendor may be contracted to write the software; or in-house personnel may be able to produce the needed products. In each case, careful planning is required.

If a commercial package is purchased, plans should allow time for thorough testing and documentation review. In addition, commercial packages still may present requirements for conversion of related data files, definition of methods for data capture, user training, establishing data communications, and implementation. Before implementation, it must be determined if changes to existing systems and operations are necessary to incorporate new software. Careful consideration also should be given to whether it is reasonable and acceptable to purchase a package that has to be modified before organizational requirements are met.

If the services of a commercial software house are being considered, there are many questions to be answered: Is the expense justified? Can the vendor perform any faster or better than the in-house staff? Who maintains control?

Software development by outside contractors, in effect, requires an outlay of on-site office space, computer time, supplies, and in-house supervisory staff. Many organizations, after considering all the factors involved with both commercial packages and contracted software development, find it more desirable to develop software in house.

Hardware considerations add another dimension to planning, that of lead time. Lead times, or the interims between order and delivery, of 6 to 24 months are not uncommon. Although most minicomputers and microcomputers are now available as off-the-shelf items, most mainframes still require 6- to 18-month lead times for actual delivery. During these periods, many of the situations involving exceptions and deviations discussed above may occur.

The development of requirements specifications for new equipment can involve a laborious and time-consuming investigation phase. A *benchmark test* often is developed to evaluate major computing equipment alternatives. A benchmark test involves a representative set of programs and processes. That is, a sample is run that includes the types and kinds of activities the system is expected to support. Often, the development of requirements specifications and the benchmark tests demand as much planning effort as the development of the rest of the project.

Calendar.   The *calendar of events* is another important part of any plan. The calendar presents time allocations for each component or phase of project activity and the sequence in which phases are to be completed. Evaluation of project progress is based upon calendar-designated control points.

Most planning calendars provide for multiple time frames for evaluation. Some project activities are best controlled on a weekly basis. Other activities are checked only at the end of each accounting period, quarterly, or on an exception basis.

Several computer-related tools are available to assist in the calendaring process. Most, like the Project Evaluation and Review Technique (PERT) and Critical Path Method (CPM), are designed to increase a manager's control over large and complex projects.

Impact on users.   The impact of a project upon involved users deserves special planning attention. People resist change by nature; this is to be expected. People also tend to resist what they don't understand. For example, many users do not understand the extended lead times typically required in the computer field. A middle manager who is accustomed to buying manufacturing machinery with one- to three-month delivery dates generally reacts unfavorably to an 18-month lead time on computer equipment deliveries. Systems analysis, design, and program development also can require extended periods that users find difficult to understand. There are indications, however, that microcomputers and off-the-shelf software may ease some of this user tension.

Another factor that impacts users involves the *chargeback* rate for computer services. Many in-house computer centers charge individual departments for services. The chargeback-rate algorithm is determined at budget time and is designed to recover operating expenses and the costs of hardware, software, personnel, and supplies. This creates a related planning need for user departments to support the purchase of the desired computer services. This topic is covered further in a later chapter.

Suppose the chargeback rate is changed to reflect internal factors of the computing center. The change may be dictated by an increase in the cost of electric power, an increase in the cost of communication lines leased from the telephone company, or an increase in the price of supplies such as paper, magnetic media, and printer ribbons. The chargeback rate also may change if the computing center acquires any new or added equipment to support new systems efforts. Regardless of the cause, a change in the chargeback rate usually impacts user departments. For example, suppose a significant increase occurs after the budget is prepared and approved. User requests for additional projects may be blocked, particularly if the increase occurs after user budgets have been approved.

Weighted Criteria For Decisions

Decision-making activities for selecting a particular plan from among alternatives frequently include a vehicle for evaluation. The idea is to devise a quantitative measuring mechanism that encompasses all the varied factors that affect the decision.

One common method is to rank alternatives according to numeric values. Each condition or factor is assigned a numeric range and is evaluated according to that range. This idea can be expressed as a question: "On a scale of 1 to 10, how do you rate the processing speed of this particular computer system?" After managers have given numeric values representing personal evaluations for all factors, the values are totaled for each alternative. Depending on how the values were defined, the alternative with either the largest or smallest value is the consensus selection.

Consider, for example, a decision-making process for the purchase of a new computer. Selection factors include base price, maintenance costs, lead time for delivery, operating system, and compatibility with existing application software. A weighted value scale is set up from 1 to 10, with 1 being best and 10 being worst. Each bid proposal is evaluated independently by selected managers. The managers work independently of one another and assign numeric values for the five factors. Thus, five numbers are assigned by each manager for every product under consideration. Each product receives an evaluation, consisting of five separate figures, from each manager. Individual totals from all managers then are added to derive a collective evaluation. That is, after all this figuring, the product that has received the lowest collective total should be the most desirable selection. Figure 1-6 presents a sample evaluation matrix that often is used to facilitate this process.

Decision-Making Hierarchies

Planning tends to be hierarchical. That is, planning proceeds through an orderly series of steps that transcend organizational levels of management and operations. For example, a plan for a new inventory system may begin

CRITERIA	OPTION A	OPTION B	OPTION C
Price			
Maintenance cost			
Delivery availability			
Operating system			
Ability to run existing applications software			

Figure 1-6. *This matrix serves, in effect, as a scorecard for alternatives evaluated during a decision-making process to aid in the selection of the best alternative.*

with an objective statement from top management and progress to an operational level. For operational purposes, the overall statement is broken down into detailed entries concerning hardware, software, facilities and space needs, conversion plans, and personnel. These entries represent line-items—totals without detail in budget requests from CIS and manufacturing departments. At this point, the budget may be redirected back toward top-level concerns. Line-item entries may be summarized to reflect major areas of responsibility, such as finance and plant management. These represent tactical-level considerations. Further, the budget figures for the new system are reduced to dollar values for use in forecast and budget reporting for the overall organization. The plan has now gone full circle, and top-level managers review the detailed plan for approval.

Plans, then, are developed to varying degrees of detail by a group of people, a committee, or by several groups and committees, the members of which span hierarchical levels of the organization. Throughout the process, each iteration of the plan is reviewed by appropriate management personnel and undergoes further changes and levels of detail. After approval by one or more of the review committees, it is forwarded to top management. Thus, final approval for budgets and, therefore, plans rests with top-level management.

COMPUTER INFORMATION SYSTEMS PLANNING

Although this text concentrates on effective planning for computer information systems, the relationships of that planning to the overall corporate plan are of utmost importance. Major topics and areas in which this relationship is evident are covered here. These topics and areas include:

- Planning activities
- Cost-center approach
- Operating systems planning
- Application systems planning
- CIS administrative needs
- Security
- Information center consulting
- Funding methods and resources.

Planning Activities

Computer information systems planning is stimulated on many fronts. One reason for CIS planning is to provide direction and support for users. Requests for particular services by user communities stem from many sources. A need may be identified during a casual conversation between a user and a member of the computing center staff. Sometimes, a user will make a direct request for service based upon discussions with professional peers, outside reading, or simply an experience-based idea for improving the operations.

Often, the CIS department consults users about a processing requirement that has arisen in other areas of the organization. The reason for this consultation may be the impact of services rendered in a related functional area. For example, plans for the engineering function to deliver a new product line impact the functions of purchasing, receiving, raw parts inventory, manufacturing, finished goods inventory, sales, advertising and promotion, shipping, billing, accounts receivable, and others. Thus, the CIS department is obliged to inform all affected areas when a request for computing service has been identified.

Cost-Center Approach

Many CIS departments are operated as *cost centers*. This generally means that user departments are charged for services received. This method often is referred to as a chargeback system, discussed earlier in this chapter. Several methods are used for implementing the cost center approach. Two of the methods are chargeback and *pie slicing*.

When either of these methods is used, the CIS department must prepare a plan (budget) that includes a *billing algorithm*. A billing algorithm provides a method of allocating costs for services provided by the computing center. That is, there should be a method for charging for the cost of using CPU memory. There also should be separate cost factors for magnetic tape usage and storage, the amount of magnetic disk space occupied, the number of lines printed, and other usage factors. At the end of each billing period, charges for services are paid with funds transferred from user accounts to CIS accounts.

A cost-center approach to CIS services increases the complexity of planning processes. A billing rate that is too high often results in underuse of computer resources. A billing rate that is too low encourages the use of service, but at the risk of exceeding the capacities of the computing center. The goal of this type of planning is a *zero-based budget*. That is, total service charges should result in a transfer of funds from user departments that are approximately equal to the costs incurred by the CIS department.

The pie-slicing method, on the other hand, involves a review of the "customers" that use the CIS center. The percentage of services required by each customer during a particular period becomes the basis for distributing costs. For example, accounting may use 29 percent of the services, manufacturing 53 percent, administrative services 8 percent, and the computing center itself 10 percent. Under the pie-slicing method, the computing center usage is absorbed by the other user departments. That is, the monthly expenditures of the computing center are divided by the appropriate percentages and billed in the resulting proportions to those departments. Therefore, assigning accounting 29/90, manufacturing 53/90, and administrative services 8/90 distributes 100 percent of costs chargeable directly to user departments.

Accounting would be charged 32 percent, manufacturing 59 percent, and administrative services 9 percent to make up for internal costs incurred by the center. A major concern associated with pie slicing, however, is that there is no incentive for the CIS manager to be efficient, since all internal costs are absorbed by user departments.

Operating Systems Planning

A general definition of operating systems includes the programs that allocate equipment resources, language compilers and assemblers, and any utility programs that meet standard user needs. System software changes at a rapid pace. Complexities are encountered because user applications depend upon the support capabilities of specific operating systems. Therefore, planning in this area may involve determinations of whether it is necessary to retain a superseded version of an operating system after a new version is introduced. It is possible, for example, for a single installation to use multiple operating systems as a basis for supporting a series of applications. This requirement would be encountered if existing applications rely upon features of succeeding generations of operating systems.

Application Systems Planning

Most computing centers deal with user needs that require the development of tailored application programs. Other requirements, however, can be met with one of the many off-the-shelf software packages available (with more packages being developed all the time). The purchase or lease of such packages requires detailed investigation and planning.

To illustrate a common situation: a user may buy a desk top computer and a particular spreadsheet software package that is not compatible with other equipment and systems already in place. Thus, this computer system fits into the corporate CIS plan only under limited circumstances. Should the user wish to expand the use of that software, the impact upon other efforts and upon user relations may be significant.

CIS Administrative Needs

The supervision and control of the services rendered by the CIS department require a well-constructed plan. Requirements include the specifications for collecting data, for comparing the actual performance to the plan, and for reporting the results.

Security

An ever-present need in the computing area is security—for both data and facilities. Planning is needed to support the development of methods to control access to data via on-line terminals and batch service requests. These plans might include studying the frequency and expense of changing access codes. Access to the computing facilities and the disposal of waste products also require extensive plans. Implementation of security for facilities may include special access locks, video surveillance, fire and smoke alarms, and paper shredders or other special equipment. Operators of computer equipment must have special diagrams and instructions covering power, air conditioning, and/or sprinkler or fire extinguisher controls. These plans and instructions can be critically important to the restart of operations or recovery from emergency situations. Reviews of these procedures and testing of these equipment items should be planned at regular intervals.

Information Center Consulting

The proliferation of personal computers and packaged software has created an additional planning burden for computing centers. Overall policies concerning which staff members are allowed to use personal computers and whether and how much they are allowed to access corporate data resources must be determined. In addition, plans for the physical support of the installation and maintenance of these devices have to be made. Also, the planning function must provide training and one-on-one, hand-holding resources to answer questions for the users of PCs.

Funding Methods and Resources

Planning for any of the above-described activities almost certainly involves a need for funds to support the activities. As stated in the section on budgets, all planning leads eventually to financial considerations. Methods for funding planned activities vary from organizational sponsorship, to chargeback procedures, to sales of equipment and services to outside customers. A combination of these methods often is implemented. Whichever method is selected, planning considerations are critical.

To accomplish effective planning, it is necessary to understand the environment in which the planning is to take place. The environment often is referred to as the corporate culture. The next chapter discusses corporate culture. First, however, a case scenario that is expanded throughout the text is introduced in light of the discussions in this chapter.

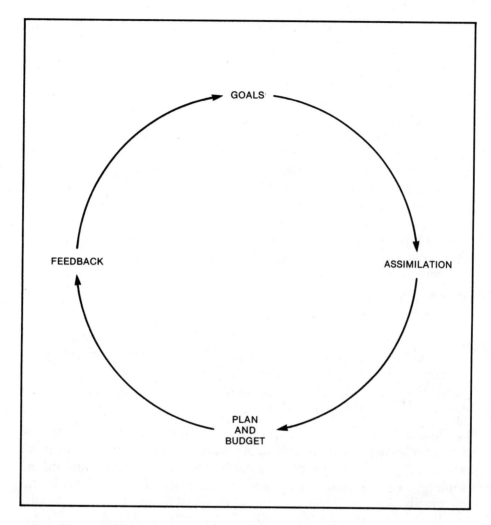

GOALS

ASSIMILATION

**PLAN
AND
BUDGET**

FEEDBACK

Figure 1-7. *A circular diagram like this one stresses the need for a continuing, cycled method for planning implementation.*

THE PLANNING PROCESS

Planning takes place at multiple levels within an organization. At each level, however, an orderly, structured methodology must be established to assure both effectiveness and organizationwide coherence of plans.

A typical, appropriate process that can be implemented for the development of plans at any level is diagrammed in Figure 1-7. The circular pattern presented is intended to stress the need for a continuum of effort, as well as a capability for iteration of a basic set of steps as necessary to derive workable, satisfactory results.

The circular pattern in Figure 1-7 indicates that contributors may join the process at any appropriate stage at which their knowledge and experience are needed. However, a sequence is implied through placement of the presentation of goals at the top of the diagram. The next step around the circle is identified as assimilation. This term implies that departments, sections, or individuals internalize and "buy into" the overall goals toward which plans are directed. Within this context, assimilation indicates that people digest a series of corporate-level goals and adapt those goals to meet their own needs. From this assimilation process comes a series of plans and budgets which, in turn, are subjected to review and feedback. The process is repeated until all participating managers feel they can accept and implement the plans. The process ends when a satisfactory level of commitment is attained.

CASE SCENARIO:
CORPORATE MARRIAGE AND CIS PLANNING

Computer-related changes that require CIS planning activities usually result from management actions or decisions. To illustrate some practical aspects of computer planning, this book will establish and track a realistic case situation that calls for application of most of the principles and techniques that are introduced, as they are covered.

In the recent and current world of corporate operations, a common, change-related planning requirement stems from corporate acquisitions and/or mergers. For the purposes of illustrating the principles of this text, assume you are involved in such a typical situation. The principals of this merger are National Consultants and Aerospace Research, Inc.

Industry observers and investment analysts applaud this merger as logical and in the best interests of stockholders and customers of both organizations. The two companies are in the same general field but are not direct competitors. One is privately held, the other is a public corporation.

National Consultants is the privately held company, with annual revenues of about $15 million. Staffing level is about 240. Work is both in the public and private sectors. Engagements handled include economic studies, organizational behavior, organizational development, and compensation studies. The founder of National Consultants, Joshua Deep, is the main stockholder, though some 40 percent of the ownership has been distributed to key personnel who bear the title of "principal." Dr. Deep has just turned

73 and is interested both in providing equity for his estate and in assuring the ongoing continuity of his company.

Aerospace Research, which is publicly held, has annual revenues in the neighborhood of $50 million. ARI employs about 800 people, mostly specialists who work in such fields as large-scale systems integration, project management, mission control, and environmental safety. A current speciality that is producing a large share of overall revenues is the monitoring and management of hazardous waste facilities. Toward this end, ARI maintains a massive database on hazardous waste facilities and the materials they store, and massive collections of readings on radiation levels in areas surrounding the controlled sites. ARI uses a consensus approach to top management, with a chairman, associate chairman, and president serving as a top management team. An attraction of ARI within the merger negotiations is that the average age of its management team is 51 years.

Computer Management Impact

Obviously, both companies have heavy commitments involving the use of computers within the mainstream of their management and operational activities. In general, National Consultants has taken a centralized approach to providing computer support to its operations. A single, central facility houses two mainframe systems and four minicomputers that perform communication and housekeeping tasks. The commitment to centralization even extends into the word processing area; most employees have access to an on-line text processor supported by one of the minicomputers.

ARI is more of a project-oriented organization. Top management thinks of staff members as belonging to a large, overall talent pool available for short-term assignments to engagements as they arise. Within these project teams, there are specialists in scientific disciplines and these groups have been strong enough to force implementation of a decentralized philosophy of computer utilization. Thus, the waste management database has twin mainframes with a minicomputer front end. Although these are general purpose computers, the software and user groups in this area are strong enough within the organization to command their own facilities. Supporting this viewpoint is the fact that government agencies have funded this dedicated facility as a separate line-item in project budgets.

The central, corporate computer facility at ARI is closely similar in configuration to the waste management database system. This equipment correspondence provides the potential for additional backup and/or load switching in support of the waste management database mission. In practice, the waste management system occasionally is off-loaded to the corporate system to assure that the backup plan will work. In part, this is because the waste management database is available on a round-the-clock basis for police and fire departments who may have to know exactly what they are dealing with if emergencies arise.

Most of the time, of course, the corporate system is available for open-shop kinds of support for scientists and engineers. User programs are stored on disk and may be called up for execution in a matter of seconds. Larger users within ARI also have a number of small minicomputers and super-microcomputers for experimental use. Decentralized thinking has led to a situation in which a group has been set up within the CIS department to buy and help install microcomputers for any qualified personnel or department with project budgets that can justify such actions. Word processing with ASI is entirely decentralized at the departmental or project level. Most word processing is done on personal computers adapted through a variety of software packages.

Case Discussion/Assignment

Assume you are assigned to the team that will develop a plan for integrated computer services for the merged entity to be formed by ASI and National Consultants (NC). As a preliminary step in this planning assignment, identify the main issues and problems associated with the assimilation of the differing approaches to computer resources management followed by the merging entities. Identify areas that should be studied and decision support information that should be gathered.

Discussion Topics

1. Define planning and explain its importance for business organizations.

2. What is a budget and how are budgets used to evaluate the performance of a company?

3. What is meant by weighted criteria for decision making?

4. What is the cost-center approach to CIS departments within organizations?

5. Explain what is meant by the statement: The decision-making process of most organizations transcends organizational hierarchies.

6. What are the big issues and dependencies linking corporate and CIS plans?

2

CORPORATE CULTURE: A PLANNING FRAMEWORK

Abstract

Corporate culture refers to the "personality" of an organization. Thus, corporate culture encompasses the attitudes and beliefs that motivate an organization. These factors establish a framework within which planning takes place. This framework is built at three levels and is reflected in planning statements at each level—corporate, CIS, and user. These planning statements define an organization's attitude toward change. Change can take a variety of forms, ranging from changes to a company's products or markets, to altered market conditions, to new laws or regulations. All levels of CIS-relevant planning must anticipate and/or react to such changes. CIS planning, in turn, also is impacted by corporate culture—regardless of whether the company presents an aggressive or conservative outlook. CIS planning should have inputs from the perspective of users and user departments. In addition, avenues for service requests either from within or external to the CIS function, methods for financing CIS services, and methods for delineating approval authority are important considerations for CIS planning. These considerations are given structure by the attitudes of the organization toward the CIS function and of the organization toward the market in general. Given these considerations, the ARI/NC case example (introduced in Chapter 1) now can be expanded to a level of increased detail. That is, planning statements that reflect the corporate culture of the merged entity can be produced at this point.

A PLANNING FRAMEWORK

For CIS planning to be effective, the CIS plan must complement the plan of its host organization. The development of a complementary CIS plan requires an understanding of corporate culture.

All plans exist within a framework comprised of the overall company, its mission, and its perception of itself. The term *corporate culture* is used to describe the sum of these factors. Corporate culture can be thought of as the personality of a company. A company's human relations activities, employee relations, community activities, and relations with other organizations all are part of this personality. Thus, an organization's mission and plans are impacted by its corporate culture.

In other words, CIS managers must know their company, its industry, and its competition. CIS planners must know what the company does, how it is done, and in what general direction top management intends to move the company.

The company mission is reflected by planning statements issued at a number of levels of the organization. At minimum, these statements are developed on three levels:

- Corporate
- CIS
- User.

Corporate Planning Statement

A corporate statement is broadly based. At this level, strategic (typically long-range) objectives and goals are defined and set by top-level management. For example, a corporate statement may call for a reduction in the outstanding accounts receivable by 25 percent before the end of the business year. Note that the statement does not say how to reduce accounts receivable. Instead, it states only that outstanding balances are to be reduced, the amount of reduction, and a time frame in which to reach this objective. In addition, the amounts of reduction and time are given in general terms—to allow a degree of flexibility.

CIS Planning Statement

The CIS plan supports the corporate statement at the departmental level. Given a corporate plan to reduce receivables, the CIS statement describes how the CIS function can support the achievement of this objective. This statement takes a tactical approach; it describes methods for implementing the corporate plan. Thus, the CIS planning statement may call for providing the user (the accounts receivable department) with more timely notifications of amounts due.

User Planning Statement

The user planning statement is the most detailed. At this level, specific actions are defined that can achieve the projected reduction in accounts receivable. The procedures outlined in this statement refine tactical considerations to an *operational* level. That is, the user statement presents procedures for contacting customers with a balance greater than $500 that is more than 30 days in arrears. The first contact is to be by mail, with telephone follow-ups every three days thereafter. In addition, the user specification defines the CIS functions that are required to support this activity. The necessary information is to be supplied to the accounts receivable department in a weekly (or daily) summary report of account status.

As an alternative, the user statement may outline reporting procedures through an existing, interactive decision support system. This procedure also may provide an additional benefit of updating account status each time a payment is received, rather than handling posting periodically, on a batch basis.

THE CORPORATE CULTURE

Every organization is an individual entity with traits that set it apart from others of its size or within its field. Corporate culture deals with perceptions—the perception a business has of itself and the perception the public has of the business. Definitions of corporate culture refer to the "beliefs" held or principles to which management adheres. One prominent computer-industry executive, IBM's Thomas J. Watson, Jr., has described corporate culture as "the way we do things around here." An example of corporate culture at work can be seen in programs adopted by many large corporations to release employees with full pay for community service work. In other words, corporate culture is the totality of the view that management and employees hold for an organization. Recall that the introductory section of this chapter describes corporate culture as the "personality" of a company.

The term *culture* often refers to a stage of development at a certain point. For example, the culture of a society may be described by anthropologists in terms of the evolutionary development of its clothing, tools, education, food preparation, shelter, and art. These criteria provide anthropologists with insights into the social skills, communicative abilities, and stature among peers of the society under study. Similarly, corporate culture often is defined in terms of stages of development and rates of growth. One characteristic of corporate culture, then, might be how a company approaches new business opportunities.

For example, if a corporation is actively seeking business acquisitions, CIS plans must be flexible enough to provide for the impact of volume surges in data resources. These potential impacts stem from integration of the CIS function of an acquired company with that of the parent company. The CIS department in such an aggressive company might elect to acquire the most industry-wide compatible hardware and software available. In addition, continual training for CIS employees is to be expected and should be represented prominently in departmental plans.

On the other hand, if the corporate attitude is nonaggressive, little change is expected and CIS plans are stable. At best, change should be slow and, therefore, can be planned effectively in advance. Equipment needs should not change rapidly and applications software should not need extensive maintenance.

One area that provides opportunities for training employees in the flexibility and responsiveness that may be necessary within a CIS function is application software maintenance. Requirements for modification of existing applications come from a variety of sources. A measure of CIS responsiveness could well lie in the attention given to requests from users for discretionary changes, as opposed to revisions mandated by governmental regulators or taxing authorities.

CIS PLANNING ACTIVITIES

To repeat a previous point, CIS planning takes place in an environment of corporate culture. Thus, the CIS planning function is affected by several factors that are directly attributable to the way a corporation (or other organization) views itself and is viewed by external entities. These factors include:

- Objectives and goals
- Corporate image
- Management attitudes about CIS resources and their use
- Where planning takes place within the corporation
- Planning responsibilities within CIS
- The process for periodic review of the corporate-wide plan
- The role of CIS in corporate planning.

Objectives and Goals

As discussed in Chapter 1, a knowledge of the corporate objectives and goals is important to the planning function of the CIS department. The perception of these objectives and goals may vary at different levels of the organizational hierarchy. For example, the board of directors might express their perception as: "The goal is to make an outstanding product that sells for a reasonable price." The chief executive officer might say: "The purpose is to make a profit." Management in the manufacturing area might target "the greatest productivity at the least cost," and so on.

To a certain extent, then, corporate objectives and goals are subject to interpretation. Within a CIS department, this interpretation is based on interaction with the overall company and knowledge of the products, policies, and people within the company. In addition, the CIS function must consider the information resources it maintains and the role of those resources throughout the organization.

Corporate Image

Corporate image, like corporate culture, is not always tangible or explicitly defined. An organization's image is developed from many sources, including the conduct of employees within and outside of corporate facilities. Perhaps the best way to explain corporate image is to say that it lies in the answers to questions such as:

- Do company personnel travel first class or economy class on airlines?
- Do most people bring their own lunch to work, eat in the company cafeteria, or go out to lunch?
- Do managers go out for two-hour, three-martini extravaganzas?
- Is there a separate, private dining facility for managers, or does everybody eat lunch in the same cafeteria?
- Do managers at all levels have assigned parking places in choice locations?
- What is company policy regarding company cars?
- What type of image is projected by advertisements for company products?
- What role does the company take in community affairs?
- How does the company view itself?
- How do others view the company?

Characteristics of this type provide indications of the way a company and its people regard themselves and conduct their affairs. Such unrelated traits as how employees travel, where they eat their lunch, or the level of democracy or differentiation according to rank within the organization are apt to be reflected in the way the company as a whole presents itself to markets or sets priorities for CIS resources.

Investors who play the stock market often are described either as bulls or bears. A bullish investor is one who believes in a free-wheeling, risk-taking, aggressive approach to investments. A bull believes that the chance of greater return on investment is worth the risk. A bearish investor believes in playing it safe, choosing conservative courses of action, and in forsaking the chance of a large payoff (and the inherent risks) for a regular, gradual pay-back on investments. In a general way, the corporate image of modern organizations can be described as either bullish or bearish. Each approach presents distinct considerations for CIS planning.

The strategic goals of a bullish organization reflect a dynamic image of rapid change and growth. This type of company often buys newly developed equipment for no other reason than to maintain "state-of-the-art" support systems. For example, there are several stories about large companies in the insurance, banking, and aerospace fields that place orders for two of every new product IBM announces—without ever seeing anything other than sales brochures. In addition, in this type of environment, approval is readily given to hire personnel for new or added applications.

In a bullish company, CIS planning tends to reflect the dynamic nature of corporate goals and objectives. For example, it may be necessary to pre-pare several, concurrent planning schemes. That is, part of the plan can be long-term and solid, based on the ongoing production and accounting needs of the company. Another portion of the plan may include a series of contin-gencies, which may be implemented in support of aggressive moves and posturing by the company.

The corporate image of a bullish company and of the CIS function within it often reflects technological leadership. Thus, CIS planning statements in such organizations often include provisions for developing new applications, encouraging users to participate in systems activities, and devising new methods for using information resources to support the organization.

Other companies base their policies upon a bearish, conservative (some-times retrenching) approach. This type of company generally seeks to main-tain a status quo. In such companies, the rate of change is safe, slow, and painstaking. Often, existing hardware and software systems are modified to avoid investment in new equipment. Such companies also tend to be slow in exploiting changing market conditions and new business opportunities. This outlook is illustrated by the classic story of a buggy-whip manufacturer who decided to wait to see whether the horseless carriage would catch on.

In a bearish company, the CIS function reflects this conservative nature. The department is governed by policies that may include purchasing all hardware from the same vendor. Systems development policies also may be fixed; policies may direct either in-house development of all application software or, conversely, the purchase of application software packages and the minimizing of development costs. CIS managers in such companies often seek to avoid serious losses by minimizing investments and other commitments.

In summary, the way a company is viewed—internally and externally— determines the environment in which CIS planning is implemented. The internal image of information systems also plays a role in CIS planning. That is, the way the overall corporation approaches the issues of information collection, storage, retrieval, reporting, and security are critical concerns for CIS planners. The section that follows covers this concept in greater depth.

Management Attitudes About CIS Resources and Their Use

Top-level management attitudes toward CIS functions often reflect the corporate image and also the prevailing practices within a given industry. That is, industry practices can provide an environment that requires a certain, minimal level of commitment to CIS. Beyond that, the aggressive or conservative posture from which management views its organization shapes the extent to which the company becomes a leader or follower. For example, the insurance field is one in which CIS capabilities have become an integral part of the products and services offered to the marketplace.

Given this environmental requirement, it follows that all insurance companies will make a heavy commitment to CIS resources. However, bullish companies within this industry will tend to go beyond minimal requirements. An aggressive insurance organization might, for instance, develop special distributed processing packages for agencies or branch offices. Others might offer telephone inquiry services directly to the public, and so on.

In general, if the overall company attitude is bullish, management takes a liberal approach to supporting information services and resources. Bullish executives expect a CIS function to be a state-of-the-art activity, and to use the most advanced hardware and software. Interactive, user friendly, rather than batch processing applications, tend to be in the forefront for a bullish company. The CIS department constantly seeks opportunities to add new and innovative applications to its list of services. New ways to use the technology are evaluated constantly. Thus, a bullish company may build its new applications upon a series of databases that implement advanced data modeling and database concepts.

In an aggressive company, computer equipment may be diversified. That is, while many companies choose to deal with a single equipment vendor, an aggressive company tends to tailor purchases to application requirements—regardless of vendor. This independence often can lead to support of a wide range of equipment by different manufacturers, including a mainframe from one manufacturer, magnetic disk and tape storage from another vendor, and terminals from still another vendor. Companies with this positive, aggressive attitude toward CIS usually are cost conscious about equipment purchases. The CIS function in these companies typically produces detailed evaluations of equipment of competing manufacturers before decisions are made.

An aggressive, dynamic corporate policy toward CIS functions often leads to decentralization of computing services. That is, several computing facilities may operate at remote work centers. These remote centers can be distant from or within the same building as the central CIS facility. For example, consider a chain of retail grocery stores. Each store has its own stand-alone computer that is linked by communication lines with a central mainframe at the corporate headquarters. Thus, each store has the capability to support real-time transaction and inventory control activities, and to send revenue and expense data to the central facility. In other types of industries, decentralization involves interactive information systems with terminals on the desks of most managers. Then, user-friendly application development packages are provided to encourage exploration of alternative solutions to problems and provide the basis for management decision support activities.

Planning in an aggressive company can be exciting and challenging— particularly challenging. The willingness of management to take risks on new technologies or methods has been found to create a level of excitement not present in more methodical approaches. CIS personnel are expected to keep abreast of state-of-the-art hardware and software developments. In this environment the CIS department often has to react quickly to change, whether changes are anticipated or unexpected.

In a nongrowth (bearish) company, it is generally assumed that existing computer equipment is adequate to handle required applications. Equipment often is made by a single manufacturer and is not necessarily the most advanced model or design available. Application software tends not to change frequently. Implementation of new hardware and application software generally follows long and careful investigation and extensive testing.

Decentralized computing capabilities rarely are implemented by bearish companies. If distributed systems are implemented, control over computing and applications development tends to remain with the centralized facility. There is little management commitment to maintaining a state-of-the-art support system.

Planning in a low growth or conservative organization takes on the corporate image—there tends to be less change, and changes that do occur are more gradual, less dynamic. Consider the situation stemming from purchasing policies: Since corporate policy dictates that equipment be purchased from a single vendor, there are few alternatives to explore.

Where Corporate Planning Takes Place Within the Corporation

As stated earlier, effective planning is broadly based, and touches all levels of supervision and management. At the higher levels of management, planning is a synthesis of many short, and often unrelated, activities. Henry Mintzberg, a noted professor of management, reports that less than 10 percent of the activities of chief executives exceed one hour in duration. In fact, more than half of the designated activities are less than nine minutes long. This is because of the conceptual nature of high-level management and because a chief executive is primarily a decision maker. Chief executives combine data extracted from many sources to form ideas or to make decisions and then delegate the responsibility for implementation.

Thus, the nature of planning is determined partly by the organizational level at which it takes place. For example, many companies hold periodic strategic planning retreats—where top managers congregate in an isolated location for a series of intensive planning sessions. The results of these sessions often define whether the company will have bullish or bearish plans. Usually, a predetermined agenda is distributed to participants who are expected to research topics, and to be prepared both to ask and to answer "what if" questions. In either case, the projected outcome of such retreats is a series of long-range objectives and goals that can be delegated to managers at lower levels for implementation.

Although ideas are communicated both upward and downward along organizational lines as a normal part of business activity, planning is most often developmental in nature. That is, administration has an idea, staff refines the idea, and lower-level departments outline specific activities that can make the idea a reality. Planning at the lower, or operational, levels of a company is generally reactive. That is, the tactical plan is produced; and an operational plan evolves in response.

In addition, the planning process is iterative. That is, planning begins when administration issues the corporate planning statement. Middle management reacts to the corporate statement, issuing the departmental statement. Operational activities required to implement the tactical objectives are produced and sent back to middle managers for approval. This feedback-response cycle may be repeated several times. When middle management is satisfied with the operational response, the plan is returned to the administrative level for final approval. At this point, several more cycles of feedback and response may be required (between middle management and administration) before a final version of the plan is published. This iterative process is discussed further in Chapter 4.

Planning Responsibilities Within CIS

Within the CIS function, development and monitoring of plans should be a specific, assigned responsibility. Implementation of CIS departmental planning can be handled on a variety of bases, ranging from part-time to multi-person responsibility, depending on the size and extent of commitment. No matter how much staff time is allocated, however, the principle should be the same: Someone must have ultimate responsibility for matching CIS directions with those of its overall organization. Areas to be encompassed within CIS planning should include:

- **Technological architecture.**   Guidelines should exist for the selection of equipment and software to support growth or development of the configuration of computing capabilities and also for the CIS organization itself.

- **Financial administration.**   Responsibility should include the setting and monitoring of capital expenditures in the CIS area.

- **Research and development.**   CIS planners should keep track of anticipated developments in computer and software technologies and should evaluate these prospects within existing architectural plans.

- **Capital management.** This responsibility involves monitoring changing costs of equipment and/or software for potential impact upon capital budgets. Increases or decreases in prices or advanced models of products should lead to modification of plans and/or commitments. Other decisions that fall within this area of responsibility include the monitoring, and possible modification, of lease vs. purchase decisions.

- **Strategic planning.** CIS planners should monitor commitments involving architecture, systems development, and operational methods in light of shifting or modification within overall organizational plans. As necessary, CIS strategies must be altered to adapt to corporate plans.

The Process for Periodic Review of the Corporate-Wide Plan

A corporate plan that has been given "final" approval by top management is not engraved in stone. That is, as a plan is implemented, changing business or societal conditions may require that the plan be altered or amended. These changes come about as a result of periodic reviews of corporate activities. Effective planning, especially corporate planning, provides vehicles for these reviews. Reviews of corporate activities are performed in two ways:

- Formal
- Informal.

Formal. Formal reviews are scheduled in planning statements and usually involve some type of documentation. A report may be produced at specific intervals, such as weekly, monthly, or quarterly. At the project level, reports often are produced daily. Consider, for example, a manufacturing company. A daily report from the production department presents figures on the number of completed units and the number of units that were scrapped that day, as well as year-to-date figures in both categories.

Formal reviews are formatted to reflect budgetary considerations. That is, activities that are presented in terms of labor hours in the budget should be presented in terms of labor hours in the review. Recall the discussions in Chapter 1 concerning the use of a budget as a measurement tool. Thus, financial information, logically, is included in reports destined for top management.

By nature, formal reports take some time to prepare. If a review report is prepared and delivered to operational supervisors with instructions to verify content and forward the document to middle management, it may be several days before data are verified and deviations are documented. Other delays may occur at the level of middle management as operational reports from departments are combined and summarized for presentation to top management.

In business there is a saying: "Time is money." Planning functions must provide a formal review mechanism that minimizes the cost of decision making and commitment.

Informal. Informal communications can provide a seemingly limitless source of review information. Informal communications include face-to-face conversations between workers and supervisors and simple, everyday observations by supervisors. That is, any time human interaction takes place, a manager may find input for the review process. Face-to-face communications can be the most positive review mechanism available to managers. For example, given an opportunity, employees often make suggestions for improvements at their level of expertise, or front-line operations.

A manager may lack the experience or viewpoint that such suggestions can provide. Thus, the cultivation of this type of communication may deliver significant benefits to appropriate managers and supervisors. Finally, when they are documented, informal observations by supervisors of employee performance are valuable in rewarding or reprimanding employees for success or failure to meet stated objectives.

The Role of CIS in Corporate Planning

Computer information systems (CIS) are traditionally a staff function. In this light, a CIS exists solely to support the primary goals of the organization. For example, top-level planners may request CIS support for data selection and analysis activities that are specific to top-level functions. Indirectly, of course, this type of support furthers the primary goals of the organization.

In this role, a CIS also functions as a consultant to other units within the organization. This role may be described as parallel to other internal service utilities. That is, the CIS now joins other utilities, such as the security force, custodians, and plant maintenance in supporting the entire corporate community. Any department or function within the organization can "purchase" their services.

Partly responsible for the changing role of CIS are the microcomputer and prepackaged software. These technologies are providing user departments with convenient, precise planning tools. With these tools, a manager can enter budget data, and then can make "what if?" entries and get immediate, projected responses. For example, suppose the manager of a manufacturing project has a hunch that the cost of a certain raw material is about to increase by 20 percent. With an electronic spreadsheet software package and a microcomputer, the manager can enter the existing budget and, with a few simple commands, enter data representing the expected price increase. Then, effects of this increase on overall production costs are automatically and immediately calculated throughout the spreadsheet.

It should be noted here that CIS functions traditionally have offered this type of service via application programs on the mainframe computer. But the turnaround from query to response is sometimes days, which discourages this type of planning support.

In the face of the rise in direct-user capabilities, CIS functions can provide input to planning processes at all levels and in all functions and departments. This input may take several forms, but usually is available from existing, historic data files maintained by a CIS. Thus, one form of input may be to provide the expected cost of continuing service at existing levels. Another form of input includes the number of hours needed to accomplish a requested application modification, or the extension of costs for a new application development. The value of this type of support is illustrated by a recent trend in which CIS representatives are asked to serve as technical resource persons on project teams involved in planning activities.

An interesting situation occurs when a CIS department supports a company that is in the business of providing computer service. For example, Lockheed has a division that markets the Dialog system. Dialog is a computerized reference service sold to subscribers on the basis of services used. Thus, the business of Dialog is computer service. But there is also a need for computer services to support Dialog internally. For example, there is a need to maintain records of computer time used by clients. In addition, billing and accounts receivable functions require extensive support. The point is that the requirements here are large and important enough to warrant the support of a computer information system. Therefore, the computing needs of Dialog require planning of two types. One type of planning concerns the equipment and software that support client requests. The other type of planning deals with providing support for the company's own administrative functions.

In summary, the nature of CIS planning is shaped by its environment. Corporate culture dictates the objectives and goals of a company which, in turn, affect the planning activities that drive the organization in general, and the

CIS function in particular. Up to this point, this text has stressed the importance of the effects of the corporate environment and the relationship of that environment to CIS planning. The next section introduces another major viewpoint on CIS planning—that of the user.

USER PLANNING FOR CIS SERVICE

In many organizations, the demand for CIS services exceeds the capabilities of CIS departments. Thus, there is a backlog of project and application development requests. User departments and functions that need these services, then, can benefit from understanding some of the needs of the CIS department. Just as CIS planning takes place in a corporate environment, the needs of users for computer support are encompassed by the requirements of the CIS function. Therefore, user departments and functions that require CIS support should consult with the CIS department to develop comprehensive and accurate request specifications. This not only helps in developing plans at the level of the user department, but also provides valuable input for CIS planning. In this way, deviations, cost overruns, and conflicts can be minimized for both a CIS department and its customers.

A set of corporate planning guidelines should be available to assist the user in planning for future CIS services. In producing these guidelines, corporate planners consider a range of factors that include:

- Sources of requests for support of a new project or changes to an existing system

- Methods for financing CIS functions

- Identification of corporate lines of authority for purchases of computer hardware and packaged software.

Requesting Service

There are several sources from which user requirements for CIS support are identified. Thus, the method by which a requirement is identified also affects the source of the request. In general, these sources include:

- User initiated

- CIS initiated

- Administrations initiated

- Results of other systems development

- Results of changes in technology.

User initiated.   Requests for CIS support may result from formal, planned user efforts. These requests often originate as alternative solutions to situations under study in the user department. In this case, the departmental study should identify a preliminary plan for the project, which includes requirements for personnel commitments and other resources to implement the solution.

CIS initiated.   A request may result from communication between CIS personnel and users. As described in Chapter 1, projects often result from reviews of historical data by CIS department or from the impact of providing CIS support to a peripheral function. That is, data resources created to support a specific department probably can be applied to support related departments. In Chapter 1, an example is given in which an engineering department plans to build a new product and the functions of purchasing, receiving, inventory, shipping, and others are affected. The data resources in this example can be shared and the processing support distributed among all these related functions.

Such requests should be accompanied by an official request or task authorization form. A sample task authorization form is shown in Figure 2-1. Appendix A describes the procedures for using this form.

Administration initiated.   An administrative requirement may generate the need for a department to request service from CIS. For example, administrators at a bank may decide to add four new customer services, all of which require automated teller machines (ATM). In this situation, many user departments, particularly general accounting and CIS, are impacted and require additional support.

Results of other systems development.   Requests for CIS services often arise as by-products of other activities. For example, a CIS function may develop a new or revised interactive inventory system. The purpose of the new system is to reduce stock-on-hand requirements. This change to the inventory system may affect several other functions. The physical plant may need less warehouse space; purchasing may have to renegotiate delivery schedules with suppliers; the receiving department may be able to reduce, or at least stabilize, its work force; and manufacturing may have to revise production and control schedules. As a result, all these functions, and others, identify new requirements for CIS support of planning activities.

TASK AUTHORIZATION

DATE ISSUED:	DATE REQUIRED:	TASK AUTHORIZATION NO.:
CLIENT:	ACCOUNT NO.:	PRIORITY: I H L
TO:		ACCEPTED:
FROM:		APPROVED:
BILLING INSTRUCTIONS:		

TITLE:	HOURS		DELIVERY DATE	
DESCRIPTION OF TASK(S):	EST.	ACT.	EST.	ACT.

NATIONAL RESEARCH ASSOCIATES

Figure 2-1. *Requests for system service should be reviewed and, upon approval, should be authorized formally through use of a document of the type shown here. This is a Task Authorization form that identifies the project involved and outlines the work to be done.*

Results of changes in technology.   To repeat a previous point, most companies now depend on computers for support. Thus, as computers evolve and offer more and better capabilities, user departments identify additional needs to apply computers. For example, many trade and technical publications, as well as general business publications, report on business uses of computers. A user who reads these publications may come across a new technology that can be applied to his or her particular business function. A request for additional CIS support often results.

Technology changes also may be brought to user attention through CIS plans. That is, an approved CIS plan to replace an existing mainframe computer with a newer, more powerful model may offer opportunities to upgrade user service. The CIS department in this case has an obligation to communicate the facts of the approval, the parameters of the new equipment, and the new features and capabilities to appropriate users. For example, a plan for including color capabilities on user terminals certainly should be outlined to users in an art department.

CIS Financing Methods

Although there are many ways to fund the CIS function, the three most commonly used are:

- Chargeback
- Pie slicing
- Overhead expense.

Chargeback.   Under the chargeback method for funding CIS service, users are charged for services they receive. The CIS department develops a billing algorithm that can be applied to any service rendered. See Figure 2-2. For each accounting period, charges for every CIS user are entered into an accounting journal. The entries in this journal provide a basis for transfers of funds from user departments to CIS to cover the applied charges.

To develop workable plans under the chargeback method, user departments must be given the rate structure for each planning period. To develop the rate structure, a CIS department reviews its own plan for that development period, reviews the historical usage records for at least the previous fiscal period, and includes the requests that have been received for service during the next fiscal period. See Figure 2-3.

Once a billing algorithm is established, a chargeback rate generally is not raised without a compelling reason. On even rarer occasions, a rate is

COMPUTER INFORMATION SYSTEMS DEPARTMENT
RATE REFERENCE SHEET FOR INTERNAL RATES
EFFECTIVE DATE _____

BATCH CHARGES:	PRIORITY	STANDARD	OVERNIGHT	LARGE JOB*
CPU second (each)				
Brand X	1.05	.70	.35	.12
I/O (per 1,000 blocks)	4.50	3.00	1.50	
Cards Read (per 1,000)*		.35		
Memory Surcharge*				
Cards Punched (per 1,000)		3.00		
PRINT CHARGES:				
Impact (per 1,000 lines)	1.50	.75	.30	
Laser (per 1,000 lines)	4.00	2.00	.80	
Inkjet (per 1,000 lines)	4.00	2.00	.80	
Special Forms*				
ONLINE CHARGES:				
TEXT PROCESSOR: CPU second (each)				
Brand Y		.0333	.0167	
WYLBUR, TIPS, and TSO:				
CPU second (each)				
Brand X		.77	.385	
I/O (per 1,000 blocks)		3.30	1.650	
TERMINAL CHARGES:				
Connect (per hour)		3.00	1.50	
Terminal Rent (per 4 weeks)		35.00		
STORAGE CHARGES:				
Datasets (per track/day)				
1–10 tracks		.02		
11th and subsequent tracks		.005		
Tape Rental (volume per bi-week)		.50		
Disk Storage for Text Processors:		.0009		
(per 512-character block per day)				
OTHER MISCELLANEOUS CHARGES:				
Setups (each)*		2.00		
Program Product Charges*				
Other Direct Charges*				
Refunds*				

— ALL CHARGES ARE PRORATED —
* See reverse side for further explanation.
NOTE: The charge for batch jobs is computed by the following formula:
Cost per job step = ((CPU sec × Charge Rate) + (I/O count × Charge Rate)) × Memory Multiplier

Figure 2-2. *This is an example of a chargeback summary for CIS services rendered to other departments within an organization. This report continues on the next page.*

Large Job Rate: In order to qualify for the large job rate the job must meet all four of the following qualifications:

(1) The <u>total</u> job must use at least 600 CPU seconds.

(2) It must be run overnight.

(3) CLASS = V must be coded on the job card.

(4) The job must be accompanied by a set-up card or message to the operator with an estimate of run time (elapsed clock time).

Cards Read: This includes both input through the Card Reader and lines of JCL input via WYLBUR or TSO. The cost is $0.35 per 1,000 card images.

Memory Surcharge: A surcharge is computed on the CPU and I/O charges based on the memory region required by each batch step. The following memory multiplier is applied to the CPU and I/O for each step:

Region:	0–1024K	1025–2048K	2049–4096K	4097–8192K
Multiplier:	1.0	1.1	1.2	1.3

Special Forms: Individual charge rates have been established for a number of different special forms used in printing. The rates vary from $0.00 to $3.77 per 1,000 print lines. This charge is in addition to the normal printing and set-up charges. Call the CIS Business Office for details.

Magnetic Tape: Magnetic tape rental and storage for customer-owned and for NRA-owned tapes is $0.50 per tape per bi-weekly period. All NRA-owned tapes removed from the premises for more than one bi-weekly period will be billed to the customer at cost.

Setups: Two categories of setup charges exist: (1) tape mount/drive use and (2) all other setups (special forms, handling, etc.). The fee for each is $2.00. A job may be charged a maximum of one charge per category, i.e. a total of $4.00.

Program Products: A charge is made for use of some of the software programs available on the Brand X system. The charge is per job step. A table of the individual rates for Program Products follows:

Program	Rate	Program	Rate	Program	Rate
ANS COBOL	$ .25	MARKINT	$1.00	DYL260	$ .50
PL/1 OPTIMIZER	.50	MARKCON	1.00	DYL280	.50
SORT	.25	MARKDUMP	1.00	SAS	.50
SORT/MERGE	.25	MARKREST	1.00	TSP	.25
MARKIV	1.00	SPSSV701	.25		

Other Direct Charges: Chargeback of the cost of special equipment rental, supplies, and services paid to outside vendors by CIS on behalf of a specific project or client. Call the CIS Business Office for a detailed breakdown.

Refunds: Approved refunds given for charges incurred by systems or operations related errors. Call the Information Center Consultant for details.

Figure 2-2 (concluded). This is the conclusion of the departmental chargeback report begun on the previous page.

COST FACTORS	UTILIZATION FACTORS
Computers	CPU Time (in seconds)
Peripherals	I/O (in 1,000's)
Data Communications	Print Lines (in 1,000's)
Supplies	Disk Space (in track days)
Labor	Connect Time (in hours)
Facilities	Tape Storage (in reel days)
Overhead	

Figure 2-3. *This table presents cost and utilization factors used as a basis for allocation of CIS charges to individual projects or departments. To implement a chargeback system, the factors listed here are quantified and processed under an algorithm that extends costs according to the services utilized. The costs are then charged on the basis of this algorithm.*

lowered. One reason for lowering a billing rate might be the lowering of hardware costs through extension of a lease agreement. Or, suppose estimated use figures that are produced in a CIS plan are significantly low. In this case, charges for CPU time are significantly higher than expected and a surplus of funds has been generated. This surplus may be redistributed to users in the form of lower rates.

More commonly, however, chargeback rates are increased because of unforeseen circumstances, such as an increase in the cost of electrical power or a change in the price of communication lines used to transmit data.

Pie slicing. The pie-slicing method is similar to the chargeback method in that the user is charged for services received. The major difference under this

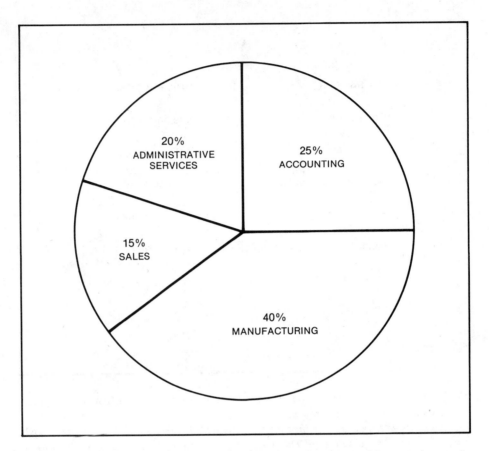

Figure 2-4. *This chart demonstrates the kind of presentation used in reporting on the apportioning of CIS costs under the pie-slicing method.*

method is that the CIS department reviews its customer base and determines the percentage of total services each has used in the past. When the percentage has been set, each user is told what its total charge will be for the planning period. An example of this type of distribution of costs is given in the discussion of the cost-center concept in Chapter 1. As pointed out in that discussion, a major concern in use of the pie-slicing method is that there is generally no incentive for the CIS manager to operate efficiently, since all funds needed are provided automatically through the billing scheme. An example of a pie-slicing distribution is shown in Figure 2-4.

Overhead expense. In some small- and medium-sized companies, CIS department services are treated as an overhead expense. In this case, user departments request services indiscriminately and expect the requests to be approved. Expenses are distributed among all of an organization's functions as part of general administration costs.

Under the overhead method, users often make many requests for service, but they must compete for the actual service. This method frequently results in political conflicts within the organization, particularly when CIS support resources are limited and demand is high.

Approval Authority for Computer Purchases

A CIS planning factor common to all companies small and large involves defining authority and responsibility for purchases of computers and peripheral equipment, such as printers, terminals, microcomputers, executive work stations, and data communication facilities. Specific guidelines for the approval of such purchases should be included within the corporate plans.

Where approval guidelines are vague or nonexistent, problems arise. In large companies, the problems may increase proportionately to the size of the organization. The signature of department supervisors in such companies may be sufficient to authorize "limited" purchases (up to $5,000) that can cover the cost of microcomputers and executive workstations. These acquisitions can result in proliferation of noncompatible equipment that impacts the types and amounts of support provided by a CIS department.

Corporate policy and planning statements, then, should delegate authority for approval of information processing hardware and software to specific people or functions. These statements also should include provisions for technical reviews and specifications for integrating computing hardware and software. The person or function with the authority for approval of purchases also should be responsible for providing users with enough resource information to support purchase decisions.

In summary, the policies, capabilities, and attitudes of user departments exert an effect on CIS planning similar to that of top-level management. Therefore, just as CIS planners benefit from a knowledge of the corporate environment, similar benefits can be had by understanding the needs of users. In the next section, another concept that affects CIS planning—awareness of the state-of-the-art in CIS—is discussed briefly. Then, the case example again is presented in light of the discussions of this chapter.

AWARENESS OF THE STATE-OF-THE-ART IN CIS

The CIS function is obligated professionally to maintain an awareness of the current state of computing technology. That is, a CIS function should be one step ahead of user requests. Recall the discussion earlier in this chapter concerning user-initiated project requests. Thus, one activity of CIS functions is research that seeks new, perhaps better, ways of providing services. This is no small task.

There are many ways for a CIS function to keep pace with the current state-of-the-art. Given the pace of computer technology, a total and complete overview is almost impossible. To deal with this problem, many CIS functions delegate areas of knowledge to individual employees, who then specialize in that subject. College and university courses, trade and technical journals, and professional or technical association meetings can be used by these personnel to update knowledge in their areas of specialization. Of course, the time and expense of maintaining this type of awareness dictates the extent to which it is maintained.

CASE SCENARIO: ESTABLISHING A FRAMEWORK

From the descriptions of the entities in the previous chapter, it is apparent that ARI and NC have both differences and similarities in corporate culture. ARI, with its stronger military background, is more centralized and authority-oriented. NC, on the other hand, seeks and secures consulting work on the basis of capabilities and backgrounds of individual consultants.

Similarities center upon the fact that both businesses can be classified as "think tanks." That is, both businesses depend upon their abilities to recruit and maintain staffs of consultants who can analyze client situations and deliver advice for solving problems and redirect, as necessary, the efforts and resources of client organizations.

Thus, the similarities in corporate culture lie in creating an atmosphere that attracts and nurtures people with the ability to consult at high organizational levels in government and business. The differences in technological or organizational specialties are less critical from a corporate culture standpoint than they are in such management areas as marketing and administrative support. The culture of the combined organization must project a feeling that people are encouraged to be truthful in their recommendations and that individuals will be recognized and rewarded according to their personal capabilities and the value of the solutions they derive for the problems with which they are presented.

In the CIS area, these sets of philosophies and policies are reflected in widely differing organization structures and procedures. NC, for example, pursues a centralized approach to delivery of computer services. Personal computation and text processing are provided through terminals linked into a centralized system. ARI, with its greater emphasis on decentralized project management, provides information center guidance to consultants and project leaders who have wide latitude in the acquisition of special-purpose hardware and software. Thus, if a project manager can justify installing a personal computer and project control software for a single assignment, he or she has a relatively free hand in making the appropriate purchases. The only constraints would be a series of guidelines about hardware and system software to assure some compatibility in reporting and to make it possible for the organization to derive meaningful operating reports to oversight agencies.

Case Discussion/Assignment

Management of the combined ARI/NC organization must articulate a statement of positions and beliefs that will serve as the basis for a corporate culture to become a driving force for the merged entity. This involves identifying the existing feelings and ambience within each separate organization, building upon the matching traits, and identifying those areas where changes or adjustments will be necessary. The presidents of ARI and NC, both aware of a need to enunciate a single philosophy, appoint a team made up of members of both staffs to come back with a suggested statement of philosophy.

Your assignment is to devise a plan of work for the team that will work on developing a document to provide a unified basis for building a joint corporate culture.

Discussion Topics

1. Describe the objectives and goals that might be included in the corporate-level planning statement of a large organization.

2. Describe the corporate image of a bullish organization.

3. What is meant by a formal review of a planning statement?

4. What special guidelines are included within planning statements governing the use of personal computers and prepackaged software within businesses?

5. What is the pie-slicing method for financing CIS services within organizations?

3

PLANNING STRATEGIES

Abstract

Planning activities are implemented in several ways within organizations and present advantages as well as disadvantages to CIS professionals. Obviously, an understanding of both the merits and pitfalls is of value in formulating CIS plans. To achieve this understanding, the definition of planning is expanded to encompass both formal and informal methods under which managers and administrators perform planning tasks. Further, planning is viewed as evolutionary and cyclical, an activity that iterates on levels that correspond to the strategic, tactical, and operational levels of organizations. At each level, planning statements reflect varying degrees of conceptual and procedural information. In general, the higher, or more strategic, the level, the less operational detail and the more financial information is included in planning and budget statements. Final approval for any plan lies at the top level of the organization, with the chief executive officer (CEO) and the board of directors.

WHAT IS PLANNING?

Administrative theorists who have been asked to produce a list of the key functions of management typically include planning at the top of the list. Henri Fayol, in writings based on extensive, top-level management experience, was one of the first to list functions that are considered basic to the process of business administration. Fayol believed that administrative ability could be acquired in the same way as technical skills, through training. He also defined administration in terms of five basic elements: planning, organizing, commanding, coordinating, and controlling. The material in this text touches on all of these elements, but the focal point is the element of planning.

Fayol (and other experts in the field of administration) wrote that the planning function involves the establishment of policies and procedures for achieving organizational goals and objectives. In effect, planning serves to create opportunities for supporting the decision-making processes and using resources to the fullest advantage.

Planning can be the basis for increasing the effectiveness of both short- and long-range activities. Plans are a tool for preparing for the future, and for measuring ongoing performance. Planning is a process for visualizing the results and consequences of business activities.

The Evolutionary Nature of Planning

Most planning is a continuing, intellectual activity that takes place in managers' minds as they perform daily business chores. That is, managers accumulate data constantly in the performance of duties; and the summarizing of this data is used to support planning activities.

In fact, most plans result from summaries of large collections of data—whether the data items are stored as documents, in computer-maintained files, or in a manager's mind. For example, consider a type of planning statement that you have probably developed—a class schedule. A catalog of data items—concerning degree requirements and an overall schedule of classes—is summarized to produce a preliminary list of choices. This list, or tentative student plan for an upcoming semester or quarter—is submitted for approval to administrative offices when you register.

Perhaps some of your chosen classes are full and your plan is disapproved. You simply select different classes, or an alternative plan, and the cycle of application, determination, and approval is repeated. After your schedule is approved, the data items within it are used by administration to support further planning and decision making. Suppose hundreds of other students also applied for one of the classes that was already full. Administrators might combine this data with data about available instructors and classrooms and plan to offer more sections of that class during the next semester or quarter.

Notice the evolutionary nature of plan development. That is, the planning process proceeds along lines made up of discrete stages. Usually, the beginning and end of each stage is marked by some type of approval or decision. Recall the discussion in Chapter 2 concerning the three levels of planning statements. At the corporate level, a decision was made to reduce the volume of accounts receivable by 25 percent before the end of the fiscal year. Then, at the tactical level, further decisions produced an outline of how this goal was to be accomplished. Decisions in the accounts receivable department (user level) served to refine the idea into specific activities for achieving the goal.

To this point then, planning started at the top and proceeded to the bottom level of an organization. The approval processes, in turn, reversed this direction and proceeded from bottom to top. Suppose, for example, that the user planning statement included requirements that exceeded existing CIS capabilities. Managers at the tactical level then have the option of disapproving this plan and sending it back to the accounts receivable department for revision. Or, these same managers could decide to upgrade the system, an activity that would require approval at the administrative level.

Thus, planning is evolutionary and involves cycles of data flows. (The planning cycle is discussed in the next chapter.) It may sound simple to produce a plan, follow it, and reap the benefits of inevitable success. In reality, however, there are pros *and* cons to planning. The section that follows discusses the advantages and disadvantages of planning that current and future CIS professionals can expect to encounter.

ADVANTAGES OF PLANNING

An organization that plans effectively has a number of competitive advantages over organizations that plan poorly or do not plan. A plan gives direction to a company. An analogy can be drawn between two runners in a marathon. One of the runners is given a map that shows the designated route and the other runner is allowed to figure out the route on his own. Obviously, the runner with the map has an advantage. Effective planning effort offers some important advantages.

Direction is provided toward achievement of a desired result.   An in-place plan enhances communication. This is particularly true when a plan is written. All participants can refer to the same information, understand the intent, and identify activities to be completed.

Planning encourages achievement.   This is true particularly in connection with specific goals or objectives. The act of evolving the plan and writing it down often provides the impetus for achievement. For example, consider the sense of accomplishment an individual athlete feels when a ''game plan'' leads to victory. The same sense of accomplishment can result for an employee who can relate a specific achievement to a plan which he or she helped to develop.

Resources usually are allocated and utilized more effectively.   Equipment and supplies can be used more efficiently because only those tasks associated with a plan require action. With the plan as a guide, only those items necessary to support authorized actions need be purchased and stocked.

Control is facilitated.   Plans encompass start and completion times for all events and elements. When these factors are known, control can be enhanced. Standards of performance can be defined and implemented on the basis of stated plans.

Plans can be the basis for identification and evaluation of alternatives.   A plan can be used to answer ''What if?'' questions. A computer model of the plan can be used to evaluate potential effects of alternate courses of action. For example, a model can be developed of a plan for a single-product manufacturing line. ''What if?'' questions then can be applied to evaluate such possibilities as addition of a second shift, adding a second product, or other alternatives.

A plan tends to force managers to visualize and understand the overall situation.   Each manager is better able to relate his or her activities to those of the full organization. All managers should be able to make better informed decisions.

Plans can be the basis for identifying the need for future changes.   A plan actually can influence the acceptance of change. In particular, a plan can be the basis for anticipating the impact of emerging technologies. For example, a CIS plan may point out the need to upgrade a mainframe computer within two years. Evaluation of the plan may reveal an inconsistency in tape densities between peripherals of present and planned systems. Conversion of files or other measures to support file maintenance can be accommodated if a plan provides a sufficient basis for recognition of the problem.

A plan tends to provide direction for the reduction of unproductive work.   With a plan in place, efforts of contributors can be directed toward accomplishment of identified results.

Efficient and effective use of facilities is enhanced.   The plan should provide a basis for scheduling the work for continuous flow through a series of established steps. The potential for matching schedules with resource allocation is improved.

Tactical decision making is encouraged and supported.   Strategic plans provide a framework for interim action and effective decision making. If a plan itself is effective, it should lead to tactical implementation. A plan that cannot be related to specific actions probably will fail. Regular review of plans encourages timely adjustment of implementation measures.

POTENTIAL PLANNING PITFALLS

A famous passage attributed to Robert Burns can be paraphrased: "The best laid plans of mice and men often go astray." The point is that a plan is no guarantee of success, regardless of its elegance. Many organizations and departments prepare a plan and then fail through lack of management support or because other activities override priorities set by the plan.

The section that follows discusses some common pitfalls that are encountered by CIS professionals who strive to produce and adhere to a plan. This list is by no means complete; it is meant only to present an overview of typical planning problems and some possible ways of avoiding problems. Twelve pitfalls of planning can be identified:

Budgets can be used to control planning.   A budget is an extension of a plan and should not be considered a substitute for a plan. The pitfall occurs when managers extrapolate last year's budget into this year's plan. The point is made in Chapter 1 that a plan is incomplete without a budget. A budget is an estimate or projection of what is needed to accomplish a stated goal. That is, a budget presents a forecast of the resources needed to achieve goals. A plan is conceptual and establishes direction. A budget determines when and to what extent a plan can be implemented. Plans may have to be modified or compromised to conform to budgets.

Therefore, planning and budgetary considerations are related, but plans and budgets differ in purpose. The most effective capabilities for dealing with change and for reviewing and controlling companies are realized when budgets are derived from well-stated plans.

Unexpected conditions may inhibit plan implementation. Unexpected conditions can impede even the most carefully drawn plans. That is, deviations and problems can arise randomly. A situation may result in which organizations and departments expend efforts and resources merely to "oil squeaky wheels," or problems that demand immediate attention. This condition, also known as crisis management, is analogous to a physician treating a patient's symptoms without attempting to diagnose and cure the disease or the source of the symptoms. Naturally, crises that do arise must be dealt with. However, an important measure of planning effectiveness lies in the degree to which crises are averted.

Inadequate corporate plans may constrain planning efforts at lower levels. CIS planning tends to be ineffective unless a corporate plan is in place. In the absence of a formal or informal corporate plan, the CIS function lacks direction. Remember, CIS planning exists within a framework of corporate planning and reflects the overall objectives and goals of the organization. Just as a house cannot be built without an appropriate foundation, a CIS plan suffers when support (corporate planning) is lacking.

Regardless of the existence of a corporate plan, however, the CIS function should use available techniques—such as interviews, questionnaires, meetings, and so on—to produce the best plan under the circumstances. The planning needs particular to CIS functions are discussed in a later chapter.

The backlog of systems projects often becomes the CIS plan. A list of systems projects slated for a CIS function makes an ineffective plan. A project list merely provides a statement of projected requirements on an individual basis. Effective planning incorporates an integrated view of all project needs as a basis for direction and control.

Usefulness of a plan is limited to the extent of the accuracy of the information it provides. The effectiveness of a plan is proportionate directly to the currency and accuracy of its information content. A plan which, by definition, anticipates future activities should not be expected always to be correct. Conditions and situations change constantly. For this reason, plans should be reviewed regularly to update status of pertinent conditions. In other words, if a plan lacks the support of current and accurate information, quality of planning suffers.

Planning can be expensive. Planning may require significant amounts of time and effort, which involve business funds. Obviously, plans are designed to provide a return on this investment. There are professionals, however, who believe that the resources devoted to planning might be better used in performing actual work. A parallel can be drawn with crisis management. Elimination of efforts and expenditures for recovery and restart measures can lead to major short term savings. Savings apparently are realized by eliminating investments in protective facilities and practices. However, when a crisis occurs, an entirely different return-on-investment picture is developed.

Emergencies are not anticipated in plans. Generally, a plan is limited in its capability for anticipating emergencies. Professionals who shun planning often point to emergency situations to rationalize their belief. It is true that emergencies are inevitable and demand immediate attention when they arise. Plans should anticipate foreseeable problems and should provide methods for avoiding or dealing with them as necessary. Planners also should incorporate recovery mechanisms that can deal with virtually any unexpected emergencies.

Any business action generally is preceded by at least a minimum amount of planning. Planning, then, helps to minimize the occurrence and magnitude of emergency situations.

Employees tend to resist change. By nature, people resist change. Thus, to many employees, plans are threatening and represent sources of pressure and tension. For these people, plans mean that future change is certain and they must prepare to adjust to new situations. Those who feel this way often believe that just the act of planning accelerates the rate of change.

Too much planning detail can constrain employee initiative. Plans and budgets must have some degree of flexibility. That is, some companies produce overly detailed plans and insist upon strict adherence. Managerial and decision-making capabilities can be inhibited in this type of environment.

Planning can be overdone.   Planning efforts may turn out to be too much of a good thing. Planners must keep in mind that their function is to produce a plan within a specific timeframe. There can be a tendency among planners to attempt to foresee and prepare for every emergency and to eliminate every risk. Such planners collect more data and require more reviews and modifications than are necessary, as well as prepare too many formal reports.

There can be a tendency simply to extend historic data rather than to plan realistically.   Plans sometimes are merely extensions of current or past activities. For example, a planner might take the budget for a successful year and multiply all entries by a certain percentage. The idea is to leave well enough alone. But a continuation of current activities is based on an assumption that external conditions remain the same, at least in proportion to the percentage applied. Effective plans are based upon an informed evaluation of actual and anticipated business conditions.

Suppose a yearly "plan" is produced in which a 5 percent performance increase is projected across the board. However, technological developments in the past year have made it possible to decrease access times by 200 percent at relatively little cost. In this situation, the new development may be overlooked if the initial projection appears attainable under present conditions.

Planning can become so theoretical that practical values are lost.   A resulting plan may be difficult to apply in a real business situation. For example, a plan may be based upon production standards that fail to reflect actual experience. Thus, if actual production regularly exceeds standards, a plan based on standards will be unrealistic.

Similarly, a plan can present too many alternatives and not enough direction. That is, a plan provides only a list of possible courses of action. In this situation, it is difficult to evaluate risks and to establish priorities.

In summary, ineffective planning may produce as many undesirable effects as no planning. There are many reasons why ineffective plans are produced or why effective plans are implemented ineffectively. The above section describes common problems that can cause planning failures. The success of plans, in turn, is best guaranteed by the support of a team of dedicated and skilled professionals. The next section discusses planning from the viewpoint of this support group—the managers and other experts responsible for producing and implementing plans.

PLANNING FUNCTION

As stated previously, every organization takes a relatively unique approach to planning. Some companies have one or more professionals assigned permanently to a planning department or function. In other companies, planning tasks are assigned temporarily to personnel in departments affected by or related to the planning project.

Organizations with formal planning structures implement specific procedures to gather source data to support plan development. In this kind of environment, evaluation activities also play an important role; and ongoing reviews of current plans may be called for in planning statements.

In organizations with an informal approach to planning, personnel receive planning assignments in what is often referred to as a "left-handed" manner. That is, managers and other professionals participate in planning projects as a sideline to their regular duties. Planning assignments of this type often are rotated throughout the organization so that responsibilities are distributed fairly. One advantage to this approach is that all supervisory personnel are involved in planning at some time and, consequently, the input to this type of planning should be comprehensive.

A drawback to this approach is that there may be a lack of formal data-collection and reporting procedures to support planning. In addition, the members of planning teams may approach planning as a "fill-in" activity and may not give it the commitment needed to plan effectively. Inconsistency of planning content results.

Both methods for designating planning responsibilities are used extensively in business. In fact, both methods may be used within a single organization. For example, an organization may have a formal planning function that consists of a number of permanently assigned personnel. Then, appropriate departmental personnel may be assigned to the planning function for a specific period or project. The point is that every organization selects a planning model according to management dictates. No matter what approach is taken, the principle is that a corporate plan should be in place as a framework for all other planning within the organization. If there is no adequate corporate plan, CIS managers and those in other functions will have to assemble sets of assumptions that function as *de facto* corporate plans.

Informal Data Collection

To rephrase a previous point, effective planning cannot take place in a vacuum. Planning is a team effort that involves every level and department of an organization. This organization-wide participation, at a minimum, includes contributions to some type of informal data collection process.

Informal data collection involves day-to-day communication among supervisory personnel and between supervisors and workers. Communication takes many forms, including departmental reports, written memos, word of mouth, and managers' personal observations. This communication supplies managers with an ongoing source of information for input to planning.

Thus, managers absorb source data for planning activities even without specific procedures in place. Henry Mintzberg, a professor of management at McGill University in Toronto, derived the following conclusions from studies that he and others conducted concerning managerial work: Managers' activities are characterized by brevity, variety, and discontinuity. Managers tend to be oriented toward action and dislike reflective activities. The plans they make seem to exist in their heads as flexible paths toward specific goals. Mintzberg also found that when managers are required to plan, they seem to do so implicitly, or within the context of daily activities.

To summarize, planning generally is a continuing activity. That is, planning often consists of solutions developed in response to day-to-day problems. Although there are situations that call for the dissemination of a formalized planning statement, planning also occurs on an ongoing, informal basis.

Role of the Annual Budget

As stated earlier, a budget is an estimate or projection of requirements for accomplishing an objective or goal. Although a budget is not meant to give direction to an organization, a budget can bring perspective to the organization's activities. The budget contains a specific, detailed breakdown of resources and activities.

A budget also contains data against which performance can be measured. In addition, a budget may provide information needed to integrate individual projects into the organization as a whole. Once a plan and its corresponding budget are in place, any activity or project can be evaluated according to budget entries. In turn, a budget reflects the scope of the information from which it is derived. That is, if the horizon of available information is short, planning and budgeting also encompass a limited time period.

The CEO Drives Planning

Up to this point, planning is discussed in light of when, where, and why it takes place. In addition, a point is made in this chapter that people represent an important support mechanism for planning activities. It also should be understood that planning is driven by people, specifically the people at the top levels of organizational hierarchies—the chief executive officer (CEO) and the board of directors.

Many of the ideas and goals expressed by top management result from communication that emanates from other levels within the organization. Then, final approval for any plan rests with personnel at top levels. Managers at this level accept and support the development of any project when they approve a plan for that project. This concept is elaborated in a later chapter of this text. For present purposes, the point is that the driving force of planning originates at the highest levels of the organization.

At the top levels of the organization, planning is a business-driven function. Plans are made in response to some type of business need. The scenario presented in Chapter 2 is an example of business-driven planning. In this example, a business need was identified—to reduce the volume of accounts receivable by 25 percent by the end of the fiscal year—and a plan was produced as a result.

Planning also can be driven by technological concerns. A newly developed technology often creates a better way of performing work. In this case, need is created indirectly. For example, a new operating system package may provide substantial improvements in throughput for a CIS. CIS managers who stay current with such developments naturally are disposed to research the new operating system. Subsequent CIS plans may be affected.

To summarize, planning involves pitfalls as well as advantages, and includes formal and informal procedures. Probably the most important facet of planning involves people, beginning with the CEO at the strategic level, and proceeding down through tactical and operational levels of an organization. The next section presents a detailed explanation of planning levels and the concerns faced by CIS professionals at each level.

STRATEGIC

Strategic plans generally address long-range goals or objectives. The CEO and board of directors produce strategic plans because they are responsible for directing organizations. A secondary purpose of strategic planning is to motivate planning activities at lower organizational levels.

In effect, a strategic plan states the corporate mission, which sets direction and provides momentum for activities at functional levels. A strategic planning statement provides source data from which departments such as CIS functions derive their particular objectives. In addition, strategic plans may include an outline of activities for reaching corporate goals, although great detail is not required. What is important is that strategic goals and objectives are communicated effectively to appropriate personnel and incorporated within lower-level plans. For example, a strategic statement might direct: "Eliminate short-term borrowing to support current manufacturing operations by optimizing cash flow from sales." At the tactical level, the goal would be: "Decrease outstanding accounts receivable by 25 percent by the end of the next fiscal year."

Strategic and tactical planning elements, in turn, may impact operational plans. In the above example, suppose there is a significant increase in text-processing requirements caused by the production of additional or more frequent collection notifications. The strategic and tactical plans contain no specification for increasing text-processing capability for the computing center. In fact, there may be limited awareness of this development at the corporate level.

Thus, this new requirement is presented to top-level management in operational-level planning statements. That is, the CIS has recognized this development and has outlined a proposal to meet it in its planning statement. If corporate management approves this plan, the CIS budget is modified to incorporate additional text-processing capabilities.

Techniques for CIS Strategic Planning

A number of established planning methodologies are available for guidance in the formulation of strategic plans for an information systems function. Each of the appropriate plans has been the subject of one or more book-length publications. Therefore, there is no room in this text to detail these methodologies. However, as a guideline, Figure 3-1 is a summary of major techniques taken from an article in *Data Management*, a publication of the Data Processing Management Association (June, 1986, p. 22). In reviewing the summary in Figure 3-1, consider that two of the most common methods used for CIS strategic planning are the Business Systems Planning (BSP) and Critical Success Factors (CSF) approaches.

STRATEGIC INFORMATION SYSTEMS PLANNING TECHNIQUES

TECHNIQUE NAME	AUTHOR	PRIMARY FOCUS	DESCRIPTION
Business Information Analysis and Integration Technique (BIAIT)	Burnstine	Organizational Information Requirements	An engineered technique which depends upon commonalities between organizations with respect to their information needs when related to a profile of similar, generic business functions. An information requirements model is built from answers to seven yes/no questions which deal with the basic trigger of all business, the order.
Business Information Control Study (BICS)	Zachman	Organizational Information Requirements	A technique which extracts the salient features of BSP and BIAIT within the context of an automated model.
Business Systems Planning (BSP)	IBM	Organizational Information Requirements	A comprehensive planning technique performed in two phases: Phase I—Top-down analysis of the organization and its business processes, and identification of how information systems support the organization. Phase II—Preparation of a long-range plan for developing a network of information systems organized by common business processes and using shared data.
Continuous Flow Approach	Gillenson & Goldberg	Organizational Information Requirements	A comprehensive technique which addresses the transition between strategic and tactical systems planning. Linkage is established between organizational business processes, application definition, and data base structuring.
Critical Success Factors (CSF)	Rockhart	Organizational Information Requirements	A technique for focusing on key business processes of an organization and related conditions which must go right for the organization to attain its business goals. While not a complete strategic planning technique, Critical Success Factors is useful in defining the information requirements of top management.
Ends/Means Analysis	Wetherbe & Davis	Organizational Information Requirements	Focuses on outputs such as goods, services, and information generated by an organization; then defines the processes which must be performed at the organizational and departmental levels to generate the required outputs.
Management by Strategies	Synnott & Gruber	Information Resource Management	A planning technique which develops strategies and tactics for acquiring and applying IS resources taking into account such factors as technology trends, nature of users, corporate policies and culture, and the role of the IS manager within the organization.
Stages of Growth	Gibson & Nolan	Information Resource Management	A technique wherein an organization is viewed as moving through stages of maturation with respect to its ability to utilize information and manage information systems resources. Each growth stage is defined in terms of organizational characteristics and IS activities.
Strategy Set Transformation	King	Strategic Business Planning Linkage	Views overall organizational strategy as an information set consisting of a mission, objectives, business strategies, and "cultural" variables. Strategic IS planning is defined as the process of transforming the organizational strategy into a corresponding set of IS strategies consisting of IS system objectives, constraints, and design approaches.

Figure 3-1. *This table presents a summary of techniques used in strategic planning for information systems. (Reprinted by permission from the June, 1986, issue of* Data Management.*)*

Inputs to CIS Strategic Planning

Although a CIS function is at the departmental level of the organization, the plans produced to support a CIS may be strategic in nature. That is, a CIS function often sets long-term goals and objectives and produces plans to meet them. As stated above, the primary inputs to CIS planning may be derived from the corporate plan. This is especially true in organizations directed by dynamic, progressive leaders.

User input.   CIS planning also is driven by the needs of users or user departments. One source for needs identification lies in annual reports that deal with future expectations rather than being limited to past results. Annual reports are prepared by most departments and functions within an organization and by the organization as a whole. These reports, usually prepared near the end of a fiscal year, summarize performance for the year and make projections for the coming year. Collectively, these reports represent the needs that are expected to arise during the coming year. A study of these reports, then, can yield important information that affects CIS services as well as strategic planning for the entire organization.

CIS planning also is motivated by user requests for service. An approved request represents an objective to be met, or a direction to be taken. That is, strategic plans for a CIS function may be derived from information within user requests. Then, additional levels of detail are added to the strategic specifications to represent tactical or operational perspectives.

Data input to support CIS planning.   The inputs described in the previous section, regardless of their source, take the form of data items. There also are external sources of data that support CIS planning. These include information services such as Auerbach, DataPro, Dialog, IDC, and others. Technical journals published by professional associations and hundreds of magazines and trade papers also provide support. Of course, it is unreasonable to expect that a planner read all the material available. Often, the tasks of planning are divided into areas of study, with each planner assigned a specific research area. Reports that result from these individual studies then are presented to the planners.

As an alternative, reports can be purchased directly from information services. These reports usually contain general information such as: the overall costs of computing, costs per byte (or megabyte) of random access storage, the feasibility of microcomputers and executive work stations, and new developments in hardware and software.

In summary, a strategic plan is characterized by its presentation of long-term goals and corporate mission. Departmental plans may be strategic in nature. Typically, a strategic plan encompasses a time frame of three or more years. Projects and tasks included within strategic plans generally require a year or more to complete, or even a year or more before project activities begin. Strategic planning, in turn, drives tactical and operational planning.

TACTICAL

A tactical plan adds a level of detail to a strategic plan. A tactical plan describes specific activities for implementing the strategic plan. Tactical planning deals with work sequences and efficient use of resources.

The difference between strategic and tactical plans can be described best in terms of the time horizons of activities described and the portions of the total organization that are affected directly by the plans.

Generally, strategic plans involve extensive time considerations. Tasks outlined in tactical plans usually can be completed in 18 months or less. In fact, tactical plans often include only tasks that can be completed within one fiscal year. Most planning that exceeds this horizon is considered strategic.

The difference between strategic and tactical planning also is indicated by the impact the plan has on the organization as a whole. From a management viewpoint, a strategic plan generally applies to the entire organization. A policy determination concerning purchases and implementation of microcomputers constitutes a strategic plan. In turn, plans for the development of an on-line inventory system are considered tactical, because they provide a means of implementing strategic plans.

There is an interesting paradox here. That is, strategic planning is performed by relatively small groups, involves limited external input, and affects the entire organization. Tactical planning, however, is limited in its effect, but is performed by relatively large groups and involves input from several sources, both internal and external.

Tactical plans also are distinguished by factors that include elements that detail the availability and use of resources, the inclusion of feasible alternative courses of action, and specifications for review and feedback processes. Of course, all considerations and activities of tactical plans are performed within a framework of strategic objectives and goals.

However, some organizations lack explicit or disseminated strategic plans. In these cases, managers of departments, such as the CIS function, attempt to determine the objectives of top management as best they can. That is, corporate goals are derived from annual reports, internal company correspondence, interviews and questionnaires, and other sources. These sources are no substitute for a comprehensive strategic planning statement, but they may be the only inputs available to managers in the absence of strategic plans.

In organizations that do not plan strategically, tactical planning tends to be reactive. The CIS function may adopt a philosophy similar to crisis management: Tactical planning occurs in response to user requests or immediate business needs. The tactical plan, then, becomes a simple projection of what services are to be provided.

OPERATIONAL

An operational plan adds another level of detail to planning. The activities described in a tactical plan are defined further to include those who perform each task and specific work schedules. An operational plan presents these definitions in behavioral terms. That is, an overall operation is broken down into smaller tasks; and start and completion dates are included, as well as quantitative criteria for completion or success.

The difference between operational and tactical planning, like the difference between strategic and tactical planning, lies in the time involved and the portion of the organization for which activities are planned. Individual tasks presented in operational plans generally involve less than a year of effort, although the time frame encompassed by all the activities may require a longer period, often a full year.

Operational plans generally are more tangible and less conceptual than strategic or tactical plans, and thus are implemented with greater ease. Operational tasks can be divided into segments; each segment can be assigned to a specific worker or functional position within the organization.

To illustrate, recall that an operational plan is an expanded version of a tactical plan. The tactical plan includes a statement of resource requirements. These requirements can be used to develop a step-by-step sequence of tasks that encompasses allocations of equipment, personnel, and facilities. As each step is completed, then, the project proceeds along a course of action first described as a strategic goal.

The portions of an operational plan that deal with personnel, time, and equipment scheduling often are prepared in conjunction with involved subordinates. In effect, management and individual employees reach agreements about the employees' projected performance in completion of operational tasks. This type of operational planning sometimes is referred to as *management by objectives (MBO)*. For maximum effectiveness, an MBO contract statement between employee and employer is built into performance review procedures. Use of MBO contracts or some form of objective statement can provide management and workers with a nonjudgmental basis for performance review and feedback.

An operational plan, like a tactical plan, also includes feasible alternative actions and methods for accomplishing the defined tasks. Often these alternative actions take the form of contingency plans designed to minimize the damage caused by unforeseen or emergency situations.

Planning exhibits similarities and differences at all levels. In general terms, greater attention is paid to details and procedures at lower levels. Goals and objectives of a conceptual nature are determined at higher levels. There are many ways of delegating responsibilities for producing plans throughout organizations. These methods are discussed in the section that follows.

PLANNING RESPONSIBILITIES

Planning responsibilities may be centralized or decentralized, depending on corporate culture. Most organizations seem to favor some form of decentralization of planning responsibilities, although neither method is more effective by nature.

In a centralized model, there generally is a specific department responsible for gathering input data and for preparing and documenting plans. In these cases, a number of employees are assigned permanently to a planning department. During periods of intensive planning, such as the end of fiscal years, personnel from other departments often join the planning department on temporary assignment. Planning in this environment is ongoing and relatively formal. Under this model, the head of a planning department has both the responsibility and the authority needed to gather source data and to produce plans.

Under the decentralized planning model, formal or documented plans are produced as they are needed. That is, as the time for submitting a plan draws near, one or more employees in each department is assigned to prepare the needed report. This task generally is assigned in addition to regular activities. Under this model, responsibilities for plan success also are delegated less formally, as is the authority necessary to gather source data. The combination of these two factors increases the chance that a completed plan will lack timeliness and accuracy. To avoid this problem, a central oversight capability should be established to integrate plans for all of the decentralized entities within the overall organization.

One alternative to strictly defined, centralized or decentralized planning models involves the establishment of quality circles. This approach, adapted from management techniques developed in Japanese companies, is discussed in a book titled *Theory Z* by Professor William Ouchi of UCLA.

Under this approach, the organization is broken down into planning, review, and feedback groups called quality circles. These groups meet regularly to discuss past and projected performance. In this way, current issues are dealt with on an ongoing basis by participating employees. Since members of these groups contribute primarily operational perspectives, plans are developed by the people who implement them. Then, results of the discussions are forwarded to the next higher organizational level for approval by appropriate managers. The result is an ongoing and effective planning and review process.

Possibly the greatest benefit of this management technique, though, concerns human relations. Employees feel that they have an active role within the organization and a say in the way things are done.

CASE SCENARIO: STRUCTURING COORDINATED PLANS

The ARI/NC situation demonstrates with ideal clarity the relationships among the steps in the formulating of corporation and information systems plans. Specifically, the relationship between the enunciation of a corporate culture and sets of plans for operating the business and its support functions is demonstrated crisply and clearly.

Given a statement of philosophy for the joined company, for example, the overall market position of the new entity can take on new flavor. On the one hand, ARI has expertise as systems integrators. This can be regarded as a transferrable specialty, even though ARI has worked primarily in the military area. NC, on the other hand, has a reputation for being able to implement systems for public and private sector entities. NC consultants, for example, have taken a number of local governments, banks, and large industrial corporations through generation-type conversions of their computer systems. Along the way, the NC staff has gained some special-industry expertise. Engagements have included conversion from audio to digital dispatching systems for trucking companies and local police and fire departments.

One approach, therefore, might be for the combined entity to seek contracts with the FBI or other federal agencies on the integration of information on populations in state and federal penitentiaries or on integrated files of wanted persons. Even in preliminary meetings among planners from the two organizations, it becomes apparent that the massive database that ARI has built for tracking hazardous wastes has applicability in other areas. For example, the NC participants point out that federal agencies are interested in establishing a central, federal file of persons who have violated paroles in any of the 50 states. The problem is that paroled persons, still under the jurisdiction of state-level corrections authorities, have great freedom of movement. Persons stopped for violations in a new state of residence are not connected routinely with parole violations in other states even though all law enforcement offices have a legal responsibility to detain such violators.

Corporate-level information planning for a merged entity has strategic, tactical, and operational implications, as discussed earlier in this chapter. At the strategic level, for example, an early consideration would center on a name for the merged organization. One strategy might be to let the two organizations continue their separate identities, consolidating only accounting and operating statements and associated support functions. Another approach, as suggested in the previous paragraph, might be to inventory the strengths of the individual entities and look for opportunities to combine these strengths as a basis for offering services to new or larger markets. In the situation described, for example, a decision to seek contracts in such areas as federal law enforcement or corrections projects could become an element of a new strategy. Before any strategy is adopted, of course, some review and investigation would be undertaken. A decision to bid on contracts in the target field, then, would represent a strategic direction. Strategic plans, in turn, would incorporate goals or targets for the type and volume of business to be sought in the new field.

Carrying this example forward, tactical plans would center around the types of staff to be recruited, the equipment to be made available, and perhaps the software packages to be installed to serve the targeted market. Note that the time dimension for each level of planning can range from the immediate to the distant future. Commitments and plans to implement them need not be constrained by timing considerations.

In this instance, for example, operational plans could be longer range in nature than either strategic or tactical plans. To illustrate, a decision to add a given capability to a computer system might have a two-to-five-year planning dimension, while the strategy for marketing to a new group of agencies might be announced in weeks or months.

Case Discussion/Assignment

Outline a study that will lead to the formulation of strategic, tactical, and operational plans for the two entities as a whole and for their information systems groups. Start by thinking about possible names for the merged entity. Describe a set of tasks or activities that would be completed in the formulation of a comprehensive set of plans. Design data gathering or interview forms that could be used in conjunction with this study.

Discussion Topics

1. What is meant by the statement: Planning is an evolutionary process?

2. What are strategic plans and how are strategic plans produced within an organization?

3. What is meant by management by objectives (MBO)?

4. What is crisis management and how can it be avoided?

5. What is business-driven planning? Give an example.

6. What is meant by this statement: An operational plan should be stated in behavioral terms?

4

THE PLANNING CYCLE

Abstract

Planning is cyclical. The planning cycle generally consists of several phases, which include the request for a plan, collection of data, preparation of planning reports, and review and feedback at ascending organizational levels. The cyclical progression moves up and down from level to level within the organization until a plan receives final approval at the top, or administrative, level. Plans may originate at any level and several cycles on each level may be required before final approval is gained. Planning for CIS requirements of business organizations involves three parallel areas that must plan independently, yet still maintain mutual support for one another. These areas include: planning for the overall organization, planning an organization-wide approach to CIS needs, and planning for the internal development and growth of the CIS function.

PLANS AND BUDGETS

Plans and budgets are developed at the strategic, tactical, and operational levels of the organization. At each level, a separate planning statement may be disseminated; and each statement usually is supported by an appropriate version of a budget. The level at which a planning statement is issued determines the amount of descriptive detail. The operational plan contains the most detailed, procedurally oriented description. The tactical plan, in contrast, presents summary information of the operational plan; and the strategic plan does the same with the tactical plan.

This is not to imply that operational plans are developed first and then summarized to produce higher-level plans. Rather, the implication is that information takes different forms at different levels. Planning development within the organizational hierarchy can be diagrammed with a triangle or pyramid structure, as shown in Figure 4-1. The section that follows discusses the planning cycle and reviews the levels at which plans are developed. Emphasis is placed upon how CIS planning is affected at each level.

Strategic

Strategy can be defined as the art or science of planning for and conducting large-scale operations. As this definition suggests, strategic plans reflect, in general terms, the long-term goals and objectives for the overall organization. These plans normally are developed and administered by top-level managers, and are used to establish an organization's direction within time frames that may cover three or more years.

A CIS function may encounter strategic planning on two separate, yet parallel, tracks. The first track involves support for corporate strategic plans in the form of information services. For example, historical data may be required by strategic planners to produce statistical projections.

The second track stems from the need within CIS functions for direction and long-range goals. Although many businesses and individual functions choose not to plan strategically, for CIS functions this choice is limited by the nature of their activities. For instance, plans involving major equipment changes or development of new application systems require time frames that place these functions within the framework of strategic planning. That is, factors such as extended lead times for delivery of computer equipment and for development of applications present elements that place these activities within an organization's strategic planning framework.

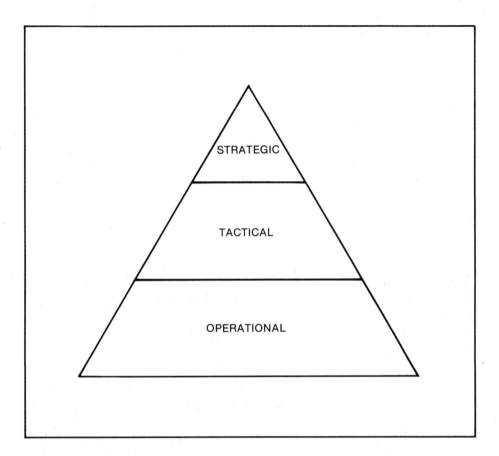

Figure 4-1. *A pyramid diagram can be used to illustrate the multilevel nature of a corporate planning structure.*

Tactical

In general terms, a tactical plan describes how a strategic plan is to be implemented. A tactical plan consists of a series of activities for achieving strategic goals. These activities involve shorter time frames than strategic plans. In addition, tactical plans generally are designed for implementation at middle-management levels.

Tactical plans also provide an additional level of detail to strategic plans. For example, tactical planning statements for a CIS department are supported by information such as schedules for implementing application development projects, figures on the availability and distribution of resources, and delivery schedules for hardware and software purchases.

Operational

An operational plan is concerned with specific tasks by which tactical activities are implemented. At this level, planning activities often include the development of alternative courses of action. Operational plans usually are developed by floor supervisors, group leaders, or other managers. In addition, it often is feasible to solicit input from and participation of line employees in developing operational plans.

In CIS functions, operational plans can include sections for the analysis group, the programming group, and the production group. In addition, there may be entries reflecting hardware needs, estimates of supplies needed, and projections of personnel requirements.

Budget

A plan is a description of goals and objectives plus the procedures and activities to implement them. A budget describes the resources that are allocated to implement a plan. Like a plan, a budget has several phases that reflect levels of detail and correspond roughly to organizational hierarchies. That is, a budget that supports an operational plan generally is quite detailed. At the operational level, budgets generally are not stated in financial values. Rather, budget items are presented as specific units of work, amounts of space, parts inventories, and so on. At upper levels, budget entries present financial summaries and reflect less detail. Major areas of discussion for budget development include:

- Who develops the budget
- When the budget is produced
- How budget costs are determined
- How responsibility for the budget is allocated
- Capital versus expense considerations.

Who develops the budget. To repeat, budgets are developed at many levels of the organization. Most organizations follow unique sequences of steps for budget development. That is, each organization tends to create its own budget development process. However, common factors can be identified. Employees usually submit some type of request for resources, supplies, or funding to first-line supervisors. These supervisors, or managers, consolidate and summarize pertinent data and submit the results to the succeeding administrative level for review and approval. At each subsequently higher level, budgets may be challenged or amended and returned to the lower level. At the lower level, in turn, employees may defend or "go to bat for" their presentations. In other words, budget development can include a good deal of negotiation, and sometimes some bartering. This activity continues until a completed budget document, which includes financial extensions of labor and resource requests, is approved at the corporate level.

When the budget is produced.   Like planning, budget development is evolutionary. Therefore, even though there are specific periods of formal budget preparation, constant attention should be paid to budgetary concerns. A formal budget document normally is prepared yearly and reviewed and/or updated regularly, perhaps at the end of each quarter. Quarterly updating of budgets commonly occurs in organizations that undergo rapid change, such as those involved in computing industries.

In many organizations, formal budgets are prepared for one-year periods and two or three additional years are budgeted in a forecast mode, usually for capital expenditures. That is, the first year is budgeted on a firm, committed basis, and additional years are projected simply to provide a general framework for the succeeding years. Budgets rarely cover periods of less than one year. However, in highly volatile industries, budgets may be developed with two quarters firm and two quarters in forecast mode. This situation often occurs in CIS functions in which large numbers of contract programmers work on short-term projects.

How budget costs are determined.   A point is stressed throughout this text that the higher the organizational level at which a budget is produced, the more financially oriented the document becomes. At lower levels, budget outlays are stated in terms of amounts of labor, square feet of space, or amounts of analysis or programming. That is, limited financial data are included in budget entries at operational levels. Cost factors are applied at higher levels at which financial considerations are addressed.

How responsibility for the budget is allocated.   As stated previously, budget development involves all levels of an organization. In turn, responsibility for budget preparation and control also is distributed along the lines of management hierarchies. As noted, floor supervisors and group leaders typically state budgets in terms of work units. At upper levels, the work units of operational budgets, especially those concerning labor hours, are presented as dollar amounts, usually through application of standard costs.

Capital versus expense considerations.   Items on budget reports generally fall into one of two categories—capital and expenses. Capital items are nonexpendables such as buildings, modifications to buildings, and large machinery, equipment, or furniture. Major software costs typically are treated as capital expenses. If an application is developed within the organization, the costs of the development project typically are capitalized. If software packages are purchased, either for systems software or applications, the cost of the purchase and of implementation may be treated as a capital expenditure. Often, capital items are designated as having value greater than a specific amount, such as $100, $1,000, or $5,000, that is dictated by the type of industry, machinery, and equipment involved. A characteristic of a capital expense is that the item involved is not consumed during the normal business cycle, but retains a value over an extended time period.

Expense items represent the costs of expendable resources, such as direct labor, supplies, and rent. These items are used up within relatively short periods. Though major software expenditures tend to be capitalized, software packages for microcomputers typically are expensed. Even though a software package will have an extended useful life, the amounts of money involved at this level usually suggest treatment as expenses. An exception might occur if a company spent a substantial sum for a site license for unlimited use of software. Licensing arrangements of this type can involve $10,000 or more. One of the authors is associated with an organization that capitalizes all microcomputer software expenditures above $750.

Expense items are the most dynamic factor in developing budgets. To illustrate, suppose a business has a 30-year mortgage on its facility. For budget purposes, the calculation of this capital item is based on a relatively stable cost factor—the mortgage payment and interest rate. During those 30 years, however, wages certainly will change; and materials and parts costs will change as well. Thus, plan and budget development activities tend to focus upon expense items. For this reason, the remainder of this discussion and the discussions throughout the text emphasize expense item considerations.

Data Requirements for Budgets

In the most basic terms, a budget is a tool for presenting data and information. Of course, these data can be applied by business managers to monitor and control businesses. This principle—that relevant information provides powerful support—also points up the importance of CIS functions for businesses. This section discusses different types of budget entries and the support capabilities they provide. Examples of data items that might be included in a budget are:

- Projected number of employees needed
- Technical management costs
- Distribution of administrative support
- Overhead expense distribution
- Estimated travel needs
- Training needs
- Per diem days associated with travel and training
- Software projects and packages
- Software maintenance needs
- New hardware and hardware upgrades
- Hardware maintenance needs
- Supplies
- Space needs.

Note that the discussions of these items are not concerned with dollar values. During the initial stages of budget development, these items represent a perceived need and are dealt with only as requirements. Costs for budget items generally are applied at the first level of management (and higher levels) within an organization and during later iterations of budget development.

Projected number of employees needed. The amount of staff-time resources represented by a budget entry may take many forms. A budget entry could be a single number that represents the total employees needed to complete a project. Or, this total can be broken down into numbers of employees needed according to job classifications and, further, according to labor hours needed within each classification. In a CIS function, these classifications include data entry operators, computer operators, programmers, analysts, and others.

Budget items in this area also might be presented in relation to various projects that require staff-time resources. This type of request, then, includes specifications for individual application development projects and the ongoing maintenance of existing applications.

Technical management costs. A technical manager participates in project analysis and design, reviews documentation, can write programs and documentation, and supervises analysis and programming activities. A technical manager's time often is budgeted to projects according to estimates of the support required for each project.

Distribution of administrative support. Administrative support for CIS or computing-center activities generally is applied as overhead. There are numerous algorithms for distributing overhead and several standard methods are covered in the next section.

Administrative costs typically are reflected on budget reports in terms of percentages of administrative time needed for projects or defined activities. For example, a budget for a new project might include a request for 15 percent of the total working time of a specific administrator. This method presents a problem, however, because of the nature of administrative work.

It is difficult to identify exactly when an administrator is working on a single, specific project. In fact, a study of managerial work by Henry Mintzberg reveals that as much as half of executive activities last less than nine minutes. Further, Mintzberg found that executives often perform administrative tasks in informal meetings—or even in discussions held during coffee breaks or other non-work periods.

Overhead expense distribution. Another important part of budget projections is the allocation of overhead expenses. Overhead refers to the costs of doing business and includes many implicit expenses such as employee fringe benefits (vacations, health plans, sick pay, and paid holidays).

Many organizations divide overhead into staff-related costs—which include facilities, equipment, and wages—and administrative support. Then, a percentage of total expenses is calculated to represent overhead. The authors are aware of one organization that calculates total overhead at 41 percent for staff-related expenses and 72 percent for administrative expenses. This means that, after all direct expenses have been included, the total budget is increased by 113 percent to cover overhead items.

Estimated travel needs. Travel requests may be stated as a single, overall estimate, a percentage of another budget item (such as training), or as a detailed list of specific travel requirements. Specific requirements might be illustrated with statements such as: four analysts to attend the National Computer Conference in Chicago, four analysts to attend the Telecommunications Conference in San Diego, or one programmer to attend the IFIP conference in Dublin, Ireland.

Travel requirements also include personal transportation for business purposes. Thus, there may be entries that reflect a projection of miles that employees travel in their own automobiles for appropriate reasons.

Training needs.   Training needs usually are stated as numbers of training days. These entries represent days spent by employees attending classes or seminars. Days spent working on projects, even if the work involves training, can be charged directly to the project. Training may be formal or informal, held on site at a college or university, or at an off-site location, such as a convention center or hotel.

Budget entries for training, then, include estimates for costs of seminars and educational sessions, payroll costs for the personnel involved, and the costs of registration at conferences.

Per diem days associated with travel and training.   Per diem entries are stated in terms of the number of support days needed. Per diem refers to allowances for travel and training expenses that are budgeted on an informal, daily basis. It should be noted that employees who attend one-day training seminars may be eligible for a partial day of per diem reimbursement.

Many organizations consider any official off-site activity eligible for per diem reimbursements. In addition, most organizations do not require documentation for expenses that are covered by per diem payments.

Software projects and packages.   Some organizations prepare budget requirements for individual application development projects. In these cases, each item discussed in this section is reflected in a separate entry for each application project. On another level, entire projects for developing or purchasing application software are budgeted in terms of total research and development (or purchase) time and dollars.

Software maintenance needs.   It is important that budgets include support resources for the maintenance of the software assets of an organization. Maintenance may be performed by in-house employees, contract programmers from commercial firms, or through purchases of appropriate, updated versions of software packages.

In addition, situations often arise in which activities that begin as maintenance operations expand into full-fledged application development projects. In these situations, budgets must be revised to reflect this new status—and then compete for approval with other project requests.

New hardware and hardware upgrades. Budgets also must be set up to accommodate new hardware developments, which include upgrades and add-ons to existing equipment. Initially, these requests may be stated in terms of numbers of devices or extensions of capabilities instead of total dollar values. For example, a request may specify 100 microcomputers with specific capabilities or an eight-megabyte increase in primary memory for the central computer.

Hardware maintenance needs. Another important budgetary consideration for any CIS function is the maintenance of computer hardware. This request often involves an annual service agreement for existing devices and for any new devices to be added during a budget period. The agreement may be with a hardware manufacturer, a hardware vendor, or a private maintenance organization, such as TRW, Sorbus, or Control Data Corporation.

Supplies. Budget entries that represent supplies generally are stated in quantitative terms. Examples include the numbers of boxes, sizes, and types of paper; specifications for business forms, such as invoices, payroll checks, and accounts payable checks; and file support needs which include the number of reels of magnetic tape and/or removable disk packs.

Space needs. The space needs of the organization also must be budgeted. These needs are reflected by budget entries for office space for people, space for computing equipment, and space for the storage of supplies.

THE PLANNING CYCLE

Budget development can begin at any of three levels of the organization: strategic (top management), tactical (middle management), or operational (line management). Remember that budgets, in effect, are extensions of plans. The planning cycle corresponds with the cycle of budget development and vice versa. Often, the path traveled by a budget document in receiving approval marks the iterative trail of planning development. The path incorporates a full agenda of planning characteristics and activities, including:

- Top-down model
- Bottom-up model
- Presentation and communication
- Decision and/or adoption
- Review.

Top-Down Model

Top-down planning originates with an idea or goal at the top level of an organization. Plans conceived at the top level are disseminated as a basis for lower-level planning activities. Top-level decisions may take the form of formal documents or informal comments. In either case, the top-level plan marks a beginning point for the planning cycle and motivates planning on a tactical level. An example of documentation containing budgeting guidelines is presented in the memo in Figure 4-2.

For example, top management might inform middle management that a 15 percent increase in production is expected for the next fiscal year. Middle managers then produce a tactical plan which must be approved by top managers. Suppose this plan includes a proposal for the opening of an additional manufacturing line. This proposal is reviewed by top management and is either approved or sent back for modifications. Upon approval by top management, the tactical plan is sent to line management for expansion into an operational specification.

Carrying the example further, line management creates a preliminary plan for achieving the tactical objectives of middle management. To add a line to the production facility, line managers create a list of people, equipment, and other resources required. Another feedback/review cycle is required, and consultation and modification meetings are held between middle and line management.

Feedback and review continues among managers at all three levels until a workable plan has been developed and approved. This is not to imply that all levels must view the plan as the best or most acceptable. Rather, a workable plan must be developed that satisfies the requirements at all three management levels.

MEMORANDUM

DATE: April 15, 19xx

TO: D. L. Fry, N. B. Arnold

FROM: Esther Producto

RE: NEXT FISCAL YEAR BUDGET PLANNING GUIDELINES

The information presented below should be used as a basis for the budgeting and planning you will do for the next Fiscal Year. This first cut is intended to give you an opportunity to suggest revisions to the guidelines. Please present your recommendations to me not later than two weeks from today. I will issue the final guidelines one week later.

The schedule for preparation of the budget is:

Today	First cut guidelines
2 weeks	Guideline revision recommendations from managers to Producto
3 weeks	Final budget guidelines
4 weeks	First round of budget inputs from managers to Producto
5 weeks	Feedback and suggestions from Producto
6 weeks	Second round of budget inputs from managers to Producto
7 weeks	Budget ready for review by Producto
8th week	Review with Producto by managers.

ASSUMPTIONS AND FORECASTS

A. General Computing

   1. The general compute load will be plus or minus 5 percent of the current Fiscal Year load.

   2. Self-service (remote) printing experiment will begin during the second quarter.

   3. Fifty (50) microcomputers will be placed into service.

   4. Total terminals in service will reach 900.

   5. An operations supervisor will be hired during the first quarter.

Figure 4-2. *This memo demonstrates a suitable method for communicating budgeting guidelines to all levels within an organization. The memo continues on the facing page.*

6. The Systems Programming Group will add a full-time person to specialize in microcomputers during the first quarter.

B. Text Processing

1. We will upgrade the Operating System by the end of the first quarter.

2. The Brand Y computer will be netted together with the Brand X computer.

3. The peak hour demand for service that is now 110 concurrent users will grow to 135 concurrent users.

4. There will be a 30 percent rate reduction, fueling the demand.

5. Training will include continued beginning courses and also more advanced courses.

6. Improvements in file backups and in archiving will be achieved.

C. Electronic Mail

1. Total support will be about 1.5 full-time employees.

2. Of the support, 80 percent will be for maintenance activities.

3. Of the support, 20 percent will be for enhancements and development.

4. This activity will be supported by Corporate overhead funds.

D. Business Office

1. Ed Brady (retiring) will be replaced by a microcomputer to do accounts payable, inventory management, depreciation analysis, and insurance reporting.

2. Further automating of the accounting functions will be supported by one full-time employee programmer.

E. Applications Support

1. The Information Center will operate at a level closer to current Fiscal Year hours than the budget.

2. The Information Center will concentrate on desk consulting and documentation.

3. The Applications Support management effort will operate at a level closer to the current Fiscal Year actual hours than the budget.

F. Engineering Services

1. We will RETIRE 50 old, hard to maintain, terminals.

2. Staffing will be at the same level as the current Fiscal Year.

Figure 4-2 (concluded). *This is the conclusion of a memo on budgeting guidelines.*

Bottom-Up Model

The impetus for plans also may originate at operational levels of the organization. Under this model, iterative cycles of review, feedback, and approval still are required before a final version is produced. But the idea or goal of the plan originates in user departments. For example, because of their "hands-on experience," line managers or engineers often devise improvements in production activities or services. These ideas are presented to supervisory personnel for study and approval and may mark the beginning point of planning cycles.

Presentation and Communication

Because plans must be presented and understood at many organizational levels, open lines of communication among levels are critical to planning projects. Communications may be informal, such as in conversations in hallways, over lunch, or as part of phone calls. As stated previously, inputs to plan preparation can come from many sources.

However, there also are points in the process where formal communication is required. For example, suppose a CIS director is preparing a budget proposal for the coming fiscal year. The director sends a memo to CIS section supervisors and requests projections of requirements for each section. In effect, the director is gathering source data. Additional data may result from projections of needs produced by user departments.

The source data are combined or summarized to produce an initial version of the budget. Because of decisions or compromises made in consolidating diverse inputs, this document may modify the requirements supplied by section or user managers. When the budget is completed, the director meets with his or her manager to discuss its content, item by item. Although a written document exists, the discussion is informal and can help to identify problem areas.

In many cases, budgets are presented formally to review groups or committees. These presentations normally occur at points of consolidation in the planning cycle. That is, the CIS director in the above example would be required to present the budget to a management committee before approval is granted.

Decision and/or Adoption

Decisions and adoptions of plans and/or budgets seldom occur until after several iterations of the planning cycle. That is, the budget report prepared by the CIS director must be approved at the succeeding level of the organization. At this level, the power of approval often lies with a controller. Further modifications may be necessary before approval is granted. In fact, several cycles may be necessary, particularly if budget requests are new or controversial.

As the plan evolves further, the controller may use the CIS budget request as input for tactical planning. The CIS budget may be combined with reports from other departments, such as general accounting, accounts payable, or accounts receivable; and a tactical plan or budget is produced. Then another approval is required, from a higher level—and gaining approval may require several more modifications and feedback/review cycles.

Although this process may seem tedious and repetitive, many managers feel it is the most efficient and powerful method available for developing effective plans. With each iteration, the plan moves toward a version that is acceptable to all of the many parties involved. Final approval, then, rests with top management. The final version usually is documented formally, with each functional area receiving only the portion that pertains to its particular function.

Review

Chapter 1 presents a discussion of the managerial capabilities provided by budgets. That is, actual performance can be compared with projections in a budget for the purpose of identifying successes or failures in meeting projections. Thus, budget reviews can increase management capabilities. In addition, there may be merit to the historical perspective gained from reviewing completed budget development projects. But such reviews are not intrinsic to planning or budgeting processes. For the purposes of this text, then, budget reviews are discussed only to provide an overview of plans and budgets. Reviews are not covered extensively throughout the remainder of this text.

CASE SCENARIO: PROFESSIONAL CONFERENCE

To reinforce the discussion of the planning cycle, the case scenario that follows presents a top-down evolution of planning activities.

Description of Requirements

The board of directors of a major professional society has decided to hold a series of technical conferences. The themes of the conferences are to center around vertical markets in which members of the society have expressed interest. This decision becomes the basis for a strategic planning statement: The board of directors proposes, in the interest of serving its members, to sponsor a series of technical conferences based on relevant themes.

Initially, the project involves a feasibility study and report. The directors appoint a planning committee, either from a group of volunteers or from the administrative staff employed by the organization. The planning committee, in effect, is responsible for developing a tactical plan for the conferences. That is, the committee is to produce a planning statement that provides enough information for the board to make an informed decision about whether to hold the conferences. This process requires several cycles of feedback and review between the board and the committee. At some point, the board either approves the project and the focus of committee work shifts to the production and publishing of a tactical plan, or the project is cancelled.

The initial study involves measuring member interest in the conferences. To make this determination, the planning committee might prepare a questionnaire for members. The questionnaire is designed to provide some indication of the amount of interest in the conferences, geographic areas in which interest is high, and topics in which members are interested.

The results are presented to the board at an initial feasibility meeting. Suppose the board decides that the questionnaire results are insufficient to begin operational plans, but sufficient to warrant further study. The planning committee is instructed to conduct further research, concentrating on non-members in the geographic areas in which member interest is high. Thus, another iteration of feedback and review is initiated.

At the same time, the planning committee is combining questionnaire results with other data derived from studies of potential sites (hotels, convention halls, etc.), the types of exhibits that fall within areas of expressed interest, fee structures for attendance and booth spaces, and promotional avenues for the conferences.

After another presentation, the board is satisfied that there is sufficient interest among members and non-members to warrant the project. The planning committee is given approval to proceed. The next step in this process is to produce and publish a tactical planning statement. This statement outlines processes for local management of conferences, defines parameters for exhibitors and exhibits, provides a list of recommended sites, describes specific areas of interest, outlines a general promotional campaign, and produces a price structure for exhibits, attendance, and advertising space in conference directories.

Tactical Requirements

At this point, the activities of the planning committee center on two topics: determining conference sites and defining a local management structure for the conferences. The planning committee chooses and gains approval for 12 sites throughout the country. Exact locations of these sites are not critical to the immediate discussion. Obviously, the conferences are held in major cities with appropriate support facilities, such as hotels, convention sites, transportation, and so on.

The planning committee also proposes to delegate local management of conferences to conference steering committees (CSC) at each location. The CSCs are to be comprised of local volunteers (including members and non-members of the association) and support staff from the administrative office of the association. The planning committee will appoint appropriate persons to CSC positions.

There is a change here in the role of the planning committee. Moving away from a pure planning perspective, the focus of the committee now centers on supervising the activities and summarizing data input from the local CSCs. That is, the planning committee now becomes a standing oversight committee, and shall be referred to as such throughout the remainder of this case example.

Operational Specifications

Another feedback and review cycle begins between the oversight committee and the CSC. That is, a CSC prepares proposals concerning specific areas of activity and submits them to the oversight committee for approval. Areas of research delegated to the CSCs include:

- The technical program
- The keynote
- Special activities
- Professional development tutorials
- Local promotion
- Identification of local staff volunteers
- Conference operations.

Because these topics relate to the Case Discussion/Assignment presented at the end of the chapter, they are elaborated upon in the section below.

The technical program.   The primary purpose of the technical program is to provide an opportunity for attendees to expand their knowledge of recent technological developments. Each CSC is to design its own program, subject to the areas of local interest and availability of appropriate speakers. Activities involved in the design of technical programs include the definition of a conference theme (which should be supplemented by conference promotions); location of speakers, panelists, and authors of papers for presentation; collection and qualification of relevant papers; and the coordination and publication of a program of conference proceedings.

The keynote.   Each CSC also is responsible for identifying an outstanding individual to make a keynote presentation. This presentation sets the tone, or theme, of conference activities. The keynote address, then, should be made by an outstanding expert with a recognized name. The session at which the keynote speech is delivered usually is scheduled for the beginning of the conference. At the same session, then, it is customary for a session or conference chairperson to present a short pitch for the educational program, a statement about the exhibits, and awards presentations for outstanding performances by industry professionals.

Special activities.   This designation usually is applied to the social and interpersonal activities that are part of every professional conference. Special activities might include mixer receptions to increase peer interaction and ongoing film, slide, and video presentations about current and developing technologies.

Professional development tutorials.   Often, a professional or scientific meeting highlights key current developments in its field or discipline by inviting prestigious leaders to lecture about topics on which they have special expertise. Such sessions offer learning experiences at depths greater than are available in the regular educational sessions. A CSC might choose to design and present a series of tutorial sessions of this type.

Local promotion.   In the early stages of the project, the planning committee measured member interest in the conference. This interest, though, is of no value unless members and others are aware of when conferences are being held and how to register. Thus, CSCs will need to use local promotion resources such as radio, newspapers, and direct mail to reach potential attendees. CSCs design the promotional campaigns because of their familiarity with local resources.

Identification of local staff volunteers.   An important support function at the conference is performed by volunteer staff workers. These workers are needed for such tasks as crowd control, registration packet stuffing, staffing information booths, monitoring educational sessions, and acting as messengers to conference committees. Each CSC is responsible for identifying, training, and supervising a team of local volunteers. The volunteers may be recruited from local chapters of the professional association, local educational institutions, and other sources.

Conference operations.   The responsibility for conference operations is assigned to a subcommittee. The conference operations committee plays a supervisory role in the assignment of office space, allocation of space for educational sessions, coordination of audio-visual equipment, coordination of volunteer services, and registration procedures.

Operational Plan

Each CSC is responsible for all of the above activities. Each produces an operational plan for its conference as a product of these activities. Recall that an operational plan presents specific activities to reach a stated objective. Thus, plans for the technical program, keynote address, local promotion, and so on encompass an operational plan. The tactical plan, then, is produced by combining and summarizing the operational plans of all subcommittees of the steering committee. The tactical plan is again subject to approval of the board of directors.

Of course, plans produced by CSCs are subject to the approval of the oversight committee. So the oversight committee is indirectly responsible for location selection, determination of conference dates, acquisition of contracts for exhibit halls, and so on. The oversight committee supports any action which is approved at its level. However, as the previous section points out, the actual performance of most of these activities is delegated to the local steering committees. For this reason, the oversight committee chooses one of its members to serve as liaison between the oversight and steering committees. In addition, the oversight committee, with approval of the board, appoints a general chairman for each conference. A general chairman is needed because the steering committees often are divided into individual subcommittees that cover specific topics.

Case Discussion/Assignment

Assume that the Data Processing Management Association (DPMA) is planning a national conference in your area or in a major metropolitan area nearby. You are asked to serve on the local steering committee to make arrangements for the convention. The convention program includes the presentation of exhibits by software/hardware vendors and also involves about 50 technical/professional sessions on hardware, software, systems analysis, and management. Consult your instructor or a local library to gather background information about the DPMA and the needs of its members. Then, develop a plan of work for soliciting and screening professionals who may be interested in participating in the conference. That is, you are to find vendors who would be interested in preparing exhibits for the conference and qualified professionals to give seminars and educational sessions. Remember, you are working at an operational level. Your plan should be specific and detailed—but need not present financial information.

Discussion Topics

1. What is the difference between expense items and capital items on financial budgets?

2. An operational-level budget report usually contains limited financial information. Why?

3. Describe the bottom-up model of planning evolution.

4. Explain what is meant by the statement: The top-down planning model is very common in organizations, although it is not always formal.

5. Why is planning described as a cyclical activity?

5

SELECTING SYSTEMS PROJECTS

Abstract

CIS planning takes place within an environment defined by corporate culture. Systems projects are the point at which a CIS function interfaces with its environment. Thus, the selection and management of systems projects and user requirements are interdependent within organizations. In effect, user requirements, in the form of application specifications, drive CIS functions. Compelling arguments can be made for the establishment of formal or semi-formal project selection methodologies. Project selection activities should be performed with a recognition of the service-oriented nature of CIS activities. In effect, user satisfaction with systems projects is one indicator of the success of CIS activities.

INTRODUCTION

One of the most demanding activities in CIS planning involves selecting projects for development and implementation. The volume of project requests in many organizations exceeds the capabilities of its CIS function. Thus, a methodology is needed to support effective prioritization and selection of projects for development and implementation. Methods vary among organizations. However, most successful methods seem to be those in which final approval for selection lies outside of the CIS function itself.

Several selection methods are discussed throughout this chapter. Selection methods, however, are contingent upon the way costs of CIS services are accounted for within the organization. Therefore, as background to the discussions of selection methods in this chapter, this initial section presents a brief summary of methods for financing CIS services. In Chapter 2, the three standard financing methods are introduced: chargeback, pie slicing, and overhead.

Chargeback Method

Under the chargeback method, standard fees for each CIS service are determined according to a billing algorithm. For organizations in which the chargeback method is used, project selection is facilitated by the capability to make uniform predictions of project costs through use of values established by the billing algorithm. Realistic planning also is encouraged because of the implicit recognition that the costs of development will be applied to the budget of the using department.

Pie-Slicing Method

The pie-slicing method allocates costs according to percentages of CIS services provided to each user department. That is, if 30 percent of CIS services are delivered to the accounts receivable department, then 30 percent of total CIS costs are charged to accounts receivable. The same percentages can be used as a basis for distributing development resources—the basis of project selection. A problem arises, however, in that this method prohibits new users from receiving CIS support. Therefore, some type of prioritization method is needed. Usually, responsibility for priority setting is assigned to a steering committee composed of high-level executives from a cross section of user groups.

Overhead Method

Some organizations treat all CIS services as part of the overhead involved in doing business. In such organizations, user requests may be selected more for political than economic reasons. A steering committee often assigns priorities to project requests and makes selections based on these priorities.

Regardless of financing method, most selection methods involve prioritizing project requests. Selection and prioritizing methods are discussed in the section that follows.

REASONS FOR INITIATING APPLICATION SYSTEMS PROJECTS

CIS departments tend to be demand driven. That is, CIS services are provided in response to expressed needs of user organizations. The reasons, or motivations, for systems projects can provide background support to guide project selection. The next section examines the reasons for initiating application systems projects—regardless of whether the projects are initiated by top management, a specific function or department, the CIS function itself, or other sources. Included in this discussion are systems projects initiated in response to demands created by:

- Organizational needs
- Environmental needs
- Developments in technology
- Growth in education and experience.

Organizational Needs

Many application systems projects result from changes in existing needs or development of new needs within organizations. Changes can be motivated by evolutionary factors, external pressures, strategic considerations, and so on. The discussion that follows presents a number of factors for change within business organizations. Of course, the reasons for change are countless and their full scope certainly is beyond the requirements of this discussion. Some of the major factors that drive change within organizations include:

- Growth
- Changes in objectives
- New products, services, or markets
- Change in operations
- Personnel changes

- Operational bottlenecks
- Opportunities to increase efficiency.

Growth.   One of the most common reasons for change is organizational growth. New needs are created as customer acceptance of a product grows and as the number of products offered by a business also increases. Application systems projects that are initiated to support organizational growth usually involve the revision and expansion of existing systems.

As an organization grows, data storage needs increase. Information processing volume also increases. Some of these problems can be solved by acquiring new and/or expanded hardware. However, other types of growth-related opportunities require modifications to existing programs and the addition of new software.

Systems projects that support growth generally enjoy a high priority. These projects often are essential to the day-to-day operations of a business, as well as to its continued growth.

Changes in objectives.   The goals and objectives of organizations usually remain relatively stable. However, when goal-related changes do occur, modifications or additions to information services often are required. These requests address the elements of newly formulated plans for achieving the organization's new goals and objectives.

New products, services, or markets.   Any time a new product or service is slated for production, or a new market is targeted, new demands are created for information services. Consider this example. In the early 1980s, banks began to offer their depositors a new service, interactive banking. To provide this service, banks installed automated teller machines (ATM) at branch offices. The service was received well and was expanded to include locations such as college campuses, retail stores, and airports.

Project teams responsible for providing these services faced many important considerations, which included maintaining the integrity and security of data. Projects such as these usually are given high priorities by CIS functions.

Changes in operations.   Operational changes within organizations often create new needs for systems projects. Consider again the above example. Traditionally, customers went into banks and stood in line until a teller was available. Customers often had to wait in line for unacceptable time periods. Computers provided some relief: Terminals were installed at teller stations. Drive-up windows, also with terminals, were set up. The idea was to provide more timely service by providing tellers with interactive capabilities and by improving the response time for inquiries.

The introduction of ATMs created needs for data communication capabilities. Competition among banks led to a corresponding need for 24-hour service in some cases. All these changes in operations, then, led to modifications of existing applications and developments of new applications.

Personnel changes. Application system projects frequently result from changes in personnel. Suppose a department or function manager has come to rely on a particular report that supports a specific assignment. If this manager is moved to another position, he or she may request similar capabilities for the new assignment.

These requests often are described as modifications to existing systems. The manager may request that the report be modified to meet the requirements of the new assignment. CIS management and evaluation teams must approach these requests with special care. A simple modification of existing report capabilities may not produce the desired results. In addition, modifications may render the report unacceptable for the original purpose.

Operational bottlenecks. As a company matures, bottlenecks may appear in certain areas of its operational activities. Many of these problems can be solved with automated devices. The development and implementation of these solutions, however, may require a systems development project for support. Project requests of this type should by reviewed and analyzed carefully, since the request actually may be only a symptom of a deeper problem.

Opportunities to increase efficiency. One of the simplest projects to prioritize stems from a perceived opportunity to increase the efficiency of a system or operation. These projects differ from project requests directed toward solving specific problems. A request for a project designed to increase efficiency should be supported by a detailed description of the existing operation and the improvements offered by the new methods. These presentations provide valuable inputs to the analysis activities that follow.

An attraction of this category of project request is that management will usually support any soundly based effort that will cut costs and/or enhance productivity.

Environmental Needs

Many projects are initiated in response to external, or environmental, demands. Such demands typically stem from two major sources:

- Competition

- Regulation or legislation.

Competition.   Systems or application development projects often are required to respond to changing conditions created by competition. Information services support the entire organization; and the organization, as a whole, must keep pace with the market. Remember the example of the bank providing customer services through interactive ATMs. A bank that declines to implement an ATM system may lose customers to banks that do provide this service.

Often, the development of such an application system becomes crucial to an organization's ability to meet or beat its competition. Information services also are crucial to the support of decision-making activities. Competitive factors often create situations in which innovative and timely courses of action are needed. The extent of CIS support may determine how well an organization can deal with these situations.

Regulation or legislation.   Application systems projects also are generated by other external forces, which include local, state, and federal governments. A change in tax laws, for example, may create new processing needs and/or additional requirements for information to support decision making.

In addition, many industries are subject to government control. For example, the makers of certain pharmaceuticals must comply with Food and Drug Administration (FDA) regulations; and airlines are governed by the Federal Aviation Agency (FAA). When such regulations are present, information systems include control mechanisms to ensure operations do not exceed or deviate from government specifications. Failure to comply may mean heavy fines or even the closure of the business.

Developments In Technology

Another reason for which projects are initiated encompasses both internal and external considerations. Technological developments are one of the most prevalent motivations for project requests. This discussion considers technological developments in terms of:

- Hardware

- Software.

Hardware. Developments in computer technology may lead to requests for new systems projects. For example, consider the changes that have occurred in data storage media. Originally, punched cards were used to store data. Punched cards gave way to magnetic tape and magnetic disk storage. These changes led to the conversion of data handling operations from batch modes to direct access orientations.

Hardware development is driven by many factors, one of which is the tendency for hardware to become less costly and to offer increased processing capabilities at the same time. That is, hardware continues to become less expensive to acquire and maintain. The economic benefits often are not readily stated in terms of dollars-and-cents returns on investments; but the benefits offered by hardware developments usually merit study and analysis.

In business organizations, acquisition of new and/or upgraded hardware usually motivates the development of additional applications or the modification of existing applications. As users become aware of capabilities that are bigger, faster, or newer than what exists, users find ways of implementing these capabilities. Usually, the requests quickly exceed the new capabilities. This drives additional hardware development and the acquisition of additional hardware on the part of organizations. There is a saying within computing industries that sums up the situation: "The work always expands to exceed available resources."

Software. The evolution of software also has seen dramatic changes. As software capabilities are developed and improved, systems projects are initiated that reflect these capabilities. For example, the introduction of direct-access capabilities created demands to modify batch processing systems. Inventory control systems and airline reservation systems were among the first to benefit. As software continued to feature efficiency improvements, users demanded additional capabilities. On-line or interactive applications still are in high demand, as is evident especially in the automated teller systems implemented by most banks.

In the late 1970s and early 1980s, a significant software development was the shift from procedural to non-procedural programming languages. Non-procedural languages provide capabilities by which nontechnical users can develop applications with statements and commands that closely resemble natural language. As these languages expand capabilities for increasing numbers of users, new and/or modified applications result.

Growth In Education and Experience

Many requests for new or revised applications result from the increased sophistication of systems users. That is, as users become more comfortable and skilled with computers, they think of new and better ways to use them. Skilled users sometimes are said to possess a degree of computer literacy. Computer literacy is a product of two factors: education and experience.

The level of education of users is a factor that affects CIS functions. Users with a comprehensive working knowledge of computer capabilities tend to request advanced capabilities and applications. That is, these users know what they want and how that service can be provided. CIS functions that are driven by this type of request are faced with a challenge. In effect, they must provide service to the most demanding and discriminating of users. Remember the point made in an earlier section, that user satisfaction is one indication of the success of a CIS function.

In addition, user experience with computers increases computer literacy. That is, users of computers receive "hands-on" training that is reflected in their ongoing requests for applications. CIS functions and planning managers should be aware that, as users become familiar with a system, their demands probably will increase and become more sophisticated.

With experience, CIS specialists also become more sophisticated in solving business problems. CIS personnel may discover opportunities for new applications or modifications to existing applications and present these opportunities to users. If users respond favorably, systems projects may be initiated.

PROJECT SELECTION

Project selection should be directed toward measuring the appropriateness of project requests and should avoid bottlenecks caused by overly detailed cost and benefit analyses. Since project requests often initiate at the corporate level, one way to screen requests is to evaluate projects in light of strategic corporate goals. In this way, priorities can be established for approving CIS development projects; and a balanced portfolio of applications can be developed and maintained.

In some cases, CIS projects can be approved without undergoing formal screening. Some projects require only limited organizational resources and affect single organizational units. These projects might be acted upon independently. Some of these projects, however, may require screening and development resources from the CIS departments. If this occurs, the CIS function may fail to provide effective support to the overall organization. Formal selection methods that incorporate the goals of the organization are required.

Steering Committee

Many organizations establish steering committees that evaluate systems projects and set priorities for development. These committees usually are made up of middle- and top-level managers. Members of such committees should carry organizational positions and personal reputations sufficient to assure respect for decisions reached. That is, the membership of the steering committee should be respected sufficiently so that management is willing to invest large sums to support their recommendations.

Conversely, committee members should make the commitment necessary to dispel any questions about the validity of their recommendations. Committee members should serve willingly and should avoid any inference that their activities represent some sort of necessary evil. Committee members should be aware that steering committees can fail and should conduct themselves accordingly.

Steering committees often are set up to evaluate application requests on a one-time basis, such as at the beginning of a planning period. However, many organizations increase the effectiveness of steering committees by having them meet for regular progress evaluations throughout the planning period.

Steering committees offer an advantage in that systems project requests can be reviewed by a group that consists of user, non-user, and CIS representatives. Under this method, priorities can be based upon the merits of a project and the strategic goals of the organization. Notice that political considerations are minimized because multiple viewpoints are considered. In addition, the CIS function participates in, but is not given authority to make, final decisions.

PROCEDURE	STRENGTHS	WEAKNESSES
SIMPLE RANKING	• Fast solution possible • Tends to provide a solution focused on key issues as interpreted by dominant participants • Full capture of information (voice tones, facial expressions, etc.) • Greatest likelihood for synergy	• Many participants may fail to express certain ideas or views • Domination by certain participants may occur
WEIGHTED CRITERIA	• Wider perspective • Less influence by dominant participants	• Slower procedure • Failure by some to express ideas or views • Some loss of synergy
DELPHI TECHNIQUE	• Provides the widest perspective • Full range of ideas or views • No chance for participant domination • Highest likelihood of innovative solution	• Slowest procedure • Difficulty in focusing or redirecting attention • No chance for synergy

Figure 5-1. *This table identifies and compares three approaches to the setting of priorities for the allocation of resources to systems development projects. Strengths and weaknesses are identified for each of three techniques: simple ranking, weighted criteria, and review under the Delphi technique.*

Priority Setting

Project selection is performed effectively by consensus. That is, final selection authority rests with a majority vote of a specific group, instead of with an individual. Project requests are reviewed and prioritized individually by group or committee members. Then, individual priority schemes are combined and summarized to derive the collective priorities of the group.

There are several ways to set priorities for proposed application systems projects. Three methods are presented in Figure 5-1 and discussed in the section that follows.

Any method used to evaluate projects should begin with a general review of the strategic plan of the organization. It is imperative that conflict be avoided between approved projects and organizational goals and objectives.

The evaluation team then reviews the organizational budget, or the portion affected by the project under consideration. Common evaluation methods include:

- Simple ranking

- Weighted criteria

- Delphi technique.

Simple ranking. The simple ranking method is perhaps the easiest to implement. Under this method, a team of evaluators is appointed. Each evaluator is given copies of project requests under consideration. The packages are ranked from most important to least important by each evaluator. These evaluations can be done independently, or without a meeting of the entire team. It may be better, however, for the team to meet and discuss the requests before ranking them. In some organizations, formal presentations for each request are made by the users initiating the requests.

This method provides a mechanism for the expedient evaluation and ranking of projects, particularly if the team meets to perform the ranking. Meetings usually provide advantages regardless of the purpose of the meeting. That is, a group of people working together can accomplish more than the same number of people working separately. Therefore, evaluation meetings are enhanced by face-to-face discussions involving multiple parties.

There also are drawbacks to this method, however. A team meeting may be dominated by the most effective public speaker or by members who are higher up in organizational or social hierarchies. More conservative or reserved members may not participate as fully as they should.

Weighted criteria. Setting priorities according to weighted criteria is a structured, slower form of simple ranking. However, this method may add a degree of objectivity to the evaluation process. Under this method, a formal set of quantitative criteria is established as a basis for evaluating projects. These criteria usually are set by consensus at a meeting of the evaluation team and represent elements that motivate project selection.

For example, separate criteria might be established for such factors as the relevance of the project to corporate goals, the potential return on costs of development and implementation, and so on. Then, the project team assigns weight factors to criteria that represent their perceived importance in the selection process.

Next, a range of values is established that represents the degrees to which criteria are met. For example, team members may be instructed to assign values from 1 to 10, with 1 being best and 10 being worst, to represent how well projects meet criteria. By definition, the number 1 can be either most or least important and sets the base of the evaluation range.

In effect, team members place scores on projects. That is, if five criteria are chosen, five values are given to each project by all team members. Individual scores are multiplied by factors that represent the weight given to criteria by the evaluation team. Thus, the evaluation team's perception of the importance of each project is reflected in the scores.

The weighted-criteria method suffers from some of the same weaknesses as simple ranking, especially in the early stages of establishing criteria and weight factors. The quiet or reserved members of the team still may be reluctant to express ideas and views. Even the most reserved members, though, are willing to express their opinions of projects on ranking questionnaires.

Delphi technique.   Under the Delphi technique, a number of people perform repeated evaluations of projects, submit comments after each evaluation, and continue until a consensus is reached. This evaluation method provides for a broad-based review of a project. Because of the repeated evaluations, it also takes longer to reach a decision on the priorities of the submitted projects.

The extended time frame for evaluation makes it impractical for a committee using this method to meet for extensive face-to-face discussions. Thus, even the most timid members of the committee usually supply input. With each additional evaluation, the individual priorities of members tend to become more congruous. At some point, a meeting may be called to resolve a few remaining decisions and to determine final priority schemes.

Under the Delphi technique, however, there is significant difficulty in dispensing relevant information among committee members. The independent ranking process inhibits members from sharing specialized knowledge with other members. In addition, if the attention of members begins to stray to unwarranted areas or activities, it is difficult to get the team back on track.

Management Style

Selection processes in CIS functions are affected by management styles. Even within steering committees, a leader or manager of the evaluation team usually is chosen or appointed. Thus, the nature of management largely can

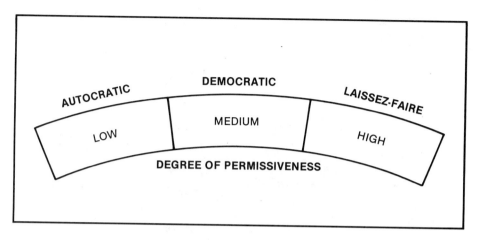

Figure 5-2. *This diagram shows the spectrum of management styles applied to oversight of systems development projects—autocratic, democratic, and laissez-faire—and indicates the degree of permissiveness associated with each.*

determine what method of prioritization is implemented, how members perform their tasks, how opinions are expressed, and to what extent opinions are shared. Figure 5-2 presents a diagram that represents the spectrum of management styles and the degrees of permissiveness for each. There are three general management styles and they are described as:

- Autocratic
- Democratic
- Laissez-faire.

Autocratic. Autocratic management style is characterized by a strong, often dominant, leader. In fact, a parallel often is drawn between autocratic managers and political dictators. The leader makes the majority of the decisions with little or no effective input from subordinates. Figure 5-3 illustrates the flow of information under an autocratic form of leadership.

Under an autocratic manager, communications are essentially downward. The leader makes decisions and delegates responsibility for implementing the decisions.

The effect of an autocratic management style on the prioritizing of application systems project requests can be dramatic. For instance, an autocratic team leader may direct and influence the process to satisfy personal biases, often without regard for stated CIS or corporate goals.

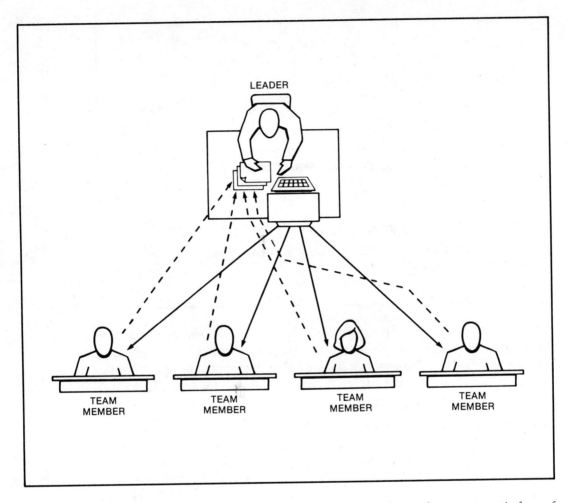

Figure 5-3. *This diagram traces the flow of information under an autocratic form of leadership for the systems development process.*

Democratic.   The democratic management style often is referred to as participative. Democratic managers strive to treat decision making as a group process. That is, all members of evaluation teams are encouraged to provide input to decision-making activities. Figure 5-4 shows lines of communication under democratic management. Under this type of management, liberal policies govern communication; and information may flow upward, downward, and horizontally throughout a CIS function or evaluation team. Democratic managers act as coordinators, or monitors, and allow subordinates, in effect, to govern themselves.

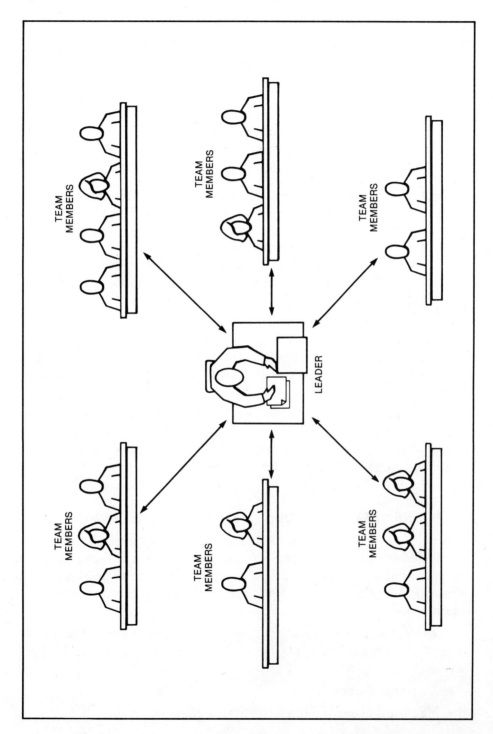

Figure 5-4. *This diagram traces lines of communication that follow the democratic approach to supervision.*

There are many ways of implementing democratic management and varying degrees to which participation of subordinates is encouraged. A manager or administrator may delegate the establishing of priorities and implement decisions made by consensus of team members. Or, a manager may solicit extensive input from team members and set priorities that reflect this input. Most democratic managers lean more toward the latter model. Of course, the manager always retains ultimate authority and responsibility for decision-making and project-selection processes.

Laissez-faire. The laissez-faire style of management is the most permissive of the three. Decision-making authority is delegated individually to members of project teams. Managers who implement this technique tend to become consultants, or sources of information, for subordinates. Communication flows through the manager, but information is shared extensively. Figure 5-5 presents a diagram of the flow of information under this type of model.

Laissez-faire management is not conducive to the setting of priorities for project selection, especially when projects affect multiple and competing functions of the organization. One of the primary purposes of this management style is to allow team members to establish and follow their individual priorities. In addition, a manager effectively abdicates authority and responsibility for project control.

This management style works best for situations in which individuals are expected to work independently on tasks that require personal initiative and knowledge. Professionals that respond well to laissez-faire management include research scientists, teachers, and sales persons.

REPRESENTATIVE PROJECT SELECTION CRITERIA

Regardless of selection method, CIS functions usually evaluate projects according to some type of criteria. Criteria may be stated formally and given weight, or may just take the form of the most important topics discussed in evaluation meetings. As stated previously, criteria are factors for consideration upon which decisions are based.

There are many criteria for evaluating application systems project requests. Common factors that often are established as selection criteria include:

- Economic benefit
- Master plan compatibility
- Project risks
- Required resources.

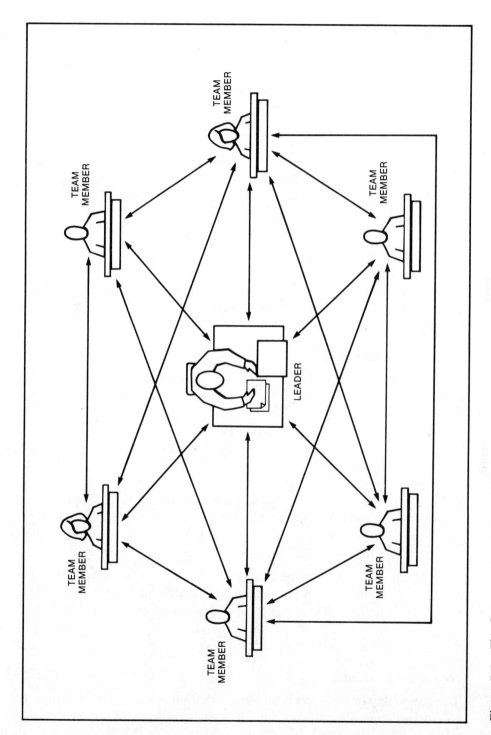

Figure 5-5. This diagram traces the flow of information under the laissez-faire method for supervision of systems development activities.

Economic Benefit

Projects that are selected for development and implementation may incur substantial costs. A common selection criterion involves evaluating costs in light of expected benefits. This is perhaps the most common and important criterion used in CIS functions. In some cases, cost/benefit analyses seem to be the only factor considered by evaluation teams. That is, if a project cannot be shown as having a potential dollar benefit, evaluation activities cease.

This thinking can be a drawback, since some projects provide significant intangible benefits that should be considered. To illustrate, a sales manager may request that a message be added to each invoice summarizing year-to-date purchases and thanking the customer for this business. It would be impossible to justify such a change on the basis of traditional return-on-investment criteria. However, customer goodwill well might override purely financial considerations.

Obviously, if a legal or regulatory requirement mandates development of a given report or addition of information to an existing document, financial considerations are not a factor.

Master Plan Compatibility

To repeat an important point: CIS planning takes place in an environment defined by the long- and short-range goals of the organization. Most CIS functions evaluate projects in relation to the overall corporate goals. This evaluation often is performed during initial stages of selection processes. Projects that conflict with corporate goals usually are scrapped.

Project Risks

Risk is an important factor for evaluating systems projects. In simple terms, a risk is a chance that the project may fail. If a project fails, funds will have been expended for which there is no return. Many evaluation teams consider the costs of failure as well as success.

Many project teams define risk as the degree of difficulty presented by a project. Difficult projects require significant amounts of resources to implement. Sometimes difficulty is perceived in areas that are not understood fully by project teams. Evaluation teams should strive to become as informed and knowledgeable as possible before making risk evaluations.

Required Resources

The availability of resources is another important selection criterion. Levels of existing hardware, software, and personnel available for implementing a project must be considered. This is especially true when a project under consideration calls for new hardware or software. The evaluation must determine if the capabilities cannot be provided by existing resources. Also, a project selected for implementation may involve man-years of effort. Evaluation teams should be certain that necessary personnel are available for slated tasks.

EVALUATION ALTERNATIVES

In addition to these common criteria for project selection, many secondary factors affect evaluation of system alternatives. For example, an evaluation team may decide that a project fits into corporate goals and provides sufficient cost/benefit performance, only to find that a needed software package is unavailable. In contrast, the same team may decide that there is insufficient in-house programming staff to implement a project, and fail to consider using contract programmers.

CASE SCENARIO: ESTABLISHING SELECTION CRITERIA

As the integration of ARI and NC proceeds, management has selected a name that reflects the decision to broaden the consulting base and competencies of the combined entity. The organization now is known as National Research Associates (NRA).

One of the early projects identified as a developmental opportunity to the CIS function of NRA involves the consolidation of communication systems. The opportunity surfaces when it is discovered that the combined organization needs a voice telephone system that exceeds the scope of either existing system. Further, a feasibility study indicates that a change in telephone systems would be highly cost-effective. Both companies are leasing telephone systems at the time of the merger. An evaluation team comprised of members from both organizations finds that a purchased telephone system can pay for itself in savings on lease costs in less than four years.

Accordingly, a decision is made to seek bids from leading providers of telephone systems with integrated voice and data capabilities. The CIS manager for the combined entity, Esther Producto, has been appointed manager of the acquisition project. Under her direction, a request for proposal (RFP) has been prepared and distributed to 18 potential suppliers. This RFP is reproduced as an appendix at the end of this text.

Case Discussion/Assignment

Your assignment is to review the RFP in Appendix C and to prepare criteria for the evaluation of bids that NRA expects to receive on its new communication system. Specifically, you are to establish six to eight major requirements or features of the new system that will affect the selection decision. These criteria will form a matrix to be used as a basis for evaluating bids. Each criterion is to be represented by a row in the table; and each vendor submitting a bid, in turn, is to be represented by a column.

As bids are received, entries in matrix cells will reflect team member evaluations (a number from 1 to 10) of how the proposals meet the criteria. Column totals, then, will represent overall ratings by team members for each proposal.

Choose your criteria from the specifications incorporated within the RFP. For each criterion you select, prepare a short statement that explains its bearing upon selection. Then, indicate the good and bad points related to each criterion that should be considered by team members.

Discussion Topics

1. What are weighted criteria and how are they used as a method of selecting projects?

2. How does the chargeback method of financing CIS services work?

3. What is autocratic management and what are the drawbacks for project selection that are presented by this management style?

4. How do developments in hardware technology motivate project requests?

5. Why are economic benefits the most commonly used project selection criteria?

6

APPLICATIONS SOFTWARE PLANNING

Abstract

Planning for software development projects is a major CIS management responsibility. An initial decision typically made in CIS functions is whether to develop applications with existing resources or to purchase commercial packages. Criteria are established under which both alternatives are evaluated. Typical criteria include factors such as time, user requirements, maintenance, costs, and staff resources. Regardless of whether a package is developed or purchased, CIS managers historically have found it wise to create standards of uniformity for development activities, especially in the area of programming conventions.

A decision to purchase a software package, however, involves some unique considerations. Evaluations must be performed to determine compatibility with existing systems, multi-user capabilities, processing capacities, and so on. Then, a package that meets these specifications must be located.

For either custom-developed or commercial software, development teams naturally place emphasis upon costs. Costs are divided into developmental and operational expenses. In addition, comprehensive documentation is required under both methods. Any development, evaluation, or testing activity usually is supported by a formal report.

CUSTOM DEVELOPMENT vs. APPLICATION PACKAGES

Computer software is acquired by businesses to meet needs and solve problems. Prior to the proliferation of commercial software packages, user requests for new applications typically were screened by a management steering committee. Approved systems were committed to extensive development projects within which the CIS staff designed, coded, tested, and implemented applications programs that met specific needs.

In the early 1980s, commercial software packages became widely available for standard business applications, such as word processing, database, transaction processing, financial reporting, manufacturing control, inventory control, and spreadsheets. Software packages were developed by computer manufacturers and independent companies that took advantage of the adage: "There's no sense in reinventing the wheel." Many, sometimes all, user processing requirements in businesses now can be met with packages purchased "off the shelf." Thus, software development for CIS planners and functions involves an initial decision of whether to develop custom applications or to purchase software packages that meet existing needs.

There are advantages and disadvantages to both methods for acquiring software. CIS professionals, then, may find it useful to set up selection criteria to support this decision-making process, as discussed in Chapter 5. Several major criteria are presented in the section that follows. These criteria include:

- Time considerations
- User requirements
- Maintenance after installation
- Cost
- Available staff resources.

Time Considerations

The time required to develop a new application has been a source of irritation for users since the earliest computers were installed. For many years, there were no shortcuts: A major system took at least a year to develop, more often two to three years. Complaints abounded that systems were obsolescent, perhaps even obsolete, before they came into productive use.

As common denominators of business programs were identified, it became possible to abridge some time elements by re-using modules, or elements, of programs that already existed. As such plans proved feasible, a major segment of the software industry grew up around the development and marketing of standard application packages.

Unfortunately, many users equate standard application packages for computers of all sizes with those they have purchased off the shelf for microcomputers. A major CIS application is a hugely different entity from a microcomputer program. Considerably more time, effort, and adaptation are needed for a mainframe system. However, time saving—and money saving as well—still are possible.

Although commercial packages usually undergo a period of testing and conversion, these periods normally are far shorter than are required for custom development projects. Under custom development, the user organization engages in the full spectrum of design, specification, programming, testing, and installation for an application, without reliance upon pre-packaged applications. From-scratch development, however, does use standard utility programs that are part of an installation's systems software.

User Requirements

A commercial package may not meet all of a user's stated requirements. Sometimes, commercial packages can be modified to provide the required capabilities, but a modified commercial package also may require extensive analysis and development efforts. When a standard package is modified beyond the limit of variables or options built in by the vendor, it becomes, in effect, a custom package. That is, the manuals, warranties, and support commitments of the vendor are lost when major modification is applied to a standard package. Also, the advantages of commercial packages can be nullified by the time and money invested in drawn-out modifications.

As another implied commitment, a user who modifies a standard package is isolated, to a large extent, from future improvements a vendor may make to a standard package. Typically, vendors offer contracts under which users receive updated versions of software packages under extremely favorable terms. When a user modifies a purchased version of a program, the package becomes incompatible with future, advanced versions of the same program. Therefore, once a commitment to modify is undertaken, the same time and effort must be expended for any future versions that the using organization wants to adopt. For this reason, most experienced managers of CIS systems functions adopt a policy in opposition to any modification; packages either are used as-is or not used at all.

Commercial packages generally are ready to use upon purchase. For this reason, in situations in which a package meets nearly all user requirements, the user requirements may be traded off, or modified, to balance the shortened development time and lessened expense of commercial packages.

For example, suppose a general ledger accounting package is needed by an organization that currently uses four-digit account numbers. A package is found that supports only three-digit, alphabetic account identifiers, but meets all other requirements. Substantial cost benefits may be realized by changing four-digit account numbers to three-letter codes. In this situation, however, the entire organization and its customers are affected. The universal nature of this type of modification may be difficult to justify.

Maintenance After Installation

An important aspect of planning for application development projects is estimating the amount and magnitude of modifications and updates that will be needed in the future. An application package, regardless of development method, must remain operational under changing business conditions. The ease with which a package can be modified affects the "develop or buy" decision. For example, a payroll/personnel application should be capable of incorporating future changes in tax and wage structures with relative ease.

Cost

Cost considerations for application packages include development costs or purchase price and ongoing maintenance upon implementation. In addition, any modifications that are required to implement commercial packages are factors in cost calculations.

Available Staff Resources

The availability of staff—or human—resources also is a significant factor in software development decisions. For example, decision makers may determine that an application can be developed by staff programmers for less than the purchase price of a commercial package. If the programmers already are committed to existing projects, however, the situation changes. Time may be lost due to delays until programmers are available. These delays may lead to production losses. Remember that an implicit goal of CIS planning is to meet the overall goals of the organization.

STANDARDS

Development and implementation projects for applications can be combinations of many types of activities performed by many different people. In addition, the people who design an application may not be the same people who operate and maintain it. Thus, the management and control of such projects may require the establishment of standards. Standards are uniform procedures and/or measurements that are used to govern the performance of people or functions.

For example, the establishment of standards creates a common ground upon which different programmer/analysts and managers can read and understand program documentation, including source code statements. That is, a manager or a programmer/analyst should be able to interpret design specifications and source code listings written by programmers. In fact, standards, called programming conventions, frequently are required in this area. For this reason, the section that follows discusses standards for program development.

Many attempts have been made to establish standards for programming and for analysis and design activities. Individual organizations often establish standards for internal use. For example, IBM developed a standardized system design method called HIPO (Hierarchical Input Processing Output). In addition, Yourdon Inc. developed a method for data flow diagramming (known as *bubble charts*) and published several books on the subject. Several private and government sector groups also are addressing this topic. For example, the American National Standards Institute (ANSI) is working to establish a set of standards for systems analysis and design that could gain wide acceptance.

Regardless of how standards are created, the important point is that effective standards should be practical and understandable by all who are affected. Areas in which standards have been developed that relate to CIS functions, and particularly to application development, include:

- Naming conventions
- Data dictionaries
- Aids for maintenance
- Organization of production and job control information
- Programming conventions.

Naming Conventions

Standards are applied effectively to conventions for naming data elements, records, files, reports, and so on. Usually, the names applied to these entities reflect the nature of the entities. For example, a common practice in application development projects is to establish a glossary of standard abbreviations, such as CUST for customer, NO for number, PT for part, and COMM for commission.

Adding these abbreviations to file identifiers establishes specific and unique references. For example, adding AP for accounts payable, AR for accounts receivable, and PR for payroll to account numbers identifies the elements as parts of specific applications.

Data files and reports also must be given standard names. Again, the purpose of naming is to describe the report or file and to give it a unique identity. The same holds for the naming and formatting of system documentation.

Data Dictionaries

For systems in which data dictionaries are created, standardization is critical. Data dictionaries are reference files that list and specify all data items within a system. These descriptors must be written in a format that remains uniform within each system. Although there may be several versions of data dictionaries created for the system, all versions must contain complete and uniform listings of data element names, attributes, and usages. An example of a data dictionary entry might be: CUST NAME (customer name), alphabetic data, 30 characters long, used in accounts payable and accounts receivable.

Aids for Maintenance

Uniform formats can be of significant benefit in the maintenance of application software. Standardized data structures and names, as well as systematic approaches to program coding, minimize maintenance and updating efforts.

Organization of Production and Job Control Information

An important concern in any CIS function is the efficient scheduling of equipment and production resources. Standard methods for requesting service and presenting job control information support scheduling activities.

Programming Conventions

Although standards are important in the areas discussed above, standards are critical for programming coding and design. The standardization of style and form used in writing programs increases the efficiency of development and the ease of modification. To illustrate this point, the section that follows presents a sample set of guidelines that may be followed in coding programs in the COBOL language.

General guidelines that apply to the writing of COBOL code for application programs include:

- Entries that identify the beginnings of the four divisions of COBOL programs (IDENTIFICATION, ENVIRONMENT, DATA, and PROCEDURE) should be given separate lines on coding sheets or in keyboard-entered source code.

- Coding for the DATA and PROCEDURE divisions should be started on new pages. This practice facilitates reviews and evaluations of program coding. Separate pages make it possible to read both divisions side by side. This assists in verifying that data definitions and procedure descriptions correspond as required.

- At least one blank line should be inserted before each paragraph name, and each paragraph name should be on a separate line. Section names should stand out and be easy for reviewers to locate.

- Comments should be used liberally throughout the program for documentation purposes. Each comment line should be identified, at minimum, with an asterisk (*) in column 7. Comments of major importance or significance should be indicated with full lines of asterisks above and below the comments.

- File names should be meaningful to all users of the application and also should describe the content of the file. A 30-character field is available for file names.

- SELECT and ASSIGN clauses that identify and deal with the same file should be written on the same line of the coding sheet or in keyboard-entered source code. Multiple SELECT and ASSIGN clauses should be aligned vertically on the coding sheet or source code listing, as shown in Figure 6-1. References or descriptions that amplify the statement should be written one per line and aligned vertically beneath the ASSIGN clause, also shown in Figure 6-1.

- Margins and indentations for statements are to be determined by the level of the statement. That is, statements of equal level should align

```
FILE-CONTROL.
     SELECT FILE-ONE
          ASSIGN TO XXXXXX.

     SELECT FILE-TWO
          ASSIGN TO YYYYYY
          ORGANIZATION IS INDEXED
          ACCESS IS RANDOM
          RECORD KEY IS ZZZ-ZZZ.
```

Figure 6-1. *Recommended programming conventions should require that multiple SELECT and ASSIGN clauses be aligned as shown here.*

vertically. Indents of two additional spaces are to be included any time a subordinate-level statement is written.

- Literals should be completed in one line. The text of a literal should not carry over from one line to the next. If a literal is too long to fit on the

  line following its identifier, the entire literal is brought down one line and indented according to established standards. See Figure 6-2.

- Section and paragraph names in the PROCEDURE division must be descriptive and meaningful and should indicate the primary, logic functions performed. Figure 6-3 shows a series of names that conform to this standard. Notice that the names resemble English sentences; they contain nouns, adjectives, and verbs.

- If a statement is too long to fit on a single line, the continued portion should be indented from the beginning point of the first line.

- Statements with implied operations should be written so that their operands, or data locations, are aligned vertically—on separate lines, as shown in Figure 6-4.

- Coding for IF statements with multiple clauses should be indented uniformly, with each condition on a separate line. ELSE and THEN statements should be aligned with the IF statements and also should be

```
05  LONG-DESCRIPTION                  PIC X(46) VALUE
         "THIS IS A LONG DESCRIPTION WITH A VALUE CLAUSE".
```

Figure 6-2. *This syntax diagram covers inclusion of literals in a COBOL program.*

```
                    100-COMPUTE-GROSS-PAY
                    200-EDIT-HOURS-WORKED
                    300-VALIDATE-EMPLOYEE-NO
                    400-READ-TABLE-RECORD
                    500-WRITE-DETAIL-RECORD
                    600-WRITE-FINAL-TOTALS
```

Figure 6-3. *This diagram covers standards for inclusion of section and paragraph names within the PROCEDURE division of a COBOL program.*

```
        OPEN INPUT        FILE-ONE
                          FILE-TWO
              OUTPUT      FILE-THREE.


        MOVE  ZERO        TO   QQQQQ
                               VVVVV.
```

Figure 6-4. *COBOL statements that implement implied operations should follow this standard format protocol.*

```
IF       X EQUAL TO Y
         AND P EQUAL TO Q
         AND S EQUAL TO T
THEN
         MOVE ...
         ADD    ...
ELSE
         PERFORM ...
```

Figure 6-5.   *Coding of COBOL statements for IF. . .THEN. . .ELSE clauses should follow this standard format.*

```
READ A-FILE-NAME
     AT END MOVE "YES" TO EOF-FLAG.

READ A-FILE-NAME
     INVALID KEY MOVE "YES" TO ABORT-FLAG.
```

Figure 6-6.   *This is the recommended format for AT END and INVALID KEY clauses in COBOL.*

on separate lines. The proper format for these statements is shown in Figure 6-5.

- AT END or INVALID KEY clauses should be indented and on a line separate from corresponding READ statements, as shown in Figure 6-6.

This list of standards for the COBOL programming language is not meant to be complete. But, in examining the standards and corresponding illustrations, it can be seen that implementing standards such as these creates uniform program listings that can be understood and utilized by more than one programmer or analyst. Uniform source statement readability is valuable for development projects in which many programmers design and write modules, and still other programmers handle maintenance. Planning for programming standards within a CIS organization through such measures can pay dividends in maintenance ease and in smoothness of ongoing system operation. The section that follows discusses important considerations for locating and evaluating commercial, or proprietary, software.

EVALUATING PROPRIETARY SOFTWARE

The initial steps for purchasing software packages are identical to the early stages of development projects. That is, a study is performed to identify the specific need to be met or problem to be solved. Then, a list of specifications that the solution must meet is produced. At this point, a decision usually is made either to develop the application or to purchase a commercial package. Available packages are evaluated according to the specifications. An evaluation plan may be outlined. It should include the definition of requirements, sources of software, and confirmation and testing procedures.

Consider, for example, a CIS function that receives a request for a new accounts-receivable application. The present system is outdated and unable to handle the volume increases caused by the successful entry of the organization into new markets. The evaluation plan calls for site visits to gather information from users of accounts-receivable packages in similar systems. Figure 6-7 shows a planning statement for a site visit, which includes a summary of the overall procedure and a list of questions for users.

A site visit can be a powerful evaluation tool. The evaluation also may be performed internally by analysts and managers. Regardless of the method used, several common factors are studied, including:

- Processing capacities
- Data handling
- Primary output capability
- Hardware
- File considerations
- Multi-user capabilities.

HOW TO MAKE A SITE VISIT TO EVALUATE A SOFTWARE PACKAGE
COMPUTER INFORMATION SYSTEMS DEPARTMENT

A. Overall procedure:

    1. Obtain user names from the vendor of the selected package.

    2. Call and set up a visit.

    3. Prepare interview questionnaire (Section B).

    4. Brief traveling party concerning content of the questionnaire.

    5. Pre-assign responsibility for specific questions to travelers and assign one traveler to be the recorder.

    6. Summarize the responses upon return.

B. Software package evaluation questions to be asked of or information to be obtained from the user(s) at the selected site:

    1. Obtain the names of any vendor personnel who have been outstandingly helpful and their specialties.

    2. Obtain exact configuration (hardware and software) required. Schematics are very helpful, along with make and model numbers.

    3. Have any hardware components proved troublesome or unreliable?

    4. What environmental or special facilities are provided for the computer?

    5. If any terminals are remotely installed, what type of cabling is used?

    6. When was the hardware installed? Who brought it up? Did vendor install the package turnkey or did user provide (grow) a programming expert?

    7. Is a hardware service log kept? How many maintenance calls were there in the last year? How many times was the system down more than four hours?

    8. How many times has software or package changed in the last year? Who installed the change? Was the changed system stable? Were changes improvements?

    9. How many software/package bugs occurred in the last year? Were they minor or major problems? How long did it take for the vendor to get the user back up? How long did it take for the vendor to supply a permanent fix?

    10. Was there any abnormal turnover in vendor's support staff?

    11. How do system environments compare?

Attribute	Ours	Theirs
a. No. of terminals		
b. No. of keyboard staff		
c. Hours/week operation		
d. Size of files		
e. No. of reports		
f. No. of pages printed		

Figure 6-7. *This memo establishes a plan for a site visit during which an application software package will be evaluated. Memo is continued on the next page.*

Add other factors deemed pertinent.

12. Sketch system overview (on separate sheet of paper) and include:
    Inputs: CRT and other
    Outputs: CRT
    Reports: Hardcopy
    Files
13. What volumes, counts, or other management information does the system produce?
14. Has the package been modified locally or is it used as delivered?
15. What would the user change in the way the package functions if feasible?
16. How often has the user had to pay overtime to catch up after an outage?
17. If the user had it to do over:
    a. Would they do it again?
    b. What would they change?
18. List names, telephone numbers, and specialties of those interviewed.
19. Include any miscellaneous notes.
20. List the names of persons in the traveling party.

Figure 6-7 (concluded).   *This is the final portion of the site-visit memo.*

Processing Capacities

The first factor deals with processing capacities. An accounts-receivable package affects the quality of service that an organization provides its customers. This factor also encompasses future customers; a software package should be flexible enough to absorb expected growth. Evaluation personnel gather background data about the current and expected rates of growth of the customer base.

Data Handling

User requirements for data handling are critical in evaluating commercial packages. Evaluations must be supported by specifications of numbers of months files remain active, numbers of days allowed for payments, procedures for dealing with overdue accounts, and so on. An accounts-receivable application involves collecting funds; thus, a package must be found that provides continuity and consistency of services. In other words, it is not feasible to expect users to change their practices to match the capabilities of a new package.

Primary Output Capability

The output capabilities of a software package also must meet user and organizational requirements. A critical output requirement is that an application package should be able to drive, or direct operation of, existing printers, microform devices, laser document generators, plotters, or other devices that are in place within the using organization. Also, many organizations place long-term orders with forms suppliers for application output documents. If an existing function uses preprinted, prenumbered invoice forms, the software chosen also should provide that capability.

Hardware

A vital determination to be made in evaluating an application software package centers on whether the programs will run on an organization's in-place hardware. Each software package makes demands on a hardware configuration. Factors to be evaluated include compatibilities of evaluated software packages with memory capacity, disk space requirements, input equipment and procedures, and processing time.

File Considerations

Since most applications require some type of data storage, another factor in evaluating software is the nature and size of files that must be maintained—at present levels and in the future. File considerations also include data integrity and security. Backup procedures also must be taken into account.

Multi-user Capabilities

Recall that the purpose of a CIS function is to provide service and support to users. Software packages must be evaluated to determine how much support can be provided to how many users. Unacceptable delays and data lock-outs often arise in systems that provide on-line service. Evaluations should anticipate these situations to avoid costly problems after implementation.

FINDING APPROPRIATE PACKAGES

Upon completion of evaluations, a project team has a detailed set of specifications and capabilities that must be provided by the package. The next job, then, is to find the package that best meets these needs.

One of the simplest ways to survey the software market is to review computer-related periodicals, of which there are literally hundreds. Even some mass-market publications now carry ads and articles about business software packages.

In addition, several research organizations perform software reviews and publish results. These sources include Data Sources, Datapro, IDC, and others. Some of these organizations also provide direct research services. That is, a client submits a specific request and the research is done by professionals for a fee. Many trade magazines, such as *InfoWorld* and *Computerworld*, include software reviews in regular or special issues.

In short, advertising and reviews of software pervade the industry. Vendors, then, become another good source of information, even though they are biased in favor of their own products. Perhaps the best source of information on software packages may be other users. In the example given above, an organization sends a team to a site with a similar system to gather first-hand information on both the hardware and the software. Other first-hand information may be gathered from everyday conversations with professional peers or at trade and professional conferences.

ESTIMATING COSTS

One of the most challenging tasks in evaluating any application development project involves estimating costs for development and implementation. Most CIS functions rely on historical data to support these estimates. That is, data are compiled that reflect development costs of similar projects in the past. These estimates usually are produced for two stages of systems projects:

- Developmental
- Operational.

Developmental

Developmental costs are related to the analysis, design, and implementation of a problem solution. Individual areas of effort in the developmental process include:

- Analysis
- Design
- Programming
- System testing
- File conversion
- Acceptance testing
- User training

Analysis. Costs associated with analysis tasks often are incurred before the project is approved for development. These reviews tend to be part of the on-going mission and responsibility of the systems analysis group within the CIS function. These services typically fall within budgets established for user consultation specifically for answering questions and/or discussing new opportunities that may be recommended by CIS professionals. Feasibility studies and reports produced at this stage provide support for the approval decision.

Costs for analysis activities, then, are estimates based on projections of man-hours of effort. These estimates generally are compiled from information concerning costs incurred during similar activities for previous projects and the experience of analysts. That is, cost estimates for analysis activities are derived from historical data and are adjusted for current situations such as recent changes in personnel costs, available software tools, modifications in available computing capacity, and so on.

Design.   Design activities also can involve cost estimates based upon historical data. In addition, there are operational factors figured into estimates of design costs. That is, design costs are affected directly by methods for file organization, types of hardware available, programming languages used, and so on.

Programming.   Many methods have been devised for estimating programming costs, although none is accepted widely. Estimating programming costs often involves two phases. A first estimate generally is based upon preliminary information generated during analysis. Then, a second estimate is produced during or upon completion of the design phase. The second estimate tends to reflect programming effort and cost more accurately. This is because program designs are more specific and provide a basis for better estimates. One technique used in planning for programming requirements at this point in a project is to count the number of modules in design documentation and to multiply this total by an average number of hours and/or cost for development of each module. Most project leaders establish rules of thumb for program module efforts that are usable for cost and resource requirements estimates.

Other costs are charged to the programming effort even though they do not involve the writing of instructions. For example, effective programming often involves investigations into the capabilities and compatibilities of existing equipment. In addition, initial tests are performed during this stage to ensure that programs run properly and produce desired results.

System testing.   During the programming phase, initial testing is performed on programs. However, further testing is required to demonstrate program performance within the overall system. That is, tests are run to measure factors such as the ability of programs to accept and process data from other parts of the system and to produce data that are compatible with other application components. These tests are performed by running a set of sample data through the entire system. This activity is called a system test.

Costs of a system test involve the preparation of test data by programmers and analysts, equipment and supplies, and personnel. Analysts and/or designers usually review output products of system tests, often with users actively involved.

File conversion.   The development of an application package may involve converting existing files to a new format. When master files are involved, backup copies and security considerations are critical. In addition, historical files also may require conversion to facilitate data security and maintenance procedures.

Also, file conversion may require a complete set of separate conversion programs. This can be an extensive, and costly, programming effort. Even if commercial packages for conversions are available, costs are involved that must be considered. These costs are figured in the same way as regular programming costs, as discussed in the section above.

Acceptance testing.   The final test that an application undergoes is the acceptance test. This is a system test that is performed by or in conjunction with users. An extensive data file is prepared and run in an attempt to exercise all conditions and peripheral activities affected by the system. Test data are provided by users and are evaluated or modified as necessary for hardware and software performance evaluations by programmers and analysts. Even manual activities are performed during the acceptance test.

An acceptance test is performed by users to achieve final validation of outputs and results. This is the point at which users finally "buy" the system as suitable for performing the jobs and delivering the services they specified in the requirements. Toward this end, tests include data representing the full spectrum of the user application. As a final step, it is sound practice to process a random stream of live data under the new system to satisfy users that the new application will perform their work. Only when all of these conditions are satisfied does the user "sign off on," or accept, the new system.

Costs of acceptance testing should be anticipated at the outset of a development project and should be budgeted to reflect the need for thoroughness, as well as the critical role of this activity in putting the new system into active use. Project costs should encompass the participation of users, including both personnel and any facilities that will be involved.

User training.   The introduction of a new application to a system probably requires some amount of user training. Training initially is performed by analysts or programmers involved in development. However, an effective training technique is to appoint a key user who has or is given extensive training in the operation of the application. The key user often has provided the greatest amount of input to the development activities. A key user within a department provides quick, accessible support to other users. Ideally, this individual or group of users will have been with the development project from its outset.

Key users should have been involved in developing and approving system specifications, in assembling test data, and in conducting acceptance tests. This same individual or group will return to the user department to implement and operate the new system. Therefore, this individual or group is in an ideal position to know how the system will impact users and to direct the preparation and administration of materials and programs that train users to adapt to their new working conditions.

Costs involved in this area are derived from information such as the number of persons to be trained, equipment requirements, man-hours for training personnel, facilities charges, and so on. An important factor that often is overlooked is the cost of backup personnel for employees involved in training activities.

Operational

Operational costs are associated with the physical installation of a software package and the routine execution of the application. Major areas of operational costs include:

- Training
- Supplies
- Computing equipment use and maintenance.

Training. In the development of application packages, two separate training requirements must be addressed. The first concerns user organizations and is discussed in an above section. The second requirement stems from the needs of computer operations personnel. Computer operations personnel oversee the routine execution of applications and should receive an operations manual that outlines specific procedures, including directions to be followed for reruns or aborted operations. In addition, operators are responsible for implementing the creation of backup files and for the implementation of restart operations as necessary. Training costs for operations generally include the preparation of training manuals.

However, the most effective training is performed on a personal, face-to-face basis. Some operational training may take place in conjunction with program, system, and acceptance testing procedures. By combining these activities, significant reductions in overall training costs may be realized.

One of the purposes of this type of instruction is to help operators understand what happens to data items as they flow through the entire system.

Operators who have an overall understanding of the system perform their jobs knowledgeably and effectively.

Supplies. Costs of supplies include estimates for design and printing of special report forms, such as checks and invoices. In addition, estimates are produced for costs of consumable supplies expended during development activities. Finally, estimates may be made to project costs of supplies needed to support the ongoing operations of the system.

Computing equipment use and maintenance. Operational costs also include the purchase, use, and maintenance of hardware. CIS planners need to consider and account for costs such as use of existing mainframes, purchases of new computers or terminals, costs involved in establishing communication links among terminals, costs of storage media, and so on.

In addition, any hardware requires at least a minimum of maintenance. The establishment of maintenance programs for equipment can be a major expense. These programs may involve agreements with equipment manufacturers, the establishment of in-house maintenance functions, contracts with third-party maintenance organizations, or combinations of these alternatives.

To this point, planning for the development or acquisition of application packages is discussed in light of decisions that involve or are made by CIS professionals. The discussion has focused on such factors as requirements analysis, cost considerations, and procedures. Usually, any decision of this type is supported by some form of documentation. The next section presents requirements for documentation in all phases of software development projects.

DOCUMENTATION

Software development begins with a request for service. The formal request may be the first document in the development process. Many CIS functions design a specific request-for-service form that users are asked to complete. The purpose of such a form is to structure the descriptions of requirements so as to expedite CIS responses.

Once a request is approved, a series of activities is required to develop, implement, and install a new or revised system. The activities for software development parallel the general structure of a systems development life cycle (SDLC). The SDLC is divided into phases, and each phase is supported

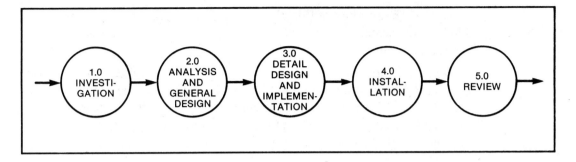

Figure 6-8. *This diagram identifies and presents the sequence of phases for a typical systems development life cycle.*

by corresponding documentation. This section on software documentation is broken down according to phases in a typical SDLC, which include:

- Investigation
- Analysis and general design
- Detail design and implementation
- Installation
- Review.

Investigation

Figure 6-8 presents a diagram of the systems development life cycle. The initial, or investigation, phase of the life cycle is concerned with requirements and specifications, especially requirements related to users. A common approach involves interviews with current users of a system and users who are requesting new or revised applications. The result of this phase is a comprehensive statement of a problem or situation and the requirements for its solution.

Of course, this statement is documented thoroughly. In fact, this statement actually may be a package of documents that includes copies of correspondence and memos, existing record and report layouts, user statements, and so on.

Analysis and General Design

Activities of the analysis and general design phase should begin with an analysis of the existing system. Analysis should be supported by extensive data gathering. The product of this phase is a determination of the feasibility of solving the problem identified during the investigation phase. Then, a preliminary, general design of a solution can be produced.

Again, documentation is critical to support the activities of this phase. Specifications are drawn up for the existing system; a feasibility statement is created; and a general design of a solution is produced. All these activities are documented on a project report reviewed by management as a basis for approval or modification of system development continuation.

Detail Design and Implementation

To be effective, computer programs also should be supported by documentation. In the detail design and implementation phase, programs are written that implement a specific solution to the problem. This phase may be the most document-intensive portion of the life cycle. In addition, the testing of programs that takes place during this phase also requires documentation. The documents produced during this phase, as well as documents produced in all phases, support the training of users and operators. Again, a progress report is presented to and reviewed by management.

Installation

Support documentation required for the installation phase includes a formal project description, a comprehensive testing description (including test data and defined results), and training and operations manuals.

An important part of this phase is the acceptance test, during which users give final approval to results of a project. That is, the acceptance test is performed in conjunction with users to determine whether the application to be installed meets specified needs. A user sign-off on test documents indicates approval; and the package then is ready to be turned over to the production group.

The installation phase also includes the activities for converting master and data files, when necessary. This activity often can be as demanding on personnel and equipment resources as the project itself.

Review

There are many types of reviews in systems development. Reviews either center around the development project or the system under development. Development projects should be reviewed at the end of each phase of the life cycle. Then, a final review takes place upon completion of the project. The purpose of this final review is to evaluate failures and successes of the project and to provide guidance for future projects.

In addition, procedures may be established for regular reviews of applications in light of user requirements. All these reviews must be documented; formal reporting procedures normally are set up by project teams.

CASE SCENARIO: WHO SWALLOWS WHOM?

When NRA was formed, one of the merged entities (ARI) was more than three times as large as the other (NC). The natural tendency, in such a situation, is to assume that the larger company's systems and sets of processing procedures would prevail. However, NRA is one of those exceptions that proves the rule.

The blending of application programs in a situation like the one at NRA must follow a practical course. Obviously, it is beyond the scope of a single project to integrate all the applications of both organizations. It is not even clear whether it is practical or desirable to integrate all applications. However, one thing is clear: Accounting reports must be restated soon after implementation of the merger. Practicality dictates that, in such a situation, accounting and regulatory reports (payroll, tax, etc.) should be an early candidate for systems integration. Certainly, this is the case at NRA. Management has called for consolidation of accounting applications at the earliest opportunity.

One of the first characteristics that surfaces in looking at this consolidation is that things are contrary to normal expectations. On the face of it, it seems natural to fold the NC system with its $15 million in revenues into the ARI system with $50 million in income. However, a closer look indicates that the two systems do not relate to one another in this way.

ARI, despite its larger size, has a system aimed at reporting on a series of projects carried out for a single, all-encompassing client. In everyday terms, ARI has one customer. This simplifies the structure of accounting systems and of the reports that must be generated. By contrast, the smaller entity, NC, has multiple clients and a complex accounting structure. NC can vary its rates and bases for billing according to individual situations. There can be flat-fee jobs, time-and-materials jobs, and even jobs with contingent fees. In the commercial systems field, for example, some companies link their incomes to the savings they can realize on behalf of their clients.

Since the NC system has a greater degree of complexity, it becomes apparent that ARI has to be consolidated into NC, rather than the other way around. In terms of computer system design, this requirement is less than ideal. It means that the smaller files have to be expanded to accommodate the larger ones and that a major hardware transition will be necessary. However, in its present state, the NC system does not have the capacity to accommodate the full ARI system. Summary data from the ARI system must be captured manually and added to NC statements to derive early sets of accounting and financial reports for NRA. Unavoidably, much tedious manual work is needed in the short term to produce adjustments to the NC system to reflect the overall NRA situation. This is the kind of requirement that can cause nightmares for accountants and auditors. It is also the kind of reality that cannot be avoided in some instances.

This situation provides the kind of practical example that demonstrates the types of adjustments and/or compromises that are needed in setting priorities for selecting and scheduling application projects.

Case Discussion/Assignment

Assume that Esther Producto and other computer professionals of the merged organization have decided to use and/or adapt a standard application package to implement the consolidation of accounting records. This approach will shorten the development cycle and also will save tens of thousands of dollars in programming effort. Now, as an early step in the search for suitable application software, you are to prepare an initial list of vendors who might be able to provide the needed software. The text of this chapter describes the resources to be used. Use reference materials in your school library to identify names of specific suppliers who might be able to meet these needs. Identify the packages to be considered and their primary features. Then, explain your reasons for listing each package. You should be able to identify at least five or six sources for meeting the need described in the Case Scenario.

Discussion Topics

1. What is maintenance and what role does maintenance play in a CIS function?

2. Why are standards established for systems development projects?

3. Are full-scale development projects needed to implement commercial software packages? If so, why? If not, why not?

4. What is an acceptance test?

5. What is a system test?

7

STAFFING

Abstract

Staffing is part of the human resources management function. Staffing involves the determining of corporate needs for human resources, as well as the hiring and training of qualified personnel. Short-term personnel needs often can be met through agreements with consultants or contract employees. In addition, management may assume a role in evaluating and meeting the individual career objectives of employees. With corporate needs in mind, managers may attempt to balance the goals, capabilities, and performance of qualified employees with available positions within the organization. In this way, employees are motivated to achieve and to further their individual careers by meeting corporate goals. Organizations also may benefit by providing for the continuing education and training of employees.

ASSESSING REQUIREMENTS

It is typical of managers who are faced with a decision to ask themselves: "Exactly what do I need?" Then, to follow a logical progression, managers might ask: "How can I get what I need?" This simple model of decision making holds for many types of decisions, including those around which this chapter is centered: staffing for CIS functions and development projects.

Planning for CIS functions involves an assessment of staff requirements. Then, decisions are made and steps are taken to meet the requirements. To assess requirements, managers should analyze projects slated for development and existing applications that require maintenance. CIS managers should have access to data for support of these decisions. Types of data items that are valuable for this support include the number and types of project requests, short- (six months) and long-term (three years) requirements, programming languages and operating systems used within the system, the working environment, and the overall pattern of growth for the organization. For each category identified, the planner must specify the number of people who will be needed.

Just as an application portfolio triggers planning for systems personnel requirements, commitments for hardware acquisition should trigger a process of planning for required operations personnel. Each time a new mainframe or major new peripheral is contemplated, staffing planners should bear in mind that the new equipment may present requirements for new people to run those devices. The degree of difficulty in finding qualified operations staff can vary with the sophistication of the equipment itself. The closer to the state of the art a new device is, the more difficult it probably will be to find experienced operators. A related problem can occur through an impact on training requirements. If there is no pool of qualified people in a given market area, it may be necessary to send established employees to special schools to acquire the necessary skills.

Toward this end, it can be a helpful planning technique to establish a personnel skill matrix for the CIS function. A skill matrix is a specialized planning document that compares required skills and the qualifications of staff members. Across the top of such a matrix are column headings identifying the skills that are currently needed within an organization or that will be required to implement future plans. The rows of this matrix are assigned to individual employees. In the cells where rows and columns meet, individual employees are rated on whether they have the corresponding skills and, if so, to what level of expertise. An example of a skill matrix is shown in Figure 7-1.

SKILLS MATRIX

	LANGUAGES					OPERATING SYSTEMS				
	COBOL	FORTRAN	PL/1	C		OS/MVS	VM	UNIX	VMS	
SAM	2	1	3			3				
JOE	3		1			2	1			
BETTY	1		2	1		2		1		

3 = HIGHLY SKILLED   1 = SOME CAPABILITY
2 = SKILLED   BLANK = NO CAPABILITY

Figure 7-1. This is an example of a skills matrix that can be used for evaluation of capabilities and development needs for CIS employees.

RECRUITING

The assessment of requirements may lead to a decision to recruit staff members. In some organizations, recruiting activities are delegated to the personnel department, with final interviews or approval responsibility assumed by CIS managers. This situation points out a need to assess requirements effectively, because the CIS manager must communicate to the personnel department exactly what qualifications prospective employees must have. Usually, the requirements are presented formally, as written job descriptions that include information on salary ranges. A sample job description for a manager of a computing center is shown in Figure 7-2.

In addition, the lines of communication between the two departments should be open enough to accommodate questions and clarifications by either party.

Regardless of whether the personnel department is involved, CIS managers may decide to support recruiting activities with a formal or informal recruiting plan. A plan breaks down an overall process into discrete steps, schedules the steps, and establishes procedures for support documentation. For staffing plans, then, initial steps involve the creation of comprehensive job descriptions for positions to be filled. Then, decisions are made concerning how and where to reach qualified applicants. Avenues that decision makers can take include personnel placement organizations; classified ads in professional journals, newspapers, or magazines; college placement offices; and others.

As applicants become involved in the process, other documents are added. At a minimum, a completed employment application which presents information concerning employment and salary history, as well as professional references. In addition, applicants may submit a resume that provides additional information on work experiences and professional achievements.

The information from employment applications and resumes is analyzed by one or more CIS managers or personnel staff members, and promising applicants usually are called in for interviews. The interview process can be time-consuming. Responsibilities for hiring decisions often are shared by an interview group. The personnel department can be a valuable support source for interview groups. In fact, the authors recommend that interviewers consult the personnel department to determine the parameters of acceptable practices under equal opportunity employment legislation.

Applicant interviews are an important part of recruiting, and carry much weight for recruiting decisions. CIS functions often find it valuable to appoint a coordinator who is responsible for scheduling interviews and for distributing information to interviewers, usually in the form of documents.

One of these documents, an Interview Coordination Form, is shown in Figure 7-3. This form outlines the extent of the applicant's understanding of the organization and the job being offered. These forms, completed employment applications, and resumes are given to each interviewer. In addition, an Interview Observation Form (shown in Figure 7-4) is given to each interviewer. This form is to be completed at the conclusion of the interview and returned to the coordinator immediately. The coordinator assembles the information package for each applicant and presents the files to the manager responsible for filling each vacant position.

COMPUTER INFORMATION SYSTEMS DEPARTMENT

JOB DESCRIPTION

TITLE: Manager of Computing Center

OVERVIEW

Directs the operation of the Computing Center, through the Managers of Engineering, Operations, and Systems, to provide cost-effective data and text processing services to the NRA staff. Participates in CIS policy-making councils, and personally engages in directing R&D in office automation. Reports to the Head of the Computer Information Systems Department.

GENERAL RESPONSIBILITIES

Subject	Percentage of Effort
1. Establishes service level measures and monitors level of service provided against these criteria.	15
2. Personally reviews security, privacy, fire, safety, and systems integrity mechanisms/software/procedures whenever they are within the Center.	15
3. Maintains close working relations with other CIS managers to ascertain how the Center is regarded through those who know its users best.	10
4. Maintains an awareness of all applicable government procurement regulations and periodic audit guidelines. Operates the Center in conformance with these rules or drafts letters requesting exceptions.	5
5. Leads efforts in assessing the need for new service offerings and the time for retirement of existing offerings.	10
6. Participates in Office Automation R&D to guide any development activity along lines that make it operationally acceptable and supportable in the NRA environment.	15
7. Reviews and monitors the execution of all plans concerning new equipment, revised configurations, or major new service offerings.	5
8. Prepares financial plan for the Center and proposes revisions when appropriate.	5
9. Participates in the rate setting process, monitors financial recovery under established rates, and calls any significant overages or underages to management's attention.	10
10. Reviews and approves all contemplated personnel actions by the Managers of Systems, Operations, and Engineering services.	5

Figure 7-2. This is a sample job description for a computing center manager. The job description is completed on the facing page.

Subject	Percentage of Effort

11. Maintains contact with peers in other local corporations through participation in professional activities or by direct personal contact to help calibrate the local labor market and to promote the free exchange of vendor experience.

5

100%

QUALIFICATIONS

Education

- B.S. or B.A. and sufficient courses to understand role of computer-based tools in research and corporate operation
- Special classes or self-study to understand the capabilities of the computing equipment used at NRA.

Skills

- General supervision, including delegation, followup, and close contact with staff
- Strong interpersonal communication, leadership, and negotiation
- Planning.

EXPERIENCE

Expected

Some combination of the following:

- Management and personnel administration
- Vendor relations
- Multi-employer background
- Computer operations
- Systems programming
- Text processing
- Engineering.

Desired

- Computer operations
- Systems programming
- Text processing
- Engineering
- Marketing.

PERSONAL ATTRIBUTES

- Integrity
- Patience
- Strong service attitude
- Self-starter
- Record keeper.

Figure 7-2 (concluded). This is the second page of the job description for a computing center manager.

INTERVIEW COORDINATION FORM
COMPUTER INFORMATION SYSTEMS DEPARTMENT

Applicant _____ is being interviewed primarily

for the position of _____ .

The interview coordinator is _____ . Other employment options developing out of interviews should be discussed in confidence with the interview coordinator.

- After the NRA orientation interview, interviewers may assume that the applicant is generally familiar with the structure, business profile, and the environment at NRA. As part of the orientation, the applicant has been given both the NRA and CIS organization charts and brochures and information on NRA benefits.

- After the job orientation interview, the applicant should have a general understanding of the type of work involved in the available position, but additional questions may arise. Honest, informed responses should be the rule in this area. Your answers will help the applicant evaluate his/her interest in the position and in NRA and can help you form an evaluation. Any unanswered questions should be noted and referred to the interview coordinator.

- The applicant has been informed of the salary range for the position. Questions regarding salary should be dismissed politely in order to focus on issues related to an evaluation of the applicant's potential for a position at NRA.

- A reference check will be made by the Department prior to any offer. You need not be concerned specifically with this area during the interview.

- Inappropriate areas of discussion should be avoided. Your good judgment is the best guide to what is appropriate, but some areas most typically not at issue during an interview are race, religion, sex, non-job related health and physical handicaps, age, marital status, political ideology and affiliation, style of dress, birthplace and origin of name, transportation, personal finances, place of residence, owning or renting, membership in social organizations, military status, and criminal record.

- Please complete the attached **Interview Observation Form** immediately following the interview and have it delivered to the person indicated within 30 minutes after the close of your interview session. There is no need to be very formal or to withhold any comments. Contact the interview coordinator if you have difficulty for any reason in completing and returning the form in a timely manner.

- Keep in mind the goal of getting the best possible match for both the corporation's and the individual's needs. An understanding of the reasons for your recommendation is the major purpose of the comments section. Be disciplined and focused, but don't try to force content into the comments section if there is no substance.

Figure 7-3.   *This form provides guidelines and spaces for schedules for multiple interviews of candidates for CIS positions. The form is concluded on the facing page.*

NRA ORIENTATION INTERVIEW

Interviewer _____ Date _____ Time _____

Place _____ Ext _____

JOB ORIENTATION INTERVIEW

Interviewer _____ Date _____ Time _____

Place _____ Ext _____

EVALUATION INTERVIEW

Interviewer _____ Date _____ Time _____

Place _____ Ext _____

*LUNCH (flexible, usually 12–1:30)

EVALUATION INTERVIEW

Interviewer _____ Date _____ Time _____

Place _____ Ext _____

EVALUATION INTERVIEW

Interviewer _____ Date _____ Time _____

Place _____ Ext _____

EVALUATION INTERVIEW

Interviewer _____ Date _____ Time _____

Place _____ Ext _____

EVALUATION INTERVIEW

Interviewer _____ Date _____ Time _____

Place _____ Ext _____

EVALUATION INTERVIEW

Interviewer _____ Date _____ Time _____

Place _____ Ext _____

*LUNCH: at _____ ; hosted by _____

Others attending: _____

Figure 7-3 (concluded). This is the final portion of the interview scheduling form.

INTERVIEW OBSERVATION FORM
COMPUTER INFORMATION SYSTEMS DEPARTMENT

Please complete and return to _____ , CIS, Room _____

Applicant _____ Date interviewed _____

Interviewer _____

As appropriate, and if you feel you have some basis to make an evaluation, please rate candidate on the dimensions shown in the following table for the position for which he/she is being considered.

Do not force the interview along the lines of this table. Use the table to organize and present the observations you are able to make as a natural part of your discussion with the applicant.

	Below Average	About Average	Above Average	No Observation/ Not Applicable
Strength of professional background				
Creative ability				
Professional assertiveness				
Verbal skill				
Writing skill				
Ability to organize (self and work)				
Ability to focus on what is important				
Growth potential				
Overall match to position				

Your assessment of the applicant's strongest area _____

_____

Your assessment of the applicant's weakest area _____

_____

Comments:

Recommendation: Would hire for position (strong recommendation)   _____
                 Would hire for position   _____
                 Would NOT hire for position   _____
                 Would consider for another position   _____

Figure 7-4.   *Individual interviewers can be asked to enter observations on a form of this type as part of the screening process for candidates for CIS positions.*

RETENTION

The staffing function also deals with the retention of employees within organizations. There are many factors involved in decisions to retain employees. In many CIS functions, the nature of projects governs retention decisions. This is especially true for situations in which programs are developed under contracts, with volumes of work fluctuating as projects are initiated and terminated.

Another factor is the potential for professional and technical growth on the part of employees. That is, determinations often are made on an employee's present qualifications and qualifications that can be gained with experience. A primary source of information about growth potential is the performance, or productivity, evaluation. Figure 7-5 presents a performance evaluation form for the position of application programmer. In addition, productivity evaluations are discussed in other parts of this chapter.

In many organizations, retention decisions are made as a part of the salary review process. Salary reviews may be performed yearly for all employees. The performance of an individual employee is compared with that of other employees with the same job classification. The purpose of such reviews is to recognize outstanding performance and to reward it. Employees with substandard performance either may be given an incentive and training to improve or a decision may be made not to retain, or to terminate, them.

Whereas hiring decisions are important, terminations are probably of equal importance. Timing is critical for terminations. That is, terminations should be timed so as to minimize disruptions within the organization. Often, terminations occur at the end of a project. In these cases, employees may anticipate the termination and the separation is amicable. In other cases, terminations are based on lack of performance, or on the occurrence or non-occurrence of some specific action. These situations are potentially harmful; and managers should take precautions to protect the facility against possible abuse by a disgruntled employee.

Many organizations hold exit interviews, regardless of the reason for terminations. Generally, these interviews are conducted by personnel department members who usually have training in the behavioral sciences. Exit interviews can provide feedback on reactions to personnel policies and practices that are not available from other sources. A person who is leaving an organization usually is less inhibited about expressing opinions than an individual participating in a normal evaluation interview. The candor not otherwise available, reported through the impartial medium of a personnel

MEMORANDUM

TO: _____ **DATE** _____

FROM: _____

SUBJECT: PERFORMANCE EVALUATION FOR _____
      FROM _____ TO _____
          (PERIOD COVERED IN THIS EVALUATION)

The Computer Information Systems Department is conducting the semi-annual personnel evaluations of its staff members. Your name has been suggested as someone who should be consulted in preparing these evaluations. Therefore, I would like to ask you to participate in evaluating

_____.

The following form is for your comments. I would appreciate it if you would fill it out and return it to the Department Secretary within two weeks of the date in the upper right-hand corner of this document. A brief explanation of each category is listed below. If a category does not apply, please indicate this on the form.

The evaluations may be read, on request, by the individual involved.

ACCOMPLISHMENTS/CONTRIBUTIONS: Describe your interactions with the individual. List his/her responsibilities, and describe the individual's accomplishments and contributions to your work.

STRENGTHS: Indicate what this individual's particular strengths are (technical competence, work knowledge, work quality, initiative, judgment, productivity, flexibility, reliability, organization, versatility). Can he/she realistically assess work schedules and meet commitments? Indicate the degree of confidence you have in the individual's ability to perform tasks independently.

PERSONAL INTERACTION: Discuss the individual's willingness and ability to work with others, to comply with procedures, and to accept criticism. Does the individual maintain reasonable contact with assigned project(s) and keep you and others informed as to progress or problems?

COMMUNICATION SKILLS: Discuss the individual's ability to express himself/herself clearly, both verbally and in writing. Does he/she document work thoroughly, understandably, and in a timely manner?

AREAS FOR IMPROVEMENT: Discuss areas that this individual could work on that would improve his/her performance and value to the project and to NRA.

OVERALL ASSESSMENT: Your overview of the employee's performance.

Figure 7-5. *Performance evaluation forms, such as this one, can be valuable in reaching decisions about retention and career advisement for CIS employees. The form is continued on the facing page.*

```
┌─────────────────────────────────────────────────────────────────┐
│                                                                   │
│                PERFORMANCE EVALUATION FORM                        │
│                                                                   │
│                                                                   │
│     EVALUATION OF: _____    │
│     ACCOMPLISHMENTS/CONTRIBUTIONS:                                │
│                                                                   │
│                                                                   │
│                                                                   │
│                                                                   │
│     STRENGTHS:                                                    │
│                                                                   │
│                                                                   │
│                                                                   │
│     PERSONAL INTERACTION:                                         │
│                                                                   │
│                                                                   │
│                                                                   │
│     COMMUNICATION SKILLS:                                         │
│                                                                   │
│                                                                   │
│                                                                   │
│     AREAS FOR IMPROVEMENT:                                        │
│                                                                   │
│                                                                   │
│                                                                   │
│     OVERALL ASSESSMENT:                                           │
│                                                                   │
│                                                                   │
│                                                                   │
│     COMMENTS BY: _____ DATE _____       │
│                            REVIEWER                               │
│                                                                   │
└─────────────────────────────────────────────────────────────────┘
```

Figure 7-5 (concluded).   *This is the final portion of the performance evaluation form.*

professional, should be examined for clues to policies or practices that can lead to longer retention of valued personnel.

PRODUCTIVITY MEASUREMENT

CIS managers also have primary responsibilities for the measuring and evaluating of CIS productivity—which is affected by the performance of both computer systems and CIS staff members. Several tools are available for measuring the productivity of computing systems. Staff performance is not determined as easily.

In the past, factors such as lines of program code and run times for programs have been used to indicate performance. These types of measurements are no longer feasible in many situations. For example, fourth-generation programming languages produce code from program parameters provided by programmers or users. The coding generated by these languages may require more object code and storage space, and may execute less efficiently, than applications written by programmers who are sensitive about processing resources. However, the relatively low cost of computer memory compensates for these shortcomings. Thus, another method may be needed to evaluate the performance of programmers who work with program generators.

One method that has been developed sets up due dates for projects as performance criteria. Stated simply, an employee who fails to complete a project by a reasonable and understood due date is not performing up to standards. If due dates are met, the quality of work is evaluated. Obviously, the criteria of due dates are more quantitative than qualitative.

As an alternative, programmers' work can be evaluated with analytical software packages. These tools identify program modules with lengthy execution times. Although the main purpose of these tools is to revise modules for maximum efficiency, they can be used to indicate strengths and/or weaknesses in programmers' work.

Finally, the work of programmers also can be evaluated in terms of the ease or difficulty with which programs are maintained or modified. Structured programming procedures often are established in organizations to ensure that programs are maintainable. Structured programming techniques are governed by installation standards.

In evaluating the work of programmers, managers should be careful not to ascribe improvements in hardware to programming efficiency. Sometimes, productivity gains occur because programs run faster on advanced hardware. Often, a new hardware device runs existing software in emulation mode. The increased capacity of the new device may appear to enhance program performance. However, the inefficiencies of the program still exist; the program simply executes with increased speed.

TRAINING NEEDS

CIS managers are responsible for maintaining the productivity of their functions. To help maintain productivity, methods are needed to evaluate performance. If performance is below standard, CIS managers may need to provide additional or "refresher" training for staff members. Also, CIS managers must provide training for new employees or employees in new positions.

A CIS staff involves many categories of employees. CIS training activities cover multiple job functions, including:

- Data entry
- Operators
- Programmers
- Systems analysts
- Supervisors and lead people
- Users.

Data entry. Training activities for data entry operators generally are a response to two related sets of requirements. The first requirement involves newly acquired equipment. Extensive training may not be needed every time new equipment is acquired. At a minimum, however, orientation sessions usually are held to familiarize operators with new equipment. Often, equipment manufacturers supply instructors and materials for these sessions, although the purchaser still incurs expenses because of personnel time lost during training sessions. These costs normally are included in budget estimates for the new equipment.

The second training requirement arises when new or revised application systems are implemented. The activities and procedures for this training should be defined in project specifications. This training typically is performed internally, often with CIS personnel acting as instructors. This type of training may represent substantial expense in terms of time and materials, and should be considered carefully by project teams and budget developers.

Operators. Training needs for computer operators are similar to the needs for data entry personnel. Purchases of new hardware or installations of new and/or upgraded applications all present needs for training. Required training may be in such areas as security and safety procedures.

A training requirement that is unique to operators involves operating systems. Operating systems may be updated several times a year. Some updates necessitate modifications to application programs. Changes in operating modes lead to additional training for operators.

Programmers.   Modifications or additions to application or system software also present needs for additional training of programmers. That is, all programmers should be given at least an informal walk-through of any and all new or modified programs with which they are involved. Programmers should be given enough information to support their participation in further modifications. This information often takes the form of written memos or updates of software manuals.

An ideal situation that many organizations shoot for is to have all programmers familiar with multiple applications. Then, should any program fail, there is no shortage of qualified troubleshooters.

In addition, programmers should be encouraged to attend outside classes at company expense. This practice can motivate programmers to stay abreast of current developments in programming languages and techniques. A secondary benefit of this practice is that knowledge gained in these classes usually is disseminated throughout the programming staff.

Systems analysts.   A typical CIS practice is to promote systems analysts from the ranks of operators and programmers. Systems analysts who follow this route usually have had no formal training in the theories of analysis and design. Of course, the "hands-on" experience that such professionals do have may be just as valuable as formal training. However, some organizations implement some type of training to familiarize analysts with the organization's standards and procedures for systems development.

Supervisors and lead people.   Training for supervisors and lead people parallels that of programmers and analysts. Training activities pertain to hardware, programming conventions, and application or system software modifications and upgrades.

However, the major content of training programs for supervisory personnel is aimed at employee and human relations. Supervisors should maintain a knowledge of current union contracts, grievance procedures, employment legislation, and the hiring policies of the organization. Additional training can be provided through organization-sponsored workshops or classes at local colleges.

This type of training is especially important when supervisors are promoted from lower levels. Many organizations have experienced situations in which staff members fail as managers after being promoted for outstanding performance in an operational-level position. In these situations, the reason for failure most often is lack of proper training. Many organizations require new supervisors to undergo fundamental training in the behavioral sciences.

Users.   Situations that require user training center around new or revised applications. This training typically is sponsored by the CIS function. Recall that the authors recommend that a member of the user department be assigned to each development team. This "key" user then may be responsible for initial and ongoing user training for that project. Once the development project is completed, CIS then acts as a support facility for the key user and user departments.

This situation has a correlation in a current trend in CIS functions. The proliferation of microcomputers and high-level programming languages has brought about increased user participation in development activities. Due to these technological developments, computing and programming are readily accessible to users. As a result, the roles of CIS functions and professionals are changing.

The CIS function increasingly is being thought of as a source of systems development assistance. Under this approach, the CIS function is responsible for the guidance and assistance of users involved in development projects, and for the coordination of diverse development activities into an integrated system. Under predecessor approaches, the CIS professional acted as a vendor. That is, a user requested an application; the application was developed by analysts and programmers; then the system was "accepted" by users. Under current concepts, the user is involved in development activities and may, in effect, "hire" the CIS professional as a consultant.

CONTRACT PROGRAMMING

CIS functions often are faced with short-term requirements for programmers. In addition, as computing disciplines become increasingly specialized, many

CIS functions are finding it difficult to maintain adequate staffs of qualified professionals. Contract programming is one answer to these needs. Contract programming is a service provided by independent programmers or programming organizations. In effect, CIS functions purchase programming expertise and service from outside contractors. Contract programming is a means of supplementing existing CIS resources for specific projects or periods. Reasons for using contract programming include:

- A short-term or peak-period requirement such as a conversion effort for a physical inventory file

- The acquisition of a new piece of equipment or the implementation of a large application in emergency situations or situations in which there is insufficient time for personnel training

- A need for a specialized capability for a short period or in an area in which qualified professionals are scarce.

A note of caution: The authors recommend that contract programmers be deployed within a team structure and that they work closely with in-house programmers to take advantage of learning opportunities. In this way, knowledge of the project remains within the organization after contract programmers leave; and continuity of service is ensured.

CONSULTING ASSISTANCE

Few computing organizations have expert personnel for every area of computing. A common method for providing expertise is to use outside consultants. Consultants provide service mainly in the form of advice. One of the advantages provided by consultants is that they generally are not inhibited by internal politics. That is, consultants often bring fresh perspectives to development projects. In addition, consultants may have experience in a wide variety of organizations. Thus, consultants may supply innovative solutions to difficult problems.

THE WORKING ENVIRONMENT

Planning for the working environment of CIS staff is similar to the planning done for other office professionals. Differences center around required tools and equipment. To deal with the special aspects of CIS work areas, the services of industrial engineers or other workspace design specialists can be invaluable. Considerations should include:

- Space
- Lighting and electrical power
- Furniture
- Telecommunications
- Heating and air conditioning
- Acoustics
- Privacy and distractions
- Use of color.

Space. Most medium- and large-sized organizations have established policies that cover allocation of work space according to the classification of the employee and the tasks to be performed. For example, private offices of senior executives may have between 150 and 600 square feet of space, depending upon the organizational level of the occupant. Administrative assistants and executive secretaries might be assigned 80 to 100 square feet, though persons at this level need not necessarily have private offices.

Varying arrangements are applied in allocating and arranging work space for CIS staff. As a general rule, computing professionals need sufficient space for a desk, a table, and a file cabinet. Minimum requirements are in a range of 64 square feet. At one extreme, organizations attempt to provide private offices for all analysts and programmers. Under other arrangements, all CIS staff members may share an open bay, perhaps divided by partitions under "landscaped office" techniques. Most typically, partitioned alcoves are provided that establish a semi-private work area, perhaps with two or three persons sharing an enclosure.

Lighting and electrical power. Two undesirable work conditions can be associated with lighting conditions: shadows and glare. Both conditions can result from traditional methods that rely on overhead lighting supplemented with desk lamps. Modern offices rely at least partly on indirect lighting that avoids both shadow and glare. Work spaces that include computer screens should be balanced to avoid distractions and eye strain associated with reflections and glare.

The introduction of computer work stations has overloaded the electrical systems in many offices. Care should be taken to make sure that each work station has a dedicated electrical circuit and that provisions are made for separate requirements of other electrical devices, which may range from pencil sharpeners, to document copiers, to microfilm viewers. The lost work or danger that can result from inadequate electrical service simply are not worth the risks.

Furniture. When programmers and analysts generated paper documents primarily, traditional office desks, file cabinets, and tables were adequate for their needs.

A computer work station, however, requires furniture designed to handle special equipment. The most common form of computer work station furniture resembles a secretarial desk. That is, there is a lowered surface for the keyboard and a raised platform for a video monitor, as well as accessible space to set up the computer cabinet itself. Other furniture used in CIS work stations also has changed:

- File cabinets have been modified to accommodate large (14-7/8" × 11") computer printouts.
- Desk chairs are designed ergonomically, with lower- and upper-back supports as well as height adjustments.
- Dust-free "white" boards and felt-tip markers have replaced traditional, dusty chalkboards.

Telecommunications. Traditionally, communication links used for voice and data transmission were separate. This no longer is true. The time is approaching when traffic over a company's telephone system may consist of significant amounts of data mixed with traditional voice transmissions. The time already has arrived when it is feasible and desirable to arrange for internal communication service that accommodates both voice and data transmissions.

Increasingly, therefore, digital circuits and switching mechanisms are being ordered to handle both voice and data. Also, desk-top devices coming into the marketplace incorporate both computing and telecommunication capabilities in the same units. Information workers can use computers to talk with other computers or to dial connections for voice communication. Voice and data messages can be stored within some integrated business communication network. Planning for CIS staff facilities should keep in mind that telecommunications support will require an integration of voice and data capabilities.

Heating and air conditioning. Comfort in the work area has come to equate to worker productivity and to a minimizing of turnover. To compete for employment of skilled, scarce people, a company needs to set up comfortable working conditions. Each area of an office should have individual thermostatic control. Direct exposure to ventilators or blowers should be avoided.

Special concern for the physical work environment is needed when facilities are housed in some form of open bay. The placement of partitions in open areas can have a great impact on the distribution of heating and cooling air flows. Expert advice should be sought and results should be monitored.

Acoustics. Particularly if open work areas are used, sounds created by activities at computer work stations may be distracting to thoughtful work. Although terminal operation is relatively quiet, conversations, the sounds of clicking keyboards, or the noise of printers may prove distracting to others. Accordingly, attention should be paid to the sound baffling potential of partitions, floor covering materials, and ceilings. Special hoods or coverings for equipment or sound-absorbing coverings for partitions may be considered.

Privacy and distractions. CIS staff members are expected to confer with peers, with members of their project teams, and with interview subjects. Often, these interactions occur in the regular workplace. Since these activities are important to the mission of the people involved, care should be taken to minimize both interruptions from others and to others in the area. In open-office situations, conference areas sometimes are provided. These areas either are isolated or in rooms with doors that can be closed. For services involving demonstration of equipment, as occurs when information center services are rendered, special demonstration centers often are created. The need for such facilities should be established during planning for staff facilities. Involvement and/or concurrence of affected personnel in planning for these needs can avoid friction or discontent after working quarters have been set up.

Use of color. Systems work involves deadlines and inevitable tensions. All of the factors described above can, if they are considered and implemented with care, help to create a relaxed, productive atmosphere. A final factor to be considered is the color schemes used for the partitions and walls in work areas. In general, bright, contrasting color schemes tend to increase tension while soft, blending colors tend to help people to relax. Choice of colors can contribute to the feeling of tranquility in any work area. This consideration, which is nontrivial, is covered further in the chapter that follows.

CAREER PATHING

CIS professionals generally have had extensive education and experience and, therefore, want a position in which growth and advancement are assured. A CIS function that fails to meet these aspirations may find its key staff members moving to better positions in other organizations. Some type of methodology should be set up to facilitate the professional growth of staff members. This methodology sometimes is known as career pathing. Some organizations document alternative promotion routes open to CIS professionals. An example of a career path is shown in Figure 7-6. Career pathing can be implemented in steps that include:

- Identification of employee goals
- Capabilities assessment
- Performance evaluation and feedback
- Availability of positions
- Training and education opportunities.

Identification of Employee Goals

In evaluating employee desires, or motivations, the goals and objectives of the organization also must be considered. Organizational goals and objectives often are less difficult to determine and may be documented. In some organizations, the gathering of information from employees takes place informally, but can be accomplished through effective communication.

When supervisors are aware of the career goals of employees, decisions can be made to help further employee goals. Supervisors have many informal sources for this information. Conversations between employees and their supervisors are perhaps the most prevalent source of information about employee aspirations. Effective supervision often requires an "open door" policy that enables employees to approach supervisors with any type of problem or request. Supervisors also may collect information during social gatherings, such as coffee breaks, lunches, or parties.

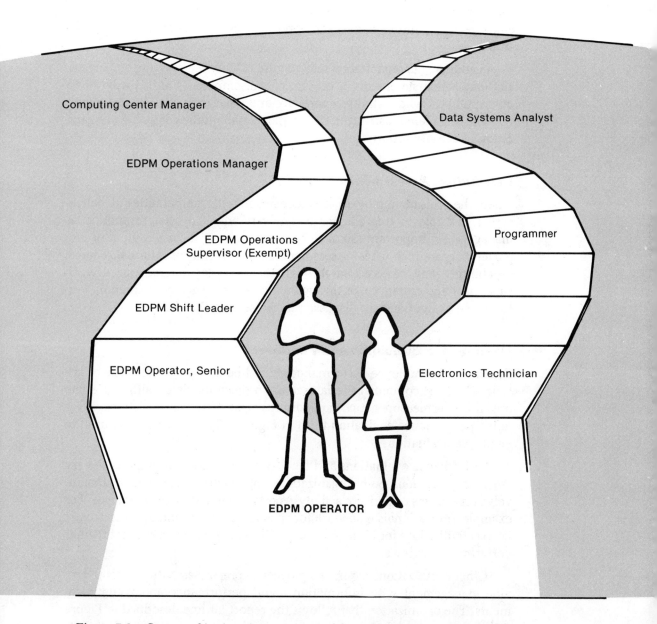

Figure 7-6. *Career pathing is an important part of the personnel function associated with CIS planning.*

A formal source of this information is employee evaluation meetings or performance reviews. Again, this method requires a free flow of communication between supervisor and employee. During these meetings, supervisors can discuss organizational needs, the strengths and shortcomings of employees, and future actions and opportunities for the organization and its employees.

In addition, an organization may require activity reports from employees, and may solicit statements of career goals of employees in this way. For a description on what activity reports are and what they contain, see Figure 7-7. This is a memo instructing CIS employees about the content and organization of activity reports.

Capabilities Assessment

Often, the goals of employees are inconsistent with their abilities. Recall an earlier example in this chapter of analysts who fail after promotion as managers. An important factor in career pathing is the assessment of employees' capabilities. These assessments may be formal or informal. That is, capabilities may be assessed through the everyday interaction between supervisor and employee, or through a formal performance evaluation. Performance evaluations are discussed in the section that follows.

Performance Evaluation and Feedback

Evaluation of employee performance should be based on some type of criteria. The most common criteria used are project due dates, although some organizations measure actual expenditures against budget projections. Refer to the performance evaluation form in Figure 7-5 for other criteria used in employee evaluation.

Performance evaluations and feedback procedures for employees vary among organizations. Some organizations implement formal methods that involve time sheets or periodic activity reports submitted by the employee. For example, professionals who work for consulting or accounting firms usually keep activities logs for billing purposes. These logs also can support regular performance reviews.

Other organizations require employees to prepare activity reports to provide management with information about performance and accomplishments. The organization that follows the report outline described in Figure 7-7 has many employees assigned to projects as consultants. These reports are submitted to project leaders and to designated CIS managers. Then, CIS

ACTIVITY REPORT OUTLINE

TO: Your Immediate Manager   **DATE:**
        (or Assistant Manager)

FROM: Staff Member and Section

SUBJECT: QUARTERLY ACTIVITY REPORT

COPIES: CIS Manager

Introduction

Assignment/project name(s)
Time period covered
Immediate supervisor/principal investigator(s)

Activities and Accomplishments

One paragraph (minimum) on each assignment highlighting what has been accomplished and what your specific contribution was.

Problems and Challenges

As many paragraphs as may be required to describe the situation, the likely outcome if no action is taken, and what you recommend.

Outlook for the Future

What you expect to be doing in the next three months, whether this will keep you fully occupied, and what you would like to do if the opportunity presented itself.

Professional Development

List any courses you are taking, any professional self-study that seriously occupies a portion of your time, and any outside professional activities in which you are engaged.

Closing Remarks

An open forum for any written input you would like to pass along plus an opportunity to request a conference if your path has not crossed ours recently.

Figure 7-7. *This is a guide for an activity reporting procedure that can be valuable in tracking the progress and career development needs for CIS employees.*

management uses the activity reports to monitor employee activities. The activity reports may be submitted quarterly, monthly, or on some other regular schedule.

Availability of Positions

After the goals and performances of employees have been evaluated, career paths must be adapted to available positions within the organization. This factor also involves communication between supervisors and employees. The supervisor should understand the desires and abilities of the employee and strive to find a position that is suitable. The employee, on the other hand, should know the goals of the organization and be willing to adapt, if necessary.

Many organizations sponsor career development seminars to facilitate this communication. The purpose of these seminars is to help employees plan realistic career paths and to provide information to employees about career paths available within the organization.

As positions become available, most companies use an established communication channel to advise employees of openings. These channels can include posting of notices on bulletin boards (visual or electronic), or publishing of notices in house organs. Any method selected should provide equal information access for all employees.

Training and Education Opportunities

Career pathing also involves encouraging improvement and maintenance of the professional knowledge of employees. Corporate policy concerning the continuing training and education of employees often is an important consideration of professionals seeking employment. In addition, the organization benefits when professionals strive to maintain current knowledge and training in their fields. There are many approaches to providing this training and education, and several may be found within single organizations.

One method is an educational reimbursement program. That is, the organization reimburses each employee who completes an approved class or course sequence successfully. The program may involve full repayment of all expenses or partial refund contingent upon a passing grade. The norm, however, seems to be a refund of from 50 to 75 percent of tuition and materials costs after successful completion of a class or training seminar.

Continuing training also may be provided to employees through internal classes or seminars. Thus, training departments may offer after-hours educational opportunities for employees who wish to upgrade or develop new skills. In these cases, the subjects of classes usually relate to organizational needs.

Another common educational avenue involves conferences and seminars sponsored by universities or private organizations. Seminars generally focus on specific topics, such as particular operating systems or application packages. Conferences provide overviews of large portions of or the entire computing industry.

For example, the National Computer Conference (NCC) is an annual event that features more than 650 hardware and software exhibits and a series of technical presentations. Attendees can compare the products of multiple vendors and attend presentations of the results of academic research and user experiences. This type of meeting encourages interaction among professionals and can be a valuable source of knowledge and support for CIS functions.

As increasing numbers of CIS professionals assume consulting roles in such assignments as information centers, a new educational requirement may be introduced: CIS personnel may require additional education and/or training in areas of general management or business operations.

CASE SCENARIO: THE NEED FOR RETAINING QUALIFIED STAFF

Management at NRA made an initial decision to minimize the disruption that would be sure to result from extensive staffing changes. In-place staff members have been instructed to continue to serve existing clients and to complete current projects under established practices and procedures. Members of the professional staff have been given wide latitude to exercise judgment in carrying out existing assignments. In general, the interim approach in the staffing area can be summed up as: "If it ain't broke, don't fix it."

In the CIS area, this means that management is encouraging staff members to continue to apply procedures and to implement systems that ultimately will be changed when operations are consolidated. NRA management is highly people oriented. Top managers realize that installing new equipment or writing new manuals doesn't produce or operate viable systems; people do. Further, top management members from each of the merged entities are convinced that each of the CIS organizations is staffed with quality people who will be an asset to NRA.

A potential problem in the staffing area lies in the need to hold on to as many members of the merged groups of computer professionals as possible. It is apparent, as described earlier, that all available systems analysts and programmers will be needed to develop and implement the new systems that will be required by the consolidated entity. Clearly, the development of new, corporate-level systems for NRA will provide at least three years of work for all members of the merged systems analysis and programming staffs. Beyond that, management expects that NRA growth will lead to a continuing, high demand for qualified computer professionals. Certainly, the identified backlog associated with the merger represents a high level of job security within the dynamic and unpredictable computer field.

Case Discussion/Assignment

Management's goal, then, is to maintain its existing CIS staff and to use all staff members effectively. Management feels that the new approaches and technologies to be applied will represent interesting challenges to all computer professionals. Given this situation, your assignment is to help Esther Producto by drafting the elements of a plan to implement this goal. First, prepare an outline of the salient points to be covered in a management statement. Then, as part of the implementation of the plan, draft a memo to computer professionals of both segments of the merged organization outlining the forthcoming opportunities and encouraging them to feel secure and needed. The idea is to encourage all of the affected people, particularly systems analysts and programmers, to stay in their present positions.

Discussion Topics

1. What is career pathing and how is career pathing implemented?

2. How is the process of career pathing similar to the process of project selection?

3. Why is it important to provide managerial training to line personnel who have been promoted to supervisory positions?

4. What is contract programming and how is it used?

5. Why is the use of numbers of lines of program code as a performance criterion being discontinued?

8

HARDWARE PLANNING

Abstract

In the area of hardware planning, CIS professionals continually change the environments in which they work and in which users are supported. A series of special, structured activities should guide and control plans for hardware changes, as well as implementations of conversions that carry out those plans. One of the first requirements is to recognize that there are differences between hardware plans that establish new facilities and plans that modify or upgrade existing facilities.

Other important requirements center around the fact that hardware planning requires relatively long lead times with many interrelated requirements, possibly from multiple vendors. Another challenge lies in evaluation of available equipment to establish correspondence between needs and performance. In turn, the considerations of lead time and capabilities are used to review the economics of CIS plans and requirements within each using organization and also to develop a realistic forecast of processing requirements for systems in operation, under development, or planned for the future.

A hardware planning process should encompass research into requirements and applicability of emerging technologies to meet those requirements. During this step, equipment alternatives are identified and recommendations are developed regarding the selection of alternatives. These recommendations, in turn, lead to equipment decisions.

Planning moves ahead with followup on decisions reached. The next step is to plan for facilities to house selected equipment. Implementation plans include activities for installation and conversion as well as for facilities. In advance of equipment deliveries, detailed plans must be set for acceptance tests. Careful plans must be made and adhered to for the startup of production on new equipment.

Throughout the planning cycle, feedback and reactive mechanisms must be in place. Feedback information should be acted upon where time permits and should be used after the fact to modify or improve hardware planning procedures.

HARDWARE PLANNING CONSIDERATIONS

There are differences between planning for a new environment and planning for the upgrade of an existing facility. Mainly, these differences center around the fact that upgrades deal with and may be constrained by layouts and capabilities that already exist. By comparison, a brand new facility can present an opportunity to start with blank walls. This text concentrates on the needs of a new environment.

Many steps are involved in planning for new computer hardware. These include:

- Lead-time considerations
- Evaluation of availabilities
- Review of economic situation
- Future requirements
- Determining capacity
- Research alternatives
- Recommendation of alternatives
- Decisions
- Facility planning
- Installation

- Acceptance test

- Production

- Feedback procedures.

LEAD-TIME CONSIDERATIONS

One, if not the most, important consideration in planning for new computer equipment acquisition is that of extended delivery dates. For example, it is not uncommon to find 12-, 18-, and 24-month delivery dates quoted for large mainframes and many minicomputers. The delivery delay is compounded by any request or need for special *components* or special *configurations* for new equipment.

In addition to delays in equipment delivery, other delays may be experienced in applications system development. As pointed out in earlier chapters, particularly in Chapter 4, acquisition of computer hardware is not the first item of consideration in the development of an application system. A preliminary equipment need may be identified during the first (investigation) phase of the application system development life cycle. But the actual equipment needed might not be determined until the third (detail design and implementation) phase. However, the order for the equipment would not be placed until actual processing needs and equipment requirements were known.

As a special equipment planning strategy, large users occasionally place tentative, or "protective," orders before final specifications are determined. This serves to put the buyer in a production/delivery queue with the manufacturer. Most manufacturers cooperate with this strategy and are willing to modify specifications for ordered equipment during the waiting period prior to production and shipment.

Users frequently are unaware of problems associated with delivery lead times. In part, this is because users tend to relate all equipment acquisition considerations to their experiences with microcomputers, which can be purchased off the shelf along with a wide range of ready-to-use software.

A further compounding of the equipment delivery problem comes from the ever-increasing rate of change that takes place in computing technology. By the time a medium- to large-scale application system can be developed, the hardware acquired, the programs written and tested, and the system placed into a production status, there will probably be several new equipment and software announcements that could affect implementation of the application.

EVALUATION OF AVAILABILITIES

An awareness of availability and capability of computing equipment is important for everyone associated with CIS plans that might require acquisition of new hardware. A person can maintain this awareness through a variety of avenues and activities, including:

- Preliminary facilities needs (to focus attention)

- Keeping up with technology

- Conference attendance

- Sharing with peers

- Trade publications and research groups.

Preliminary Facilities Needs

In terms of equipment planning, the term *facilities* refers to the space occupied by and the structural requirements for computer operations. New computing equipment is becoming increasingly smaller. Hence, less physical space seems to be needed for the equipment. In reality, however, space needs may only be shifting. For example, instead of a large mainframe computer in a central computer center, an organization may have many smaller, individual minicomputer or microcomputer work areas. Total area occupied by the computer equipment may be equal even though the space is distributed differently. Changes of computing locale may introduce new problems. One type of problem arises when microcomputers and associated equipment are superimposed upon an office area that originally housed clerical functions. Overcrowding, inadequate lighting, and inefficient operations can be just some of the results.

By contrast, the environment of a central computer facility always has required stringent controls. Electrical power, air conditioning, humidity control, fire safety, physical security, and accessibility of the hardware present requirements not needed at distributed sites. To deal with these variations in requirements, the planner must be aware of the implemented and planned changes to facilities.

Keeping Up With Technology

Computer technology changes constantly. The CIS planner must keep current continuously. Awareness must encompass hardware announcements, innovations in software and applications design tools, telecommunications, and changes in support materials. Announcements are made at special, invitation-only receptions, at conferences, at press briefings, and in newspapers and trade publications. A planner should allocate time to maintain the currency of his or her knowledge.

Conference Attendance

One of the more common methods used for reviewing the state of the technology is conference attendance. Regularly scheduled conferences encompass all aspects of CIS technology. Some, like the National Computer Conference (NCC), the Telecommunications Conference (TCA), and COMDEX have a heavy hardware orientation; others are software oriented. There are shows devoted to a particular vertical market, such as the medical or retail marketing field, and seminars that provide instruction for a specific software package.

Among the benefits of conference attendance is the opportunity to view many similar pieces of equipment in a concentrated area. For example, if an organization is considering increased printing capability, conference attendance can provide an opportunity to view impact, electrostatic, ink jet, and laser printers from several manufacturers, on the same day, in a single location. In fact, if necessary, the planner can view competitive units several times by walking between them and asking leading questions. With the same convenience, conference attendance provides an opportunity to monitor overall industry trends.

In addition to the hardware exhibits, most conferences provide a series of technical educational sessions. Sessions typically cover new products or methods and offer evaluations of hardware and/or software. Demonstrations often are included.

Sharing With Peers

Much state-of-the-art knowledge is gathered from exchanges with peers. Information shared in this fashion can be the foundation for further research or data gathering.

Another source of information interchange with peers is provided by professional associations. In the computer field, prominent organizations include The Association for Computing Machinery (ACM), The Data Processing Management Association (DPMA), and many others. Some associations have a narrow focus of interests and industry activities while others have broad industry appeal. Some have special interest groups that concentrate upon a single subject area, such as a specific programming language. If a group or groups can be found that focus on topics of interest to a CIS planner, participation holds potential rewards through interchange of relevant information.

Trade Publications and Research Groups

Professional literature can provide resources that enable a planner to compare his or her needs with the experiences of others. To the extent that appropriate precedents or experiences can be identified, research can lead to valuable guidance or significant savings through problem avoidance. Some sources for such references and research include the trade press, Data Sources, Auerbach Reports, Data Pro, International Data Corporation (IDC), and the Gartner Group.

Trade publications, such as *Computerworld, Datamation,* and magazines or newsletters from the professional associations, present articles on timely topics by both professional journalists and industry users. Of particular importance are the in-depth studies of hardware and software and of new theories and concepts. Topics for this kind of coverage might be use of data dictionaries, software performance, and the value of subsecond response times.

REVIEW OF ECONOMIC SITUATION

Economic factors often hold make-or-break sway over CIS plans, projects, and/or operations. CIS planners should become familiar with these key economic factors, including:

- Cost of operation
- Projected useful life
- Technical and economic trade-offs
- New-used equipment trade-offs
- Lease-purchase trade-offs
- Continual change.

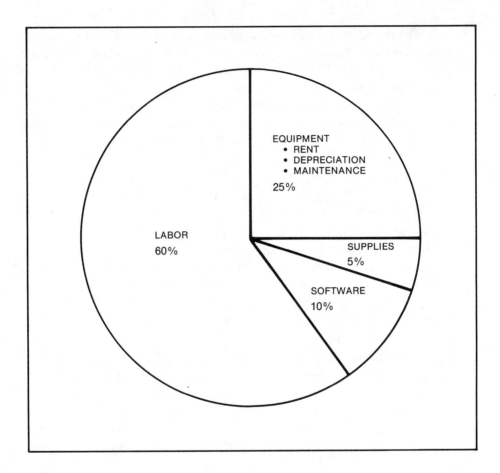

EQUIPMENT
- RENT
- DEPRECIATION
- MAINTENANCE

25%

LABOR
60%

SUPPLIES
5%

SOFTWARE
10%

Figure 8-1.   *This pie chart reflects expense distribution for a typical computer center.*

Cost of Operation

An awareness of costs is a vital part of planning knowledge. CIS planning must encompass cost-benefit analysis. To plan for tomorrow's expenditures, a CIS manager needs to be intimately familiar with today's costs. Areas of cost familiarity should include operations, distributions of costs to users, systems analysis, facilities, environmental control, power monitoring and failure protection, and others. Some organizations establish fixed, or standard, values to be used in CIS planning. A typical distribution of computer center costs is shown in Figure 8-1.

The other major CIS cost is for supplies such as continuous form paper. Requirements may include stock forms and special forms such as invoices or checks, magnetic storage media such as tapes and disks, and printer ribbons. Regardless of where supplies costs apply, they must be considered within CIS plans.

Beginning in the early 1980s, packaged software also became a major source of operational costs—for the individual user department if not the central computer center. Another software cost includes support software such as operating systems, sort programs, and other general-purpose utilities.

Projected Useful Life

Each hardware device and/or application system has its own projected useful life. The CIS planner should be aware of these figures for existing equipment and systems. This information provides a basis for projections of replacement schedules and costs. In addition, of course, knowledge of life expectancies for existing hardware and application programs can be valuable in projecting payout periods for planned equipment installations and systems. The costs associated with developing a computer system or installing a major piece of equipment must be amortized over an extended time period. Familiarity with past experience and useful-life expectations can provide important decision support for future CIS planning.

Technical and Economic Trade-Offs

Computing equipment almost invariably is considered as a capital investment. This means that depreciation schedules must be set up and followed for accounting and financial reporting purposes. Since the earliest days of computer use, there have been conflicts between technologies that obsolete computer equipment rapidly and accounting practices that require a longer period of depreciation. It is commonplace for CIS planners to demand equipment replacement on technological grounds while the company's books of account still show a hypothetic useful life of several years. For example, a new product announcement may outmode a device in two or three years while mandated accounting practices specify depreciation over five years. Since accounting records guide the financial destinies of a company, a question may arise about whether it is feasible to acquire hardware or develop application software if these actions will cause a write-off in financial reports. As a reference, Figure 8-2 shows a typical depreciation schedule for various types of computing equipment. In many instances, computing equipment will be superseded technologically before it is fully depreciated financially.

NRA MASTER TABLES
TYPE CODE TABLE

TYPE CODE	DESCRIPTION	ASSET LIFE IN YEARS	RESID VALUE %
801	CARD READER/PUNCH	10	10
802	COMPUTER, MICRO	03	0
803	COMPUTER, WORK STATION	03	0
804	COMPUTER, MINI	06	10
805	COMPUTER, MAINFRAME	06	10
806	COUPLERS, ACOUSTICAL	08	10
807	DISK DRIVE/WORK STATION	03	0
808	DISK DRIVE/CONTROLLER, MAINFRAME	10	10
809	DISK PACK, 100 - 300MB	06	10
810	DISK PACK, <100MB	06	10
811	KEYPUNCH/VERIFIER/ INTERPRETER	06	10
812	MODEM, <4800 BAUD	08	10
813	MODEM, >4800 BAUD	08	10
814	COMMUNICATION INTERFACE	06	10
815	MONITOR, CRT DISPLAY	08	10
816	MULTIPLEXOR, DATA	08	10
817	PAPER HANDLING EQUIPMENT	06	10

Figure 8-2. *This is an example of a depreciation schedule for a typical computer center. This schedule is completed on the facing page.*

TYPE CODE	DESCRIPTION	ASSET LIFE IN YEARS	RESID VALUE %
818	PRINTER, IMPACT, HIGH SPEED	12	0
819	PLOTTER, GRAPHICS	06	10
820	PRINTER/CONTROLLER, IMPACT, LETTER	05	0
821	PRINTER, LASER	06	10
822	TAPE DRIVE/CONTROLLER	06	10
823	TERMINAL, DUMB ASCII	08	10
824	TERMINAL, GRAPHICS	05	10
825	TERMINAL, HARD COPY	06	10
826	TERMINAL, HARD COPY, PORTABLE	06	10
827	MICROCOMPUTER SOFTWARE	03	0
828	FACILITY IMPROVEMENT CONSTRUCTION	10	0
829	FACILITY IMPROVEMENT EQUIPMENT	10	0
830	TAPES, MAGNETIC	10	0
831	COMMUNICATIONS CONTROLLERS	06	10
832	MOTOR GENERATOR	10	0

Figure 8-2 (concluded). *This is the final portion of the sample depreciation schedule for a computer center.*

New-Used Equipment Trade-Offs

At times, a hardware need may be satisfied with used equipment that can be purchased for substantially lower cost than new devices. This may be particularly true for individual work-station terminals and for situations in which the installed equipment is technically capable but does not have enough capacity. In cases such as this, a second, often used, machine is secured and the workload is absorbed through the addition of this new capacity. Also, the second machine can provide much-needed backup: If one of the machines is not working properly, the other can handle the more important processing until repairs are completed.

Lease-Purchase Trade-Offs

Early computing equipment was almost always leased. At this stage of industry development, leasing offered some clearcut advantages, including:

- Leasing was preferable to the high purchase costs then in effect.

- Leasing was a reliable way to secure and assure ongoing maintenance for trouble-prone equipment and rapidly changing software.

- Leasing provided protection against equipment obsolescence. Leased equipment could be returned to the manufacturer for replacement after relatively short lifespans.

A fourth reason, not relevant today, was that IBM, the major vendor, only leased equipment prior to a 1956 consent decree that settled an antitrust action brought by the Department of Justice.

In the late 1970s and early 1980s, large scale microtechnology impacted the balance of lease-purchase decision making. Microchips made all computers more cost-effective. In part, this was because the popularity of microcomputers made it feasible for suppliers to undertake mass production of microchips. Lower relative costs, in turn, brought computer system costs down to a level at which it became practical to purchase rather than to lease.

Another early barrier to purchase was the incompatibility of different makes and models of equipment. During the late 1970s and early 1980s, the ability to connect equipment from several vendors provided the planner with a new development tool: a broader competitive base from which to select.

Many organizations have adopted policies for lease and purchase of computing equipment according to capabilities and costs. For example, a mini- or mainframe computer that serves many users and costs more than ''X'' dollars would be leased while standalone work stations, terminals, and microcomputers costing less than "Y" dollars would be purchased.

Continual Change

The continual increase in computer hardware capabilities through the years has been counterbalanced by demands of increasingly sophisticated user applications. As memory and processing technologies have been enhanced, users have been quick to find ways to apply the expanded capabilities. A push-pull relationship has evolved. As new capacities are introduced, system and software techniques stimulate a backlog of new demands. Under these stimuli, changes in hardware configurations have occurred frequently enough so that change is regarded as a constant in the CIS field.

Fortunately, this type of change can prove to be economic and beneficial. Consider the organization with a Brand X, model 3, CPU that is leased from a third party (a leasing company), for $3,500 per month. The user organization finds it needs more computing power. Discussions with the leasing organization reveal that a Brand X, model 4, CPU can be leased for $2,500 per month, leading to a current reduction in expense but extending the total contract over an additional time frame for the new lease. The user gains an increase of approximately 100 percent in computing power, along with a cost saving of $1,000 per month. Significantly, all peripherals and existing software will operate on the new CPU without change.

Announcements of manufacturer upgrades often are accompanied by decreases in prices for earlier-generation equipment, which usually has been depreciated by the leasing organization. Therefore, the old CPU continues to have a viable market among smaller organizations with proportionately lower budgets. Such situations, in turn, make it necessary for CIS equipment planners to be aware of their current requirements and to update forecast needs continually.

FUTURE REQUIREMENTS

Perhaps the most common requirement is the growth in demand for information processing service. This growth often occurs as a result of the changes in technology and the increased awareness of computer capabilities. Growth of this type often is subtle and difficult to anticipate. One way of tracking this kind of growth is through preparation of equipment utilization charts or graphs. To illustrate, Figure 8-3 is a utilization chart showing the gradual growth in demand for CPU capacity.

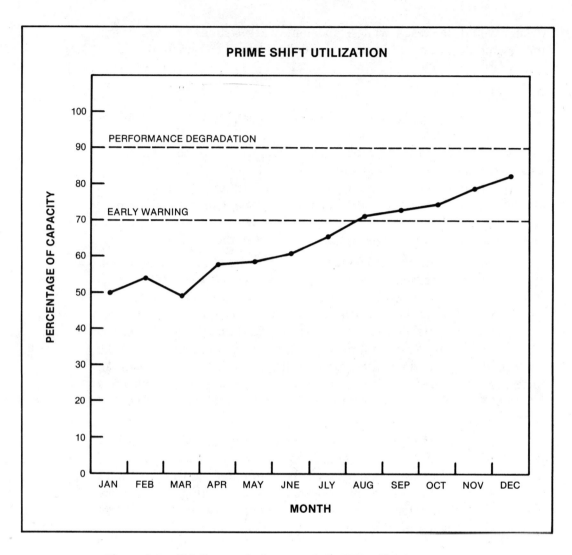

Figure 8-3.   *This line graph shows trends in CPU utilization.*

An example of subtle growth might be encountered in the use of the equipment for text processing. This application generally begins with a limited usage and expands, almost geometrically, to become one of the major equipment and data storage requirements. This increase in use is significant because it is not generally accompanied by a request, either formal or informal, for the additional capacity. At times, it would seem that the planner must be a detective to project requirements for service.

Growth of the business itself can be another important CIS planning factor. As a business grows, its production activities and transaction processing requirements are bound to expand and can generate additional demands for CIS services. Growth that impacts CIS services also can come in the form of a merger or an acquisition. As a business conglomerates, demands for data communication and computer time for processing of consolidated reports also expand.

The microcomputer has had a great effect on the growth in requests for information processing services. New, young employees have received at least minimum training in the use of computers in their formal education, sometimes beginning as early as elementary school. Employees with this background come to their jobs with an established understanding of how computers work and some idea about what they can do. Growth in overall demand for computer services often begins when an employee is assigned a microcomputer as a standalone tool for a specific application. Through exposure, dependency upon computers increases and demands often are generated for access to central data files.

DETERMINING CAPACITY

An important part of hardware planning is the determination of capacity requirements. Several of the areas that should be considered are:

- Real memory
- Magnetic tape
- Magnetic disk
- Draft and letter quality print needs
- Computing capacity.

Real Memory

The amount of internal (real) memory (as distinct from virtual memory) available on a given computer configuration can have a significant effect on processing capabilities. Internal memory is, of course, the fastest means of storing and accessing data and program segments, including system and application software.

Frequently, a particular program will require a minimum amount of internal memory. For example, certain spreadsheet and word processing packages used on microcomputers load only limited modules at any given time as a method for minimizing memory demands, and will rely upon slower disk references to provide program modules and data that cannot be accommodated in memory. Peformance capabilities are compromised by the need for frequent disk references.

Conversely, the more frequently a computer can find necessary program modules and data in its memory, the greater its throughput will be on any given application. In general, each application package will have specifications on the amount of memory needed for software, as well as recommended allowances for data files. Often, a new application system for which new hardware is requested may dictate requirements for main memory capacity.

As part of memory planning, the potential for coordinating memory operations with external storage should be considered. Instructions must be in internal memory to be executed. Therefore, instructions held on external storage devices must be brought into internal memory for execution. A determination must be made whether each new application can be supported through use of secondary storage as an extension of memory.

Magnetic Tape

Magnetic tape storage is a standard medium for storage of computer data. The amount of data that can be stored on a single tape, usually stated in the number of bits that can be recorded on one inch of the tape, continues to increase.

Data stored on magnetic tapes are organized sequentially. That is, the records are stored end to end over the length of the tape. Generally, the records will be in an orderly sequence according to values in one or more of the fields of data. The fields that are used to identify records for file organization are called *keys*. For example, the records on a tape containing the weekly time cards for all company employees may be recorded in sequence by employee number within departments. In this case, the department number would be used as the first basis for establishing sequence: The primary key. Employee numbers that establish sequence within departments would be a secondary key.

A drawback to the use of magnetic tape is that retrieval of records is slow because the entire file must be processed each time data are accessed. To retrieve a record representing a single time card, each record must be read and compared with the desired employee number. If the record sought is in position 5,000 on the file, the 4,999 records in front of it must be read and checked.

For applications in which the entire file is processed during each updating cycle, as well as for applications with low activity and high volume data needs, tape can be an ideal storage medium. For instance, data stored on other types of media may be copied to a magnetic tape for backup purposes. Such backups are necessary as a protection against equipment failure and disasters that might destroy the working version of a data file or operating system.

Magnetic Disk

Magnetic disk performs a function similar to that of magnetic tape—providing a medium for secondary data and program storage. Data within the files on disk may be organized in several ways. The more common are sequential (as on tape), indexed, and direct. Indexed organization permits the retrieval of a record through an initial reference to a computer-maintained table of key fields and addresses to find its disk location.

Planning for utilization of disk storage involves evaluation of storage requirements for a number of different types of files that may require varying levels of support. The types of files include the operating systems, program libraries, data files, work space, and space for growth. Operating systems require large amounts of storage to hold multiple programs that supervise and control hardware and software functions. Program libraries contain the operating versions of the application programs to be used to process data.

Storage requirements for data files are subject to many variables of program structure and record volume. Volumes, of course, relate to the size of the using organization and its CIS dependence. Data file storage requirements would be different for each organization. Work space is necessary for processing outputs. Sorting of data files, temporary files, and space to record summary data and form communication links between system steps are included in this space. Finally, a computing system must have space to grow as new application systems are requested and developed.

Draft and Letter Quality Print Needs

An important capacity consideration is concerned with printed outputs. In general, three types of printing capacities should be considered. The first is a high-speed output used to produce large-volume reports. The second is somewhat slower and produces draft quality documents. The last is a device to produce letter quality documents for correspondence purposes. The latter two are most often used with desk-top work stations. High-speed devices are used with medium- and large-sized equipment configurations.

Computing Capacity

A common method for determining the productive potential of a computer is to create benchmark tests in which known volumes of processing are executed. The processing time for the benchmark represents a capacity rating for the computer. Many organizations conduct benchmark tests as a basis for selection of new hardware and software. To benchmark, an organization develops a set of functions that the desired hardware or software must be capable of performing. Each vendor is asked to perform the functions and to document the results. Considerations such as ease of use, length of time needed to accomplish the task, accuracy of the output, whether the process is machine or software supported, and whether the desired output was derived are part of a benchmark test. Careful consideration must precede a benchmark test to avoid situations in which the costs for the tests are out of line with the decisions being made.

RESEARCH ALTERNATIVES

Any significant hardware or software acquisition should include consideration of a number of appropriate, potentially viable alternatives. In this sense, alternatives include different ways to do the same job, as well as selections among multiple vendors. For example, there may be trade-offs between hardware features that accomplish the same function as a software package. A given device may be slower than its alternative but might deliver substantial cost savings in an application that can accommodate the delivery delays. One software package may be more expensive to purchase and operate than a competitor but may offer offsetting advantages of ease of use and operator training.

Information upon which to base the selection of alternatives can be collected from friends and peers in the industry; trade publications; research organizations such as Data Sources, Datapro, IDC (International Data Corporation), Gartner Group, and Auerbach; and from personal experiences.

RECOMMENDATION OF ALTERNATIVES

The evaluation of alternatives should lead to a recommendation. The recommendation may be a chart showing the alternatives and the criteria used in the evaluation. Each point in the chart matrix will indicate the results of an evaluation process. Although the planner may indicate a recommendation, the chief decision maker can draw conclusions from the chart.

The recommendation may present a series of alternatives ranked in a priority order with supporting documentation for each statement. An example of this type of recommendation might be the acquisition of a new computer. The alternatives might include purchase from the manufacturer, lease from the manufacturer, lease from a third party, or purchase from a used equipment dealer.

Presentation of the alternatives and recommendations may be in a written report read by the decision maker. Most often, however, the written report will be presented to the decision maker by the planner at the same time that an oral presentation is made. This gives the planner an opportunity to explain the reasons for making the particular recommendation and to answer questions for the decision maker.

DECISIONS

Multiple decisions may result from the presentation of a recommendation. After consideration, the organization may decide to:

- Postpone any action
- Request more study and another report at a later date
- Select two or three alternatives for further study
- Select one of the alternatives for development and implementation.

When the decision is finally made to move forward, the planner can issue a request for a purchase order.

FACILITY PLANNING

Planning for the facilities needed for a computing device or devices can be a major part of the acquisition effort. Required tasks include the development of a detailed procedure accompanied by a time line showing the expected completion date for all steps. An implementation plan must take into account the time necessary either to define and write or to purchase and test the software that will be used. Special care should be taken to schedule and coordinate the delivery of the hardware and availability of the software so that a return on these investments is realized as soon as feasible. Development of the detail task list and time schedule should include a plan for how the software will be tested. Some vendors provide test time on their own in-house equipment.

Local service bureaus may provide a good source of support for system and application test activities. A short-term contract for use of specific equipment may be advisable. Additional sources of assistance for testing software may be found among other users of the same kind of equipment. In fact, there may be a users group whose members are committed to supporting others with installation testing and catastrophe backup. The planner should remember to allot funding for the travel and per diem expenses associated with any off-site testing. Some of the areas of concern for planning a computing facility to meet specific organization requirements include:

- Space
- Power
- Air conditioning
- Security
- Safety
- Access
- Communication links.

Space

Space is among the early and more important areas of concern in facility planning. Space must be provided for equipment and people.

If a mainframe or minicomputer is to be acquired, a representative of the manufacturer normally will schedule a site visit to assist in the design of physical facilities. For smaller equipment, this task is generally left to the computer planner or the user. Regardless of the size of the equipment, the physical space needed must include room around the equipment for adequate cooling and service. Space must be provided so that all panels can be opened for maintenance. A document listing typical space requirements to support a new computer facility is shown in Figure 8-4.

Consider the space needs for an executive work station, a word processor for a secretary, or a work-station terminal for a computing professional. Each of these will take at least twice the space necessary for a normal typewriter, particularly if a printer is included. Remember, too, that the secretary may not give up the typewriter for some time (if at all). It may, therefore, be necessary to provide space for both a microcomputer and a typewriter.

In the past, few executives have required either terminals or typewriters. So, the space needed for them is all new. This situation may be the easiest to solve because the executive will have the larger office and some available space.

The computing professional generally will be replacing a simple terminal with a multiple-unit device such as a microcomputer. Desk-top space requirements typically will be doubled. If a printer is to be included in the work station, remember that space must be allocated both for the blank paper and for the printed report as it is output.

Often, as described in the previous chapter, the policies of an organization for allocation of space by job classification do not provide enough space to accommodate the replacement of typewriters with microcomputers. Without proper planning, crowded conditions may result and may lead to low use or misuse of equipment, employee dissatisfaction, and, in extreme cases, employee turnover.

Power

Planning for the electrical power needed to support computing equipment has always been important. This factor has become even more important with the widespread installation of microcomputers. The standard for medium- and large-scale computer equipment has been a conditioned line. A conditioned or clean line is one that supplies a constant, nonvarying source of power. A dirty line is one where the power fluctuates and is not constant. An example of an unacceptable power source might be a line that services a large number of devices that are turned on and off frequently.

The planner should secure accurate, up-to-date diagrams of the circuits to be used. Next, each outlet should be checked to validate its use. All devices

NEW FACILITY REQUIREMENTS

1. Equipment requires 5,000 square feet.

2. The Engineering Support Laboratory requires 1,000 square feet.

3. Computer Center is to be on two levels, one level directly over the other.

4. Computer Center needs 70 tons of air conditioning from central plant.

5. Spare air conditioning capacity during maintenance, etc., must be equal to normal requirements.

6. Facility will require 300 KVA of conditioned power plus 15 minutes of standby power (battery).

7. All floor levels must be serviceable by freight elevator.

8. Loading dock with wide doors is needed. It must be positioned so that 55-foot trailers can be backed up to the dock.

Figure 8-4.   *This listing identifies typical space requirements for support of a new computer facility. The listing continues on the facing page.*

9. Tape vault of 500 square feet with automatic fire
   door and separate Halon or CO_2 system is required.

10. Zoned Halon fire protection with integrated smoke
    and heat detectors is necessary.

11. Data network must be prewired into all staff
    working areas of the building.

12. Each staff office should have at least two double-
    outlet power receptacles.

13. Office space is required for 40 applications
    programmers and 10 systems programmers (includes
    text processing support).

14. Office space is required for eight programming
    consultants.

15. There should be three to five public terminal and
    printing rooms of 180 to 200 square feet each.

16. Forms and supplies storage requires 600 square
    feet.

Figure 8-4 (concluded).   *This is a continuation of the listing of computer facility space requirements.*

connected to the circuit should be recorded on the circuit diagram, along with their projected use and power needs. Power usage should be surveyed on a regular basis, perhaps once or twice each year. Power surges, often called spikes, can damage the internal parts of a computer and peripheral devices. Also, low power is sometimes as damaging to a computer as a power spike.

All breakers in an electric control box should be labeled clearly. The labels should be inside the door of the control box and a copy should be kept in a secure area, such as an office safe. All operations personnel or direct users should know where they can turn off the main power switch in case of an emergency. Often, a computer center will have an emergency power-off switch, generally called the *EPO*, that controls all power in the facility.

The great speed and processing capability of computers, particularly large-scale computers, means that a power failure or interruption, even for a part of a second, can cause loss of large volumes of data. For this reason, many organizations install surge-protection devices or an auxiliary power supply in the form of either a battery system or a generator system. Methods used are similar to those installed in hospitals, police facilities, and telephone central offices. For computer centers, battery systems called *uninterruptable power supplies (UPS)* are used most commonly.

Air Conditioning

Medium- and large-scale computers require controlled environments—particularly air conditioning. Computing equipment in these size ranges will not work properly if the temperature varies more than a few degrees. Many computers generate large amounts of heat and must be cooled to prevent equipment failure and damage. The CPUs of some large computers are water cooled.

The planner must provide computer center management and shift supervisors with schematics showing the location of the humidity controls, air handlers, and air ducts. Also, there should be a written procedure specifying actions to be taken if the air conditioning fails. The authors can recall instances in which large fans blowing over garbage cans filled with ice were used to support critical processing when air conditioning failed.

The best systems are designed so that air conditioning is shut down automatically in the event of fire to prevent spreading the products of combustion throughout the building.

Security

Computer center security measures should protect hardware, software, and data—and should control access to locations where these assets are stored and used.

A human guard is probably the most used form of security for controlling access to critical areas. This form of control often is supported by a sign-in/sign-out log sheet and a badging system. Some badges contain an encoded magnetic strip that opens electronic locks for qualified people.

To implement physical security, some computer centers use double locked doors with a vestibule between them. The person must enter through the first locked door, wait for it to close, then open the second locked door. When this form of security is used, there is often a closed-circuit television observation of the vestibule area. The use of closed-circuit television with two-way communication and electronic releases for locked areas also is used extensively.

Another vital security concern is the storage of software programs and data file backups. An operating version of software and data files must, of course, be available in the computing center. In addition, a backup copy must be stored somewhere off-site in case of an unforeseen disaster. Methods used for off-site storage include the rental of a safe storage facility at a location such as a bank, or the exchange of backup copies with other users. Use of fireproof safes is by far the most secure and protected. Trading storage space is probably the least expensive—and also the least secure.

Organizations frequently use a combination of these methods. An internal safe is used for storing operational backups of operating systems and critical files. An external source is used to store a secure copy of these same files. There are services that specialize in providing safe storage resources. Noncritical data may be consigned to public warehouses or exchanged with a cooperating user.

A complete security plan should include provision for an alternative operating site. Such a site plan may be an agreement with another organization that has compatible equipment, with the equipment manufacturer, or with a service that provides hardware for such purposes. Such an agreement may require that a retainer be paid to insure that the resource will be available if and when it is needed. Plans for this type of security are necessary in case of "acts of God," such as earthquakes and floods, or acts of fraud or sabotage or vandalism.

Safety

In planning for the safety aspects of equipment acquisition and installation, a good place to begin is with a checklist of the regulations that must be followed. These should include local, state, and federal safety rules governing such factors as the number of fire extinguishers necessary and their locations. These rules also dictate how the extinguishers will be marked and their color. Often, extinguishers are required even though a complete Halon (inert gas) extinguishing system is in place.

If water sprinklers are used, care must be taken to protect against electrical damage to computing equipment. In general, water systems are not recommended as protection against electrical fires, except as a last resort to protect the building itself.

Other rules by regulatory agencies concern locations for the storage of hand trucks and carts, the direction (in or out) for opening doors, and the placement of ramps that replace stairs.

Planning for the safety of people and resources in a computer center requires attention to a myriad of details. Some other elements of this area of responsibility are described below.

Location of magnetic media. Media should be close enough for effective processing and far enough away from electrical transformers and other devices that can destroy their magnetic records.

Placement of smoke and heat detectors. Smoke detectors should be located in relation to potential sources of alarm. Placement patterns should be established to assure efficiency in detection as early as possible. Smoke detectors and other such devices should be connected to the company central alarm systems. That is, when the smoke detector senses trouble and sounds an audible alarm, the security office and the local fire department also should be notified.

Provision for electrical outlets. There must be enough lines and outlets to avoid overloading the electrical system at any point.

Forms handling. Removing the carbons from multipart paper and bursting continuous-form paper can create a great deal of highly combustible dust. Dust can cause equipment malfunction if it gets into the internal workings of the computer. New paper supply storage and the area for handling the output from the computer should be placed with care to avoid these problems.

Avoiding water damage. Plant engineers generally are responsible for plans to avoid damage from plumbing systems—including sprinklers. The memories of many large-scale computers are water cooled. As with any plumbing, there is the danger of pipes bursting or, at least, leaking. Computer centers are particularly vulnerable to water damage because they often use raised floors that cover extensive electrical cabling networks. Moisture detectors generally are placed in the crawl space under the raised floor. However, even with the detectors, great damage can occur from leaking pipes before the detectors sound an alarm.

Access

Determination of access authorization should be part of the planning for new hardware. Access control techniques and measures must be determined before the equipment and its applications are put into operation. Many of the needs and concerns of access are covered in earlier paragraphs. To summarize, however, access considerations must be identified, documented, and the documentation made available to all potential users of the hardware.

The two areas of concern about access identified most often are physical and electronic. Physical access, covered above in the section on security, encompasses the procedures and devices used to authorize and implement access to computer hardware. For example, most medium- and large-scale computers are housed in a secure environment and only certain people are allowed into the computer room.

If the equipment provides for electronic access, the planner must document the procedures for approving access, training users, and monitoring the activity. Electronic keys in the form of account numbers and passwords must be defined.

Communication Links

Two areas of communication within the computer center itself must be addressed as part of facilities planning:

- Voice

- Data.

Voice.   Provision must be made for giving verbal instructions to the people who operate a computer center. Any piece of computing equipment will occasionally malfunction and need service. There must be procedures to tell the operators whom to call for service. When input/output terminal devices are connected to a computer from remote locations, there must be a central location for reporting trouble. Organizations often provide a "help" or "hot" line service for such reporting. Users call the service to report equipment problems, to seek help in using either the hardware or a particular software package, or to inquire about expanded use of the resources.

Data.   Considerations associated with data communication are primarily with defining the needs and transmission rates. The defined need is associated with the discussion of access and security. That is, when data are available for access from remote locations, the plan must provide methods for approving user requests for that access. Authorization levels include access to look at data, to change or enter data, or to manipulate data. For example, a bank customer using an ATM can check (look at) the status of his or her account, make a withdrawal (change or enter data), but cannot manipulate the data.

Terminals operated by users, such as ATMs or terminals for airline or hotel reservations, generally can be supported by relatively slow transmission speeds. Voice-grade lines typically are used for these data communication links.

On the other hand, a bank teller or an applications programmer would normally need faster responses. Some equipment can support both low- and high-speed transmission. Many manufacturers provide networking capability for their equipment to enhance cost-effectiveness of high-speed data access.

INSTALLATION

Implementation is an important part of any hardware plan. The implementation portion of the plan should contain statements describing the actions to be followed, from development through operational conversion, in the areas of:

- Hardware
- Software
- Personnel
- Training
- Supplies.

Hardware

The implementation plan for the hardware would include:

- A calendar for the events leading up to the delivery of the hardware and the activities leading to operational status
- A schedule of the physical site development activities
- Specifications for setting up and using the new equipment, including location, power, etc., while old equipment still may be in place and in use
- Necessary agreements for use of either the manufacturer's or other leased equipment for early program and system checkout
- Specification for overlapped processing procedures if conversions are to take place in parallel.

Software

Perhaps the most important part of the software portion of an implementation plan lies in choosing which operating system and which programming language or languages will be used. These decisions may be dictated by a vendor if off-the-shelf software packages are to be installed.

The schedule for development of systems and applications software should establish the sequence in which the systems and applications programs will be designed, coded, and tested. For example, all application programs that control daily data input functions may have the highest priority while monthly, quarterly, and annual reports would have the lowest priority. Schedules also should be established for the sequence to be followed in conversion of existing files.

Personnel

The implementation plan for personnel should specify the types of personnel needed, the number of each type needed, and when they will be needed. Job descriptions and salary levels often will be included.

The heavy workloads associated with system conversion often are subcontracted to specialized outside organizations. Although personnel expenses may be high for the specific tasks performed, overall costs may be reduced because overtime expenses or the costs of hiring, paying fringe benefits, and terminating temporary personnel are avoided. In addition, specialized contractors will have employees who are trained in the specific work to be done. Thus, subcontracting reduces otherwise-unavoidable training and startup costs for the using organization.

Training

At least three major levels of training must be considered in connection with the implementation of a new system. These are for CIS personnel, users, and management. Training also is necessary to enable computer professionals to keep up with changing technology. Such specialists as computer analysts, programmers, and equipment operators require training to enable them to master new automated design and development tools, new and revised programming languages, and database management tools.

Analysts must be trained at two separate levels, both at an early stage in the development cycle. First, the analyst must have enough knowledge of the new concepts to make decisions about their use. This training may be received through reading trade publications; attending conferences, seminars, and local meetings of professional associations; and/or by talking to peers in the industry. After the decision is made to use a particular design concept or theory, a more intense level of training is required. Sometimes, the only way an organization can acquire this level of expertise is to hire from outside. As an alternative, established employees can be trained at vendor facilities or in local schools and/or colleges.

If a new programming language is to be used, programmers must receive enough formal training to write reasonably efficient programs. One alternative for acquiring such training is attendance at a technical school or university. If the number of personnel is great enough, it can be cost-productive to hire an educator to conduct on-site classes. As further alternatives, self-study materials can be used, with employees given working time to acquire these new skills.

At another level, training is needed for end users of a new system. This training should concentrate on specific, user-implemented input and output operations. In many instances, a user manual with instructions and sample figures is prepared. The earlier this training can begin, the better the chance that the user employees will support the new system.

Training for computer operations personnel may involve hands-on practice and special instructions for data entry personnel. For console and peripheral operators, special manuals on setup and on the meanings of *prompt* or error messages usually are required. Job scheduling instructions are, of course, critical to all operations personnel.

Supplies

The implementation plan should include a recommendation for the acquisition of supplies. This includes expendables such as paper and ribbons, nonexpendables such as disk packs and tapes, and one-time purchases such as copies of manuals.

Paper can include continuous forms on plain white stock or with horizontal bars. Paper requirements also may include special-purpose forms such as preprinted invoices, accounts payable checks, and payroll checks. The major concern with this type of supply is cost, even though quantity discounts usually are available. On the surface, discounts can look very attractive until the cost of warehouse space is computed. Also, an inexperienced planner might not be aware of the frequency of change within the organization. If systems have an average life cycle of three years and the usage of accounts payable checks is 5,000 per month, a purchase of 500,000 to take advantage of a 2 percent discount would not be wise. Many organizations have large quantities of old, obsolete forms occupying warehouse space. It is not unusual to find that the person who purchased these forms has left and that no one has been willing to make the decision to scrap the unused forms.

In other cases, there is a problem with shelf life. For example, NCR-type carbonless paper can have a relatively short shelf life. Shelf life also is a problem with inked ribbons for printers.

The relatively high cost of magnetic storage media such as tape and disk packs requires a special effort by the planner. There must be enough tapes and disks to hold live data plus backups, as well as a reasonable number of spares. It is not uncommon for an organization to need several thousand floppy disks. Even though a floppy disk may be low in cost, large quantities can add up to sizable investments.

ACCEPTANCE TEST

Acceptance test criteria form an important part of every hardware plan. The easiest test would be no test at all. That is, the manufacturer delivers the hardware and the organization accepts responsibility for installation and checkout. More often, however, the planner will prepare a set of tests that must be passed before the hardware is accepted. Some examples of criteria might be:

- All equipment components are received.
- All equipment components must operate free of errors for a period of 30 production days.
- Hardware speeds are verified through execution of a selected series of programs.
- Defined levels of storage capacities, both internal and external, are verified.
- Specified applications and operating system software packages must operate at predefined levels of performance.

PRODUCTION

The primary reason for acquiring new hardware is to produce defined outputs. Therefore, it is necessary for an implementation plan to define the conditions that must be met for equipment productivity. Some of these are covered above in the section on acceptance testing.

However, the plan also should establish a series of steps for putting the equipment into production after the acceptance test criteria have been satisfied. These steps should include:

- The conversion of historical master files
- Loading necessary databases to on-line storage
- Ensuring that all necessary communications lines are in place if distributed processing is to be supported
- Checkout of physical security procedures
- Checkout of data security procedures
- Ensuring that necessary supplies are on hand
- Testing data capture procedures and processes
- Setting up the new equipment in its permanent location.

FEEDBACK PROCEDURES

Just as there must be a process by which an application system is evaluated continuously with results reported to users, there also should be an evaluation process for operating hardware. Feedback on hardware performance should describe operating and processing efficiency.

One of the methods used to check on the operation of equipment is to prepare a report of the amount of time the equipment is down because of hardware or operating system failure. Another is an operations log that shows the time each operation started, the time the operation stopped, the peripheral equipment used, and the amount of internal memory required.

A reporting process should be developed to maintain a record of the amount of expendable supplies used. The manager of the information resources activity should be interested in a comparison of the current supplies usage with figures for past periods. Comparisons can include the cost for each printer of paper forms, ribbons, and toner. Comparisons of costs for electrical power and air conditioning also should be reported.

PERFORMANCE MONITORING

Performance monitoring measures the level of user satisfaction with services rendered. In a batch system, performance monitoring centers around the ability of a system to complete processing and deliver outputs to users within established parameters. For example, a bank must process checks received by tellers overnight and have on-line reference files ready for the start of business each morning. Also, a bank must be able to support ATM and teller terminals with, typically, a turnaround of two to four seconds. Thus, if a bank is crowding its deadlines for setting up customer files by 8 A.M. or if turnaround for on-line transactions occasionally (during busy lunch hours) slips to six or seven seconds, improvement may be necessary.

Each CIS organization should check performance against an established standard or, at least, should have a mechanism that responds to user complaints about the level or quality of service. Any slippage in performance quality should lead to a study that isolates the reason for the problem. To illustrate, a batch processing delay at a bank might be caused by growth in the size of the customer file that requires overnight processing. Given established software and hardware constraints, it could be possible that the daily sort operation takes two or three times longer than when the system was implemented. Such a problem could be solved by making additional disk hardware available and installing a more powerful sort program. The additional sort work space made available by new disk devices could reduce sort time and bring the application back into line with initial performance standards.

As an on-line example, a study might show that transaction volumes have grown at major branches because of new factory openings or new clients who run their payroll accounts through the bank. Another typical reason could be contention for communication capacity between teller stations and ATM units. A study might show that a number of branches share a 2,400-bits-per-second *bps* communication line. Conversion to a 4,800- or 9,600-bps line could make the problem disappear.

Within a planning context, any deviation from service standards for throughput and quality should trigger a study to identify causes. If service has fallen off, performance analysis may be the basis for identification of hardware or software solutions. Bear in mind that a growing number of software diagnostic programs are available to analyze performance and to identify causes of given problems.

JOB ACCOUNTING

Job accounting uses a data accumulation program to monitor and report on hardware utilization by job or job step. As applications are run, the job accounting software counts and keeps track of increments of system utilization, such as CPU seconds, printer lines, disk space occupied, input/output executions, memory utilization and other parameters that can be identified within individual systems.

Outputs of job accounting can provide a tool for measuring and evaluating the capacity of system capabilities that are being used. For example, the cumulative results of job accounting can report on percentage of available CPU time used in the overall application mix of an installation. As expected utilization approaches a saturation level, planning is required to provide capabilities for handling the expanded workload.

In this respect, use of job accounting data in hardware planning is reactive and is of little value to the strategic aspects of planning. However, job accounting outputs can be valuable inputs at the tactical and operational levels of hardware planning. Data on capacity utilization, for example, can be of value each time a new application is being added to an existing installation. For instance, suppose current utilization levels of CPU time are 65 percent and a new application would bring utilization to a level of more than 90 percent. Simply on their face value, these data indicate that additional hardware capabilities are needed.

Consider this situation further: The 90 percent utilization figure is, at best, an estimate. There could be an estimating error in projections for the new system. Errors also could creep into the current measurement figures through rounding of CPU seconds and other factors, or due to the level of accuracy of the measuring tools themselves. Over and above these potential errors, it is sound policy to provide for some measure of growth in every computer installation. A projection of 90 percent utilization would provide inadequate growth capacity for most computer facilities.

USAGE AND CONTROL OF SUPPLIES

In the total spectrum of computer center planning and operation, expendable supplies such as paper, ribbons, and microfilm rolls or sheets can seem a trivial concern. Don't be lulled into disregarding seemingly trivial supply items. Remember that these trivialities can, literally, put a computer center out of business in some instances.

At the same time, this criticality should not be construed as advice to overstock all supply items as a point of principle. Rather, planning activities should identify the necessity for a smooth, controlled flow of supplies into and through a computer center.

Particular attention should be paid to supply items unique to a given organization, such as checks, invoices, or other preprinted forms. Careful purchasing of such relatively high-cost items can pay attractive dividends. For one thing, anticipating overall required volumes can lead to attractive pricing. That is, it is far more advantageous to project a year's requirements and to work with a supplier to provide a continuous flow of needed forms than simply to order afresh each time on-hand stocks are low.

This doesn't mean that it is necessary to keep a storeroom full of preprinted forms to secure a favorable price. Arrangements can be made with forms suppliers to optimize print runs. A number of forms houses will hold stocks of ordered forms for future delivery to meet customer needs. Also, it may be possible to save film or plates to expedite reprinting. As long as installation managers and suppliers are aware of the need to plan for and monitor utilization of key supplies, dividends can be realized and a continuity of supply can be assured.

Be aware, above all, that planning for expendable computer supplies should be a responsibility of computer installation management. Suppliers are more than willing to take on this responsibility and to plan for and deliver multi-part, preprinted forms on a scheduled or individual demand basis. Such agreements, however, bring with them a loss of control by the using organization. Suppose, for example, a company changes banks or modifies an invoice form. Investments in otherwise-valuable supplies can be lost because the forms no longer are useful.

The need for internal planning and control over supplies can become particularly important as increasing numbers of organizations install nonimpact printers that can create form imprints as an integral part of the output function. In particular, the ability to include graphics in tabular outputs is reducing the volume of purchasing of preprinted and multipart forms for internal use. Nonimpact printers with capacities of up to 20,000 lines per minute can create multiple copies of outputs, fully imprinted with graphics elements, with greater economy than is possible through use of preprinted forms. Since such devices use a continuous flow of blank paper, printer setup time also is reduced substantially.

Formatting flexibility of xerographic processes in nonimpact printers also can compress data content and reduce costs for spreadsheet-type outputs. With impact printers, 132-column reports must be printed on extra-wide paper. Printers that use xerographic output can compress the size of the type and get the same data on standard, 11-inch-wide sheets, with considerable savings.

CONTINGENCY PLANNING

The name of the game in contingency planning is "You bet your company." Doing nothing risks disaster. The record is clear on this point. Each year, hundreds of businesses cease to exist because their business records are destroyed by fire, flood, or accident. Loss of information resources simply makes it impossible to continue doing business.

Between disaster and planning that provides for immediate, total recovery are several levels of contingency programs. For example, management can decide to accept power interruptions of up to two days without trying to replace computing capabilities. At other extremes, extensive amounts can be spent for power generators that turn on if a normal supply is interrupted, for off-site storage of programs and files, and for contracts that assure the availability of backup equipment on a rental basis if a computer facility is damaged or destroyed.

For several reasons, a full discussion of contingency planning is beyond the scope of this book. Among those reasons is the technical complexity of the problem. However, just as compelling a reason for avoiding this discussion is that few managers or planners heed warnings about the need for backup and recovery plans. Disasters are regarded widely as problems that happen to others. Suffice it to say, then, that dangers from natural and accidental catastrophes are real and that hardware planning should encompass the development of a formal policy that establishes the level and degree of protection to be incorporated into CIS plans. Without an edict supported by top management, there is little likelihood that definitive plans will be formulated and even less likelihood that anything will be done about implementing backup and recovery programs.

CASE SCENARIO: INTEGRATING THE INCOMPATIBLE

Though the lines of business of the entities merged into NRA are highly compatible, the same cannot be said for the separate installations of computer hardware. ARI and NC came into the merger with different brands of computers, each incompatible with the other. ARI, remember, was largely decentralized in its approach, except that a vital asset—perhaps the company's largest asset—is a database on radioactive waste disposal sites. On the other hand, NC, the smaller entity, had a centralized computer-facilities philosophy. Thus, even though ARI was five times as large as NC financially, the main computer centers of the two organizations were approximately equal in capacity and value.

On the one hand, ARI has a database which is, in effect, its stock in trade or the main operational asset. On the other hand, NC has centralized software and application programs that are more suitable to the setting up of a centralized facility. The obvious, major decision facing the task force studying computer integration lies in determining which brand of computer to adopt for the merged entity.

It becomes apparent, very quickly, that the merged company will be served best by selecting one of the two current suppliers to provide the mainframe for the new computer center. Also, to maintain the interest and loyalty of available staff, a decision is made to avoid integration through emulation. An emulator, of course, is a hardware-software approach that causes one computer to behave like another—albeit at a sacrifice in throughput. Computer professionals almost invariably aspire to work on systems that are on the leading edge of technology. Most systems analysts and programmers abhor the very thought of being associated with any form of emulation.

Another factor affecting hardware consolidation is the great importance accorded to the ARI database. Even though the NC application programs might be better suited to operational computing and management information systems, a decision is made not to cross manufacturing boundaries with the database. This means, in essence, that NRA management commits itself to an expanded version of the ARI system. It is hoped that the NC application programs, which are written primarily in COBOL, can provide a basis for the systems that will serve the unified organization.

Case Discussion/Assignment

NRA is about to launch a project aimed at specifying and installing a new central computer configuration. Based on the information provided above, write a brief statement of objectives for the project.

As an added, optional assignment to be completed at the discretion of your instructor, prepare an outline of the activities to be performed and the end products of each that are to be delivered by the hardware task force.

Discussion Topics

1. Explain this statement: In accounting for major hardware purchases, discrepancies often arise between the views of CIS technical personnel and budget makers.

2. What are contingency plans and why are contingency plans important to businesses?

3. What is an acceptance test?

4. What is benchmarking?

5. Describe the special requirements that CIS planners must address for facilities in which processing is distributed to remote locations.

6. Explain what is meant by the statement: CIS planners are involved in monitoring and review in two ways.

9

THE DECISION MAKING PROCESS

Abstract

Planning and decision making for equipment and software purchases (or leases) require the same kinds of step-by-step procedures and approvals that are involved in systems development projects. Regardless of the purpose or application, decision making benefits from an approach that incorporates an organized structure. A systems approach to decision making involves step-by-step procedures for stating objectives, identifying and evaluating requirements, generating and selecting alternatives, and implementing a chosen course of action. All phases and activities should be supported by documentation in the form of statements of objectives, specification statements, feasibility reports, cost analyses, and implementation plans. In addition, checkpoints should be incorporated throughout the system to provide a monitoring and review mechanism. At these checkpoints, presentations of data are made to appropriate managers, who evaluate and challenge the data. The continuation of the process depends upon the checkpoint approvals of these managers, who also retain the right to cancel the project.

A SYSTEMS APPROACH TO DECISION MAKING

Decisions made by planners in CIS functions often lead to major development projects. Depending upon the size of the organization, CIS or IRM (information resources management) managers may authorize expenditures of millions of dollars annually to update hardware and software. Decisions of this magnitude require approvals from corporate or organizational capital budget mechanisms.

Planning and decision making for equipment and software purchases (or leases) require the same kinds of step-by-step procedures and approvals that are involved in systems development projects. That is, an organized structure is needed. There must be checkpoints at which extensive presentations are made to and challenged by managers with capital budgeting responsibilities. Approvals (or cancellations) should be sought at each checkpoint and continuation of any given project should be subject to specific commitments.

In this sense, then, experience or education in the area of systems development should be applicable to decision making for CIS functions. The similarities are striking. Differences arise when decision-making techniques are applied to equipment planning. Therefore, the discussions and examples in this chapter emphasize decision making as applied to hardware planning.

The differences between decision making for systems development life cycle projects and for equipment planning center around the form of the project and the functions involved—and around the fact that the partnership with end users present in well-managed systems development projects is absent in hardware planning and installation. That is, when it comes to plans for equipment and system software, the CIS or IRM executive stands alone. In systems development projects, computer professionals can establish a common cause with end users who have initiated requests for service. In turn, these users can be held accountable for the values and justifications associated with development of an application to meet their needs.

Decision-making processes for equipment planning often can involve the same kinds of expense and equal time periods as systems projects. But there is no support or sharing of responsibility in reporting on and justifying the expenditures associated with a systems development project. The CIS function carries the full burden.

Figure 9-1 diagrams a series of steps and a management/feedback mechanism that comprise a typical decision-making process. As is true for

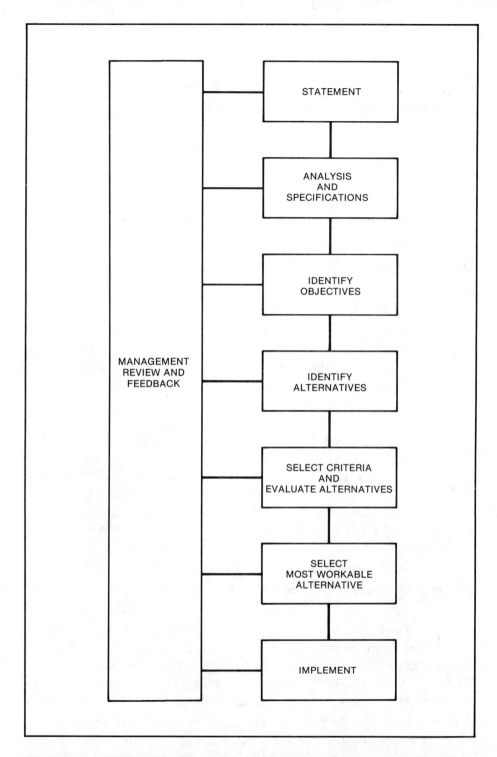

Figure 9-1. *This chart shows the steps in a typical decision-making process. Note the continuing presence of a feedback and monitoring mechanism throughout the process.*

any developmental process, these steps lead to a desired result. For the types of decisions involved in the CIS area, the following steps are appropriate:

- State decision objective(s).
- Perform analysis and develop specifications.
- Identify objectives.
- Identify alternatives.
- Establish decision criteria and evaluate alternatives.
- Select the most workable alternative.
- Implement the chosen alternative.

STATE DECISION OBJECTIVE(S)

Before any significant project is undertaken, directions and/or desired end results should be established. Given the magnitude of equipment planning decisions in IRM, the setting of objectives requires some formality. That is, a written statement should be produced to specify operations and goals.

One purpose for the written statement is to ensure that targeted objectives reflect actual requirements. The analysis of requirements often can be complex and difficult. What is perceived as a problem may be only a symptom of an underlying situation. Effective decision making addresses the foundations of any situation, rather than dealing only with possibly misleading surface indicators. The statement of objectives, as long as it addresses true causes of the situation under analysis, provides a tool for guiding decision making toward an appropriate solution. To illustrate, consider the case scenario that follows.

DECISION STATEMENT SCENARIO

Esther Producto, in keeping with her new position as CIS manager at NRA, has been approached by a few key users who feel that the organization's open-access text processing system is reaching an overload. At peak hours, response times for file access operations seem unacceptably slow. Producto has received reports from the operations manager of a disturbing number of head crashes and file-reconstruction requirements and of failures by users who attempt to access the system.

Some 300 individuals access the system through "dumb" terminals. Text files are maintained centrally. Printed outputs are produced by high-speed printers at the central facility and placed in user mailboxes for pickup.

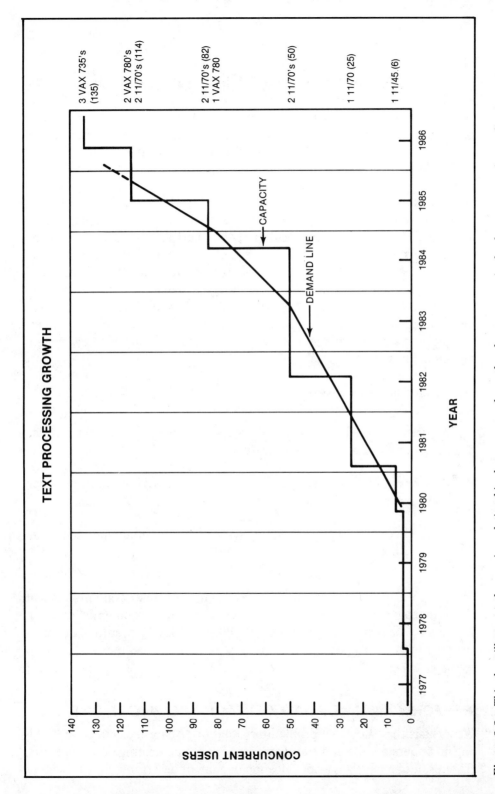

Figure 9-2. *This chart illustrates the growing relationships between user demand and system capacity for the text-processing application at NRA.*

Producto is aware that the situation is not yet acute. She feels that the existing system has some months, perhaps a year, of useful life. But experience has shown that it is best to plan, particularly within a growing organization. Producto knows that planning is most effective when efforts are applied to anticipate needs, rather than waiting for inevitable situations to develop into major problems.

In fact, this approach to planning is part of the basic philosophy at NRA. Producto described the problem to users in a memo that included the chart shown in Figure 9-2. Dissemination of the chart reassured users that the problem had been identified and also established a basis for communication about solutions. The chart shows that system capacity at NRA has increased incrementally over a number of years through installation of additional components and mainframes. The chart also shows that on-line terminals have been added to the system at a rate that has exceeded support capacities. Producto concluded the memo by outlining her intention to review system enhancements.

Given this situation, Producto prepares an initial list of objectives for submission to the organization's capital budget committee:

- Assure continued reliability and accessibility of text processing service for a period of at least three years.

- Provide simultaneous access for at least 150 users 24 hours daily, seven days per week.

- Assure backup and protection for active files containing up to four gigabytes of text.

Since reports and study documents are among the primary end products at NRA, management immediately expresses concern over potential drops in the quality of service given to clients. Producto is given authorization to proceed with the project.

PERFORM ANALYSIS AND DEVELOP SPECIFICATIONS

Analysis is the study of a problem or situation. Analysis is aimed at building an understanding and stating a purpose or at describing desired results. The result of analysis is a specification document describing the problem or situation and the general steps that can achieve the stated objectives. Analysis is necessary to understanding. Analysis of a decision statement should deliver answers to six basic questions:

- What?
- Where?
- When?
- Who?
- How?
- Why?

What?

As an initial step in problem analysis, CIS planners determine what procedures and capabilities already exist. The purposes and values of these procedures and capabilities also should be established. Planners may discover procedures that have been followed for long periods of time that have no apparent purpose. For example, reports may be produced and delivered to a long list of users who immediately discard the documents because the original requirements met by the reports have changed. Recipients of the outputs may not even be aware of how, when, or why the service was initiated. Analysis can assist in defining what the actual problem is and how the problem developed.

Within NRA, the problem is analyzed first by listing specifications of the existing system, which include such factors as: installed text processing hardware (including terminals), network configurations, and processing statistics according to days of the week and hours of the day.

Where?

Included in the specifications document are locales of operations under study. In addition, alternative locales may be explored and evaluated. Further, reasons for using existing locales may be presented as well as the pros and cons of distributing processing capabilities.

When?

Analysis activities collect information about existing processing schedules. Further, the study should help determine why the procedure is being performed according to these schedules and whether more efficient timetables can be produced. Finally, specifications should identify hours of peak or overload conditions. Thus, the specification document should present answers to questions such as: Is text processing support needed 24 hours a day? Seven days a week?

Who?

Performances and capabilities of operating personnel are evaluated. Again, planners must consider alternatives—such as recommending reassignment of personnel to make better use of individual abilities.

As an example, consider file backup. Suppose an inquiry by a systems analyst at NRA finds that backup copies of files currently are made by system programmers. The analyst also finds that backups are made randomly, or whenever system programmers have the time.

The systems analyst identifies some weak spots in the existing process. First, files should be backed up on regular schedules rather than sporadically. Second, the making of backup copies of files is too trivial a task for system programmers. Finally, the analyst has been trained to watch for the need for separation of duties in the handling of information assets. Persons with access to system software should not handle file media. Accordingly, this aspect of the existing system is highlighted on the specification document as requiring corrective action.

How?

The specification document presents the results of analyses of existing procedures. Emphasis is placed upon the physical aspects of equipment and procedures, rather than on logical elements of the system. Specific tasks for each procedure are evaluated. This analysis should answer questions such as: Why is the procedure performed in this manner? Can it be performed more efficiently or more economically?

Why?

Notice that in each of the above sections, analysts consider alternatives. In effect, analysts continually ask themselves: "Why can't this be done another way?" That is, analysts should challenge existing systems and procedures. This challenging attitude can provide an endless source of alternatives.

CASE SCENARIO: SPECIFICATION STATEMENT

Answers to probing questions serve to develop a picture of what is happening and what is needed. These answers, in turn, become the ingredients for a statement describing elements of a solution. For the text processing system at NRA, a preliminary statement might include the following specifications:

- The system must achieve 99.5 percent "up" time and must protect user files with the same level of reliability.

- The system must be able to accommodate at least 200 concurrent users to provide for anticipated expansion for the next three years.

- On-line files must be protected to a degree that assures users that no more than four hours' work will be lost, even under worst-case scenarios.

- Any user should be able to acquire access to the system within 20 seconds, at any hour.

- Users with files in excess of 500 kilobytes should receive weekly statements showing their level of utilization. This service will be aimed at encouraging users to purge unneeded files or to transfer them to inactive storage.

- Turnaround on printed documents should be enhanced. A messenger service that delivers finished documents within three hours of a request should be initiated. Rush service should be available at premium charges.

FEASIBILITY

The specification statement, then, presents a solution in general terms. As the project proceeds, this solution is evaluated according to its feasibility, or the possibility of implementing the solution under current conditions. The evaluation is presented in a report. The report should document prevailing conditions and describe workable alternatives in increasingly detailed terms.

The alternative solutions presented in the report should provide decision makers with enough data to support conclusions. The alternatives listed in the left column of Figure 9-3 demonstrate this concept. In this case, there are 10 possible alternatives. It is important to note that any alternative listed must be a workable solution to the problem.

A feasibility report is not always necessary. In some instances, the solution may be a modification of an existing system and only one alternative may be needed or possible.

RELIABILITY ALTERNATIVES

OBJECTIVES

ALTERNATIVES	RELIABILITY	NETWORKING CAPABILITY	OPERATING SYSTEM	HARDWARE COST PER USER	SOFTWARE COST PER USER	ELAPSED RESPONSE TIME	ON-LINE USERS CAPACITY
Fix 11/70	Yes	Yes ($)	No	<	>	>	114/150
Sun (NFS)	Yes	Yes	< VAX	> =	>	>	30/37 ea.
Brand X: Gould, Pyramid, CCI, Sequent	?	Yes	< VAX	<	>	> >	>32/40
DEC 8600	?	Yes	Ultrix	<	>	> >	134/168
IX/370 (UNIX/370)	Yes	No	No	<	> >	> >	?
Micro's	Yes	Yes ($)	No	> > > >	=	> >	300
VAX 780 (one)	Yes	Yes	Yes	=	=	=	96/120
VAX 785	Yes	Yes	Yes	<	=	>	107/136
VAX 785 + Upgrade 1 780	Yes	Yes	Yes	<	=	>	122/152
VAX 785 + Upgrade 2 780's	Yes	Yes	Yes	<	=	>	135/168

Figure 9-3. This is a decision evaluation matrix of the type that can be used in evaluating and selecting alternate hardware configurations.

IDENTIFY OBJECTIVES

The primary purpose of studying any problem is to find a solution. In development projects, data from feasibility studies break down this overall objective into levels of detail.

The column headings of the matrix shown in Figure 9-3 are examples of detail objectives for a problem solution. Objectives in this case include:

- Equipment reliability
- Networking capability of the equipment
- Operating system
- Hardware cost per user
- Cost of software per user
- Elapsed response time
- On-line users capacity (good response/maximum users).

IDENTIFY ALTERNATIVES

An alternative is a viable solution to a problem. However, although an alternative may solve an identified problem, it may fail to satisfy established criteria. For example, the first alternative solution in Figure 9-3 involves replacing the old, worn disk drives with new disk drives. While this measure would improve reliability, it would not provide the maximum reliability possible; and new disk drives would do nothing to improve response time for concurrent users.

One of the reasons for developing alternatives, then, is to establish criteria for selecting an appropriate solution. Remember that the selected alternative also must be approved by other managers. Selection criteria also provide a means to justify a selection. For example, the alternatives are evaluated and presented as follows:

- **Replace the worn disk drives.** As discussed above, this solution only deals with part of the reliability problem. Disk drives themselves would do nothing to resolve problems of concurrent service.

- **Replace the existing computer with a new one.** The proposed replacement equipment is a system with which personnel at NRA have previous operating experience. The reliability criteria would be satisfied, as would the objective of operating system compatibility. However, the model chosen would not increase capacities sufficiently or support projected expansion.

- **Supplement existing capacity through installation of remote, standalone microcomputers.** This approach sidesteps the identified problem, since microcomputers alone would not alleviate reliability problems in the existing system. Microcomputers also introduce new operating systems and word processing software, complicating maintenance and requiring users to master new procedures. Finally, processing costs for microcomputers are higher because each work station must be supported fully even though it is used only intermittently. For example, a mainframe system designed for 150 users might be capable of concurrent support for 50 terminals. By comparison, microcomputers would provide support for all 150 users at all times.

- **Replace the existing computer with a new computer that is compatible with the existing system.** This satisfies the reliability and operating system criteria but does not add capacity necessarily.

- **Replace the old computer with a new computer that is compatible and faster.** This approach satisfies the objectives for reliability and operating system compatibility. The capacity problem also is addressed.

At the outset, the selection of alternatives addresses the underlying problems that have led to the study. Specifically, the most important reasons for selecting the listed alternatives is to devise ways to improve system responsiveness and reliability. However, the choice of alternatives for consideration is never totally open or uninhibited. There is never an infinite supply of alternatives. Inevitably, there are constraints to be considered.

ESTABLISH DECISION CRITERIA AND EVALUATE ALTERNATIVES

Constraints on configuration and equipment selection can take many forms, depending upon the organization and the application involved. However, all decision constraints tend to fall into two broad categories:

- Resources
- Timing.

Resources. Constraints associated with resources can involve financial considerations, physical conditions, or personnel capabilities. Financial constraints center around budgets and capital investment policies. Managers in any organization should have stated, clear-cut expectations for returns on investments. These constraints apply to any decisions involving additions to computer configurations or acquisition of new equipment.

Physical constraints are set by limitations of facilities or services. Examples include limitations on floor space, air conditioning capacity, electrical power, or support functions such as media storage.

Major constraints involving personnel include the extent of experience or capabilities of systems programmers or users. Systems programming concerns center around the ability of technical personnel to handle the system software and hardware under consideration. Studies should determine the applicability of past experience and the need for retraining. Among users, determinations should be made about the compatibility of existing skills with systems under consideration, and about retraining needs.

Timing. Timing constraints are set by schedules and availabilities. Implementation programs usually present specific deadlines. New accounting systems, for example, generally are slated for implementation at the beginning of a fiscal year. Another facet of timing involves the ability of prospective vendors to deliver hardware and software on time. The computer industry abounds with stories of vendors that failed to deliver products as promised.

Because constraints represent working boundaries for selecting new system elements, they are the focus of attention in establishing decision criteria. In effect, a constraint is a boundary. Alternatives that exceed boundaries set by established constraints are disqualified.

Other decision criteria tend to sort themselves into requirements and preferences. Requirements are necessities such as file capacities, instruction execution times, benchmark performances, and so on. Preferences encompass features that are desirable but not rigid requirements. Examples of preferences include minimal consumption of power, limited heat output, no software revisions, and so on.

To summarize, the common denominator for decision criteria is that they should be stated clearly and in advance of the final decision. Vendors and decision makers should negotiate under the same set of rules. The decision criteria are the rules discussed in the following section.

SELECT THE MOST WORKABLE ALTERNATIVE

Decision making in the systems area is a process that inevitably involves compromise. That is, a selected alternative usually is the one that meets criteria most closely. Rarely is there an alternative that meets every requirement and preference for the selection.

Similarly, there are no sure-fire techniques for selecting the most appropriate alternative. However, a structured approach to weighing, or quantifying, decision elements can provide a measure of guidance for and confidence in selection procedures. Weighing decision elements involves evaluating each alternative against a collection of requirements and preferences. This process is discussed in an earlier chapter.

Under this approach, requirements are "must" factors. Every eligible alternative must conform to all requirements. Failure to meet any one requirement results in disqualification. Those alternatives that satisfy this screening then are evaluated according to stated preferences.

For each preference, every qualifying alternative is given a quantified rating, or score, typically from 1 to 10. All ratings are collected, and totals are developed for each alternative. The totals provide a guideline for the final decision. All things being equal, the alternative that meets all requirements and scores highest on preferences is the logical choice. However, many decision makers find it profitable to perform a final evaluation: the consideration of the negative consequences, or risks.

Simply stated, this final evaluation involves a walkthrough scenario of the consequences of implementing each alternative. The process should uncover any previously unforeseen drawbacks. The final choice, then, should be the alternative with the least significant negative consequences and the highest score in meeting requirements and preferences.

As part of the final selection process, decision makers also should remember an immutable alternative of any decision-making process: to do nothing. This alternative should be given the same consideration as any other. That is, the existing system should be evaluated against the stated requirements and preferences. An existing system always offers one feature that the alternatives cannot provide: It is in place, available, familiar, and probably comfortable for users.

On the other hand, if a replacement study has been launched, there must be some dissatisfaction. These negative factors should be evaluated objectively in terms of financial and personnel consequences. If a study gets as far as this evaluation, a change is probably in order. But, evaluation of the status quo helps to insure that a selected alternative provides improvements upon implementation.

IMPLEMENT THE CHOSEN ALTERNATIVE

Some highly publicized methodologies for decision making end with the selection of the most workable alternative. However, many bitter experiences have proven that unimplemented decisions have no more value than unfulfilled promises. Promises are not service. Delivery of service involves the application of careful planning and effective action *after* the selection process has been completed.

In terms of a decision-making mechanism, the main point is that the process is not complete until a thorough and acceptable plan for implementation is in place and has been accepted by all involved parties. In other words, planners and managers must follow through and deliver promised solutions. Since this discussion is not aimed at technical aspects of system implementation, no more need be said here—other than to remind readers that an accepted decision implies a commitment of resources for which decision makers may be held accountable.

CASE SCENARIO: IMPLEMENTATION

To illustrate the nature and extent of planning that is appropriate for implementing a decision, the following are some key elements of an implementation plan for NRA:

- An implementation plan and schedule should be prepared. To do this, all events associated with implementation must be identified, listed, and planned to establish a workable schedule. At NRA, critical path techniques are used to manage implementation of projects of this magnitude.

- Contracts with vendors should be prepared for delivery of equipment, software, and support services.

- The schedules of vendors and in-house organizations must be coordinated. Included are the lead times necessary to test all elements of a system, up to complete system tests.

- Facilities preparation requirements must be defined, and time and other resources must be allocated. It is axiomatic, though exceptions seem to prove the rule, that the site should be ready when equipment arrives.

- Operator and user training requirements should be determined and scheduled so that personnel are prepared for the arrival of the new system. Effective training programs can help to allay fears and avoid resistance to changes that are inevitable with the implementation of any new system.

- A conversion plan should be developed and accepted by all involved parties. Conversion methods (discussed elsewhere in this text) include immediate cutover, parallel operation during a phase-out period for the old system, or phased implementation in which departments or sites are converted individually and the entire system is implemented gradually.

- Network or other communication capabilities should be specified and integrated into the management system that will monitor implementation. It is worth bearing in mind that communication services often have inhibited the implementation of new systems.

MANAGEMENT REVIEW AND FEEDBACK

Recall the model of the decision-making process in Figure 9-1. Under this model, a separate review and feedback mechanism parallels the entire process and interfaces project activities at each step. The diagram illustrates the need for effective communication with managers who are responsible for approving—and funding—projects.

CIS professionals—present and future—should heed the first rule of management interaction: Know your managers and their expectations. Another important rule is to recognize the relative importance and magnitude of decisions. This knowledge base, together with personal relationships and experience, helps CIS personnel to determine what managers expect of reporting and reviewing processes.

In most cases, sound strategy calls for periodic update reports, both written and oral, for each phase of the decision-making process. In this way, managers are kept advised throughout the process.

These reports should be brief, but never overly simple. Decision makers should outline problem areas as well as successes. Experienced managers understand that there will be trade-offs in any major decision. The handling of these trade-offs determines the quality and appropriateness of decisions. Communications with management should identify and describe the handling of trade-offs and the reasons for actions taken.

However, reports that are too lengthy or detailed usually result in as many negative consequences as reports that are insufficient. That is, decision makers and management should strive to find an acceptable, workable balance in length and detail for reports.

Case Discussion/Assignment

It has been decided to adapt the method of text processing used within NC to all of NRA. The enlarged user population will include many persons who now use standalone microcomputers. Your job is to prepare a user training plan for users who will be added to the system. The same training program will be administered to newly hired employees. In formulating your plan, make special provisions for two categories of user: executives and executive secretaries. Bear in mind that it is generally considered to be politically unacceptable within organizations to schedule executive secretaries into the same class sessions as general clerical workers. Also, persons at the level of assistant vice-president and higher generally will not participate in group sessions. Levels of absence tend to be high because of travel and appointment schedules (and egos as well). Executives will have to be trained on an individual basis and programs for them will have to be abbreviated. As a strategy, it is best to train executive secretaries first, letting them provide ongoing assistance in building executive proficiency.

Discussion Topics

1. What is meant by a systems approach to decision making?

2. What is the difference between decision making for hardware acquisitions or facilities planning and for full-scale systems development projects?

3. Explain what is meant by this statement: The monitoring and review phase of decision making parallels the entire process.

4. Describe a feasibility report that is produced under the systems approach to decision making.

5. Why is it important to produce a formal statement of objectives for decision making?

10

INFORMATION RESOURCES FOR PROFESSIONAL KNOWLEDGE

Abstract

Information resource management (IRM) implements a new conception of the functions of computer systems and CIS personnel. As computer systems increase in sophistication, the information they handle increases in value to the organization. Information is now viewed as an asset, or a resource, of the organization. The traditional role ascribed to CIS functions, that of internal service facility, is being enhanced to encompass responsibilities for the efficient and effective management of a valuable business resource: information. The nature and capabilities of IRM professionals also are expanding. These professionals possess an added dimension of knowledge of business and management science as well as systems and computer technology. Professionals, by definition, cultivate a body of knowledge that supports their activities. Knowledge is derived and distilled from information. The ability of IRM professionals to maintain a competitive edge in businesses may depend on the currency and comprehensiveness of their body of knowledge. In turn, the technology used for business applications usually is slightly behind the most current developments of hardware and software. IRM professionals acquire knowledge from external sources, and then bring that knowledge to bear in solving existing problems or situations.

INFORMATION: A BUSINESS RESOURCE

In the past, effective managers were thought of as having an intrinsic quality for leadership. This philosophy could be expressed as: Managers are born, not made. As businesses and demands for managers grew, management was studied and specific attributes of effective managers were identified. Management skills were subject to being learned through training.

Modern theories describe management as a profession. A professional cultivates and brings an extensive and current body of knowledge to the performance of his or her work. Professional accountants, for example, regularly review information about new tax laws and market analyses to maintain their professional knowledge.

The basis of professional knowledge is information. Information is produced by processing data. This transition, from data to information to knowledge, is the framework for effective business planning. That is, data are processed and presented to planners as information. The information is evaluated by managers to support decision making. Evaluations are conducted according to the existing knowledge bases of managers. In turn, decision-making activities are accumulated as experience and integrated into knowledge.

The key word in this discussion is information. Information is the basis of planning, management, and knowledge. The importance of information has grown to such an extent that modern, computer-oriented societies are described as information societies. Consider this quote from a statement by John Diebold:

> *Information, which in essence is the analysis and synthesis of data, will unquestionably be one of the most vital corporate resources in the 1980s. It will be structured into models for planning and decision making. It will be incorporated into measurements of performance and profitability. It will be integrated into product design and marketing methods. In other words, information will be recognized and treated as an asset.*

This quotation illustrates an important change in the nature of CIS. An asset is something that has value to an organization. A bank could not exist without financial assets. Accordingly, the reliance upon and support of information resources has grown to such an extent that many businesses have ceased to exist when data and information files have been lost due to some catastrophe.

The CIS professional and other professionals in computer-oriented businesses, then, must adjust and incorporate this concept as part of their knowledge base. In fact, these adjustments in perceptions have initiated a new term for the CIS function: information resource management (IRM).

The adjustment of CIS professionals to this new view of information is evidenced by the use of the term *information resource management (IRM)* to describe the function responsible for information processing. (To familiarize you with this concept, IRM is used in place of CIS throughout this chapter.) IRM professionals are responsible not only for processing data and distributing information, but also for the efficient and effective management of information resources. This new role incorporates knowledge in the areas of business theories and administration, telecommunication, and others. Of course, this knowledge is distilled from information, of which there are numerous sources. Information sources are covered in the sections that follow.

INFORMATION GATHERING

As stated above, planners and systems analysts are faced with a constant and ever expanding need for information about business in general and about computing disciplines specifically. Some of the sources available to planners and analysts for gathering information with which to maintain current professional knowledge include:

- Professional press
- Conferences
- Seminars
- Associations
- Peer contact
- User groups
- Research publications
- Analysis groups
- Bibliographic services
- Sales representatives
- Advertising
- Consultants
- Electronic bulletin boards.

Professional Press

Perhaps the most common source of information for IRM professionals is publications, and this source continues to grow explosively. Consider that in 1650 there were only two scientific journals in publication. By 1850, the number had grown to roughly 1,000. In 1985, there were more than 100,000 publications for professional audiences and thousands more that emphasized technical subjects—and in both areas the numbers were growing weekly. Of course, the magnitude of this proliferation should arouse a degree of suspicion about the quality and accuracy of content. Judgment should be applied by individual professionals to evaluate the degree of care that goes into the screening and validation of content for published articles.

There are three basic categories of publication—journals published by the professional associations primarily for their membership, publications circulated free to qualified individuals, and trade publications.

Professional associations.   Most professional associations publish journals with articles of interest to members. Examples include *Computer* published by the IEEE Computer Society (Institute of Electrical and Electronics Engineers, Inc.), *Communications of the ACM* published by the Association for Computer Machinery (ACM), *Data Management* published by the Data Processing Management Association (DPMA), and *The Journal of Computer Information Systems* published by The Society of Data Educators.

As a point of interest, *Computer* and *Communications of the ACM* articles are very technical and often are targeted at computer scientists. *Data Management* is slanted toward business concerns and emphasizes management and administration. A significant feature of many scientific journals is that articles are contributed by appropriate, recognized experts.

Free publications.   Many publications are distributed at no charge to qualified organizations or individuals. Requirements for receiving such publications may include the job classification of manager or purchasing authority for computing equipment and supplies. Qualifications generally are reviewed annually.

The best known publication in this category is *Datamation*. This magazine is published twice each month by Technical Publishing, a part of the Dun and Bradstreet Corporation. Other publication examples include *The Office* and *Hardcopy*.

Articles in these magazines generally address current topics and may be written by external contributors or staff writers. In most of these publications there is a section that contains a series of short comments on current events and outlooks for the future.

A valuable source of information in these magazines is advertisements. A brief scan of advertisements usually provides a general overview of trends in hardware and software. IRM professionals also may use advertisements to locate vendors and/or specifications for products.

The trade press.   Many publications specialize in computing and information system topics. Popular examples include *Computerworld, BYTE,* and *PC World. Computerworld* is a weekly newspaper covering the computing industry. In each issue, a specific topic is given extensive coverage. Often, an interview with an expert in the featured area is included. *BYTE* and *PC World* appeal to users of microcomputers.

Conferences

Trade shows and conferences are another source of current information for IRM professionals. Many trade shows and conferences are sponsored by one or more professional associations. Topics of these conferences vary in content and in degree of technical depth. That is, some shows are generic, or overview presentations. Others are vertical conferences that focus on specific technical topics of individual industries or disciplines.

Depending on the size of the association, regional, national, and/or international conferences may be held. Common features of conferences and shows include exhibits of computing hardware, software, and/or support items; technical presentations; workshops; and tutorials. In fact, many professional organizations hold smaller, regional or special-interest conferences.

For example, DPMA conferences concentrate on business applications of computer technology. ACM conferences explore the technical aspects of computing and are targeted at computer scientists and systems programmers.

The IEEE-CS emphasizes scientific concepts and directs technical sessions and materials toward engineers and computer scientists. The TCA (Telecommunications Association) specializes in voice and data communications.

Interface Group is a private organization that presents technical conferences, such as COMDEX, that attract builders and marketers of computing equipment. The American Federation of Information Processing Societies (AFIPS) is an umbrella organization of eleven associations for computer professionals. AFIPS conferences present hardware, software, and applications sessions for the attendees. AFIPS sponsors the National Computer Conference (NCC) and the National Computer Conference—Telecommunications (NCCT).

Seminars

Seminars are similar to conferences, but differ in that seminars tend to feature specific topics. Because seminars generally focus upon a single topic, IRM professionals can obtain concentrated instruction in specific subject areas. Most professional associations, such as ACM, DPMA, and IEEE-CS, sponsor technical seminars open both to members and the general public. For example, the DPMA sponsors regular one-day seminars designed to increase the attendees' personal capabilities, such as listening skills.

Several private organizations also sponsor seminars. Examples include The Interface Group, The Wang Institute, and The American Management Association.

Seminars and conferences motivate *technology transfer*. That is, these gatherings are opportunities for IRM professionals to seek answers to pressing questions, to hold individual findings up to the scrutiny of other professionals, and to reap the benefits of this synergy. In other words, the development of knowledge is enhanced by the give and take of information at seminars and conferences.

Associations

IRM professionals, by definition, should strive to maintain currency in their knowledge and experiences. Throughout this chapter, professional associations and the services they provide have been discussed. Active participation in one or more of these associations can provide significant benefits to IRM professionals. Meetings are held regularly and provide opportunities to maintain regular contact with professional peers. Newsletters that detail important events and/or conferences and seminars usually are sent to members.

Meetings may be the most valuable function of professional associations. In effect, meetings are a forum for explanations and discussions of common problems. In addition, IRM professionals can accumulate a list of professional contacts who can be reached by telephone for exchanges of ideas and information. Meetings also communicate the interests of members to association leaders. Subjects that are of interest to members may be slated for a conference or seminar at a later date.

Peer Contact

Notice the references to peer contact. Peer contact cannot be stressed enough as a source of information for IRM professionals. Input from peers is universal and may come from sources as diverse as fellow workers, friends, neighbors, fellow association members, and religious or fraternal organizations. Peers provide input based upon their own experiences or knowledge of the experience of others. The benefits of this input are twofold. That is, information can be gathered about possible solutions to current problems and about the difficulties that can result when other problems are solved.

User Groups

The computing industry has spawned many *user groups.* User groups generally are organized according to common interests of people who have installed particular equipment. The advent of the microcomputer has spawned a great number of user groups. Members of user groups meet periodically to share ideas and information on how to use the equipment more effectively. These groups also may be a source of software for particular equipment.

Occasionally, user groups form a network; members are given access to electronic bulletin boards or mailboxes to exchange information. Large groups of this type often are sponsored by manufacturers. Examples include SHARE and GUIDE for users of large IBM computers and DECUS for users of Digital Equipment products.

Research Publications

In addition to the sources discussed in other parts of this chapter, many professional research organizations now specialize in publishing reviews and summaries of hardware, peripherals, software, and services. Some of the reports are extensive and detailed and may involve considerable effort to maintain. Updates may be sent regularly to subscribers for accumulation in a binder or file.

Other reports of this type may contain only a list of the main attributes of a device or software package. Specifications such as speed, capacity, and price are included in research reports. Most reports of this type are indexed to facilitate the location of specific pieces of information. Examples of prominent research organizations include Auerbach Reports, Computerworld Quarterlies, Data Sources, and Datapro.

Analysis Groups

Analysis groups are private research organizations that focus on areas of interest rather than specific products. Leading organizations of this type include The Yankee Group, International Data Corporation, and The Gartner Group.

Analysis groups research topics, such as computing or communications, and distribute results to clients through publications, seminars, executive briefings, or telephone query services. Telephone query services provide IRM professionals with immediate access to comprehensive information about a variety of topics.

Bibliographic Services

Another source of information for IRM professionals is bibliographic retrieval services. These organizations differ from analysis groups in that bibliographic services provide professionals with possible locations of data. Professionals then use these references to gather needed data. Some organizations that offer bibliographic services include Lockheed, Systems Development Corporation, Source, and the Computing Reviews of the ACM.

Sales Representatives

Vendor representatives also are a valuable source of information. Naturally, vendor representatives are biased toward the products they represent and IRM professionals should evaluate information from salespeople in this light. But sales representatives usually are knowledgeable about their products, products under development by their organizations, the competitive market in general, and future trends. Further, vendor representatives are backed by resources that include research and development capabilities and support capabilities that include seminars and training sessions. Each computer user represents a segment of the market for sales organizations. Therefore, the feedback provided by customers can affect the shape and capabilities of future products.

Advertising

Planners should review promotional advertising regularly. There is no shortage of source materials for this task. Recall the previous discussions of technical publications, and publications of professional organizations. Many of these publications rely on advertising revenues and dedicate large portions of space to advertising.

A careful review of advertising also can indicate trends and developments in hardware, software, and other areas of interest to IRM professionals. In addition, advertisements and announcements of seminars and conferences are a good indication of future developments in any area. This is because seminars and conferences often emphasize subjects on the leading edge of technological evolution.

Consultants

Consultants often are hired by IRM organizations for their expertise. However, IRM professionals need to study their requirements and the capabilities of consultants to make sure they are appropriate.

The use of consultants provides many advantages, including their experience on other systems, cost savings from not having to retain a permanent employee, and the short-term nature of the agreement. Disadvantages arise when IRM functions rely too heavily on consultants. In this situation, IRM functions are vulnerable when the work is finished or if the relationship is terminated. Historically, systems designed and built with the assistance of consultants have presented maintenance difficulties.

Electronic Bulletin Boards

Electronic bulletin boards are introduced in the section on user groups. Electronic bulletin boards are public or private forums in which participants are linked through telecommunications. To use bulletin boards, IRM professionals dial into a connecting number and then enter questions and queries to which other users respond. Often, public messages on electronic bulletin boards provide the professional with sufficient information from which problem solutions can be derived.

Case Discussion/Assignment

You are associated with a small company that handles most of its business transaction processing and financial reporting on a microcomputer. The company uses an integrated accounting application package to generate invoices and to produce aged trial balances of accounts receivable. In addition, there is a general ledger package that produces income/expense statements, balance sheets, and statements of changes in financial position.

This system has been in place for a number of months. The management team of which you are a part is making plans for handling its first year-end on the existing system. One of the opportunities put forth is to use the accumulated files from the in-place application as a basis for preparing next year's budget. It is suggested that the only requirement is an off-the-shelf spreadsheet package. You feel there may be more to the task than the purchase of the first spreadsheet package encountered. Based on your comments, you are given the job of surveying the market and coming up with the best spreadsheet for this situation.

Your assignment is to use business magazines, catalogs, and other resources available in your school library to research spreadsheet packages. Refer to and cite at least five sources that provide comparative information on at least three different packages. Based on this research, prepare comparative lists of strengths and weaknesses for three different spreadsheet packages.

Discussion Topics

1. Describe the concept of information resource management (IRM).

2. What is an electronic bulletin board?

3. Why is it important for IRM professionals to know about and use various external sources of information?

4. How can consultants enhance the knowledge of IRM professionals?

11

CONVERSION PLANNING

Abstract

Conversion planning can be a make-or-break factor for the implementation of CIS operations. Planning for systems development is ineffective unless it is followed by effective implementation, which requires more planning. Implementation usually involves some type of file, hardware, or software conversions—or some combination of the three. File conversions are a logical starting point for any conversion activities. Before any conversion can take place, the needed files must be created and available. Hardware and software conversions, then, are implemented to handle and maintain the new files. Methods for conversion are selected according to the special requirements of the project at hand. Parallel conversion involves running both new and old procedures for an interim period—until final installation and approval criteria are met by the new component. A phased conversion proceeds one component at a time until the entire system is changed over. Often, conversions are slated for a specific date, such as the end of a fiscal year, and systems are converted during down times such as weekends or holidays.

ESTABLISHING THE SCOPE FOR EACH CONVERSION

During the late 1960s and early 1970s, conversions of information systems and equipment were relatively standard or generic. The term *conversion* tended to refer to one of the final steps in systems development. Conversions were described in terms of the care and the trepidation necessary in going from a manual to a computerized system. Considerable distress also surrounded conversions from one generation of computers to another that required complete reprogramming and restructuring of files.

This is no longer the case. For the purposes of any discussion on CIS planning, a conversion is assumed to be an action or activity instituted by CIS management as part of overall considerations for system support, facilities upgrading, or software modification.

Given that CIS is the initiator of a conversion, the following types, or categories, of conversion can be identified:

- File conversion, manual to automated
- Hardware upgrade involving processing equipment or peripherals
- Hardware vendor change
- Software modification, system or application.

Plans vary for each of these types of conversions. In each instance, however, CIS personnel should begin with an overall plan covering the full scope of the activity.

OVERALL PLAN

The first requirement in a conversion plan is to understand what is to be accomplished. As with any type of operational adjustment, a conversion may well encompass two or more separate items or requirements. With uncomfortable frequency, you may find that conversions involve requirements for changes in both hardware and software. At the outset, the need is to identify and isolate all components. A CIS facility should heed the first, and most important, rule of conversion planning: CHANGE ONLY ONE THING AT A TIME.

Further, if both hardware and software are involved, change the hardware first (assuming you have established that the old software will run on the new hardware). If more than one item of hardware or software must be converted, handle each job separately if possible, testing thoroughly at each step along the way. There may be conditions under which hardware or software changes must be made to more than one system element at a time. However, these are rare and should be examined with some skepticism. For best results and minimum agony, change only one system element at a time; and, whenever possible, operate old and new system elements in parallel.

Other elements of the overall plan should deal with requirements involving timing and training. In this context, timing can involve two separate factors. One deals with the needs of the overall business. Conversions frequently center around business needs, as is the case, for example, when a decision is made to install new accounting software at the beginning of the fiscal year. The other timing consideration focuses upon company and CIS operations. An example might be a decision to convert files over a weekend when the system normally would be idle.

Training requirements should be reviewed in terms of the full gamut of personnel expectations. Training programs may or may not involve users. Certainly, technical support and computer operations personnel will need to be aware of new constraints and/or opportunities. The overriding principle behind and reason for planning in the training area is to avoid surprising people who are expected to use and support a given system.

In the training area, a basic principle of systems development should be involved any time a conversion affects expectations from users. That is, if users are expected to change the way they do things, they must be involved in training their peers. The standard method in such situations always should be to train a cadre of key users to use a new or altered system, then have this group assume responsibility for training their peers and/or subordinates.

FILE CONVERSION

Within the context of this discussion, a file conversion includes either creation of new files or modifications of existing files that may be in active use. Conversions can be from manual records or from computerized systems that may exist in older or noncompatible formats. No matter what the situation, however, conversion plans should consider the following factors:

- Files for new or expanded applications

- One-time programs

- Parallel file maintenance

- Historic files

- Providing for an audit trail

- Providing for backup and recovery

- System test plans

- File conversions and phased cutovers.

Files for New or Expanded Applications

The special consideration for file conversions that support new or expanded applications is the user dependencies involved. These must be checked carefully for appropriate cutover timing and for appropriate times to perform both data capture and operational cutovers. For example, if an inventory control system is to be introduced and/or changed, it would be appropriate to find out when the next physical inventory count is to be made. A seasoned systems person knows that a prerequisite for any file change is the availability of control totals or similar items used to validate the new or altered file. An inventory count would serve as a basis for balancing both old and new file records.

Even if a change is relatively simple, such as the addition of fields to an existing file, user dependencies are involved. An understanding of needs and any urgencies must be developed and schedules must be established and agreed to by users and others involved.

Conversion methods also can be a factor. In some situations, an entire file may have to be keyboarded. If so, it may be necessary to rent equipment for this operation, to plan to use existing terminals during off hours, or to subcontract to an outside service. This activity is far from trivial. A number of comparatively large "off-shore" operations have been set up specifically to bring in files of new data at low costs. Operations exist in such areas as Singapore, Hong Kong, Manila, and Taiwan. Many methods are available, but are not germane to this discussion. The point, rather, is that methods must be evaluated and selected and that time requirements must be identified and treated seriously.

One-Time Programs

Conversions from one computer-maintained file to another may require writing of a special program to handle format conversions, edits, or validations of data fields and records. Too often, this requirement, since it is of a one-time, temporary nature, is shunted aside until it is almost too late. Then, to catch up, programming shortcuts are used. Such practices court disaster.

Planning for such needs can be highly profitable. For example, if a database management system is in place, a condition encountered with increasing frequency, there may be available data loading routines that reduce the work significantly. Also, many machine-to-machine conversions, if they are analyzed in light of existing resources, may be able to make profitable use of portions of production programs that are to be discarded. It may be possible to combine portions of the "old system" programs with some elements of the new system to accomplish the conversion. With this approach, new program-writing may be reduced to a few "pass-through" modules that transform data formats between old and new programs. Using available resources in this way can impart a dimension to conversion planning that is both creative and profitable.

At the very least, any time an existing file is computer-maintained, planners should be aware of the need to provide for conversion programs, some of which may have to be written especially as a one-time job.

Parallel File Maintenance

A parallel conversion is one in which both the old file and procedures and the new ones are operated under conditions as close to normal as possible for some period of time. There can be a lot of comfort in this approach because it avoids the fear of unknowns among users who are comfortable with the methods they have followed and services they have been receiving. Conversely, there may be situations in which parallel operation is impossible or undesirable. CIS professionals are well advised to enlist users and top managers in the process of deciding on whether and for how long to use parallel processing. The rule of thumb is that a new system should have credibility on its own and provide comfort for its users before its predecessor is discarded.

Whatever decisions are made in this area should be planned, documented fully, and applied as guidelines or constraints for conversion planning. Planning contingencies may involve computer system capacities, the use of additional terminals or peripherals for short periods, and user groups that follow different procedures. It may be necessary to transfer or hire some employees temporarily to handle the dual workloads concurrently. For planning purposes, be aware that users will not be able to master and operate two different systems at the same time. Plan and schedule accordingly.

Historic Files

There can be a temptation to think of a conversion as a fresh start and to ignore all but immediately essential portions of existing systems. This type of thinking can create a discontinuity that penalizes a new system. In many applications, for example, users expect or require the inclusion of historic data for past periods as essential for reporting of the comparisons that support many business decisions.

To illustrate, when a merger occurs or an accounting practice is changed, it often is necessary to restate financial data for previous years. When appropriate historic data are available, such adjustments are simple and straightforward. If historic data have not been carried forward, catching up can be costly. The point, then, is that planners should develop and apply scenarios about the kinds of outputs a new system may be expected to generate, as well as sources for all data. Support for these expectations should be included in file conversion plans.

Providing for an Audit Trail

The audit trail associated with file conversion has limited content and scope. Its purpose is to assure the integrity of file conversions themselves, nothing more. The measure applied is that controls created prior to input must balance or validate the content of the new file after conversion is completed and before implementation takes place.

Planning for this requirement centers around identification of the key points at which processing steps can be recorded and documented. In days gone by, the procedure was known as run-to-run balancing. The principle still holds: At any point of data transformation, records should be created and validation measures applied and documented. Planners should identify these points and specify the files and documents to be created for file conversion validation.

Providing for Backup and Recovery

Concerns and requirements in providing for backup and recovery during file conversions parallel those associated with maintaining an audit trail. The major difference lies in the need to bridge the discontinuity between files of the previous and new systems. That is, copies of old-system files must be maintained until the new system produces enough generations of protection to provide its own backup and recovery capabilities.

One requirement in this process is to protect and maintain the integrity of the source and input media used to create the new file. The equipment that supports an old system also may be involved. For example, suppose a conversion involves a transfer of input responsibility from a central data capture function to users operating distributed, on-line terminals. To provide necessary backup during a parallel conversion period, it will be necessary to operate both the central and distributed input functions concurrently. Further, the equipment to handle the old input method may be retained for a period against the possibility that a challenge to the integrity of the new file requires reconstruction and a repetition of the conversion process.

Planning, by definition, must provide for contingencies. In planning for file conversions, the CIS function must be prepared to deal with the possibility that a file conversion may prove unacceptable and have to be repeated.

System Test Plans

System test is an essential activity within any conversion process. Every system will require its own test data and files, which should be separate and distinct from the "live" data to be carried from a previous system to a new one. However, some data within the test bank may actually be live data collected from an existing system. Conversion planning must account for all of the obvious needs of a system test.

Test data and files are constructed specifically to test the ranges of data acceptability, the validity of data content, and the appropriateness of the formats of items presented to a database. In addition, test data must exercise all modules of each program that will access or update the files. Planners must verify that test data provide these checks. The test plan also should be checked to be sure that all modules are tested individually and that systems of programs are tested fully as operational entities.

File Conversions and Phased Cutovers

When new systems are developed, it is not always possible to pause to capture all of the needed transaction and support systems. Some businesses simply do not lend themselves to these conversion methods. An example is a hotel reservation system going through a transition from manual to computer methods. Reservation systems operate around the clock and through the entire calendar. There are no down times available for file conversion.

A workable technique might be to look to some future date, say three months from the startup of the computerized system. From this date onward, manual reservation files would be converted and new reservations would be booked under the computer system. This can be done with some comfort because future reservations experience a lower activity rate than current bookings. There would be comparatively little disruption and/or duplication involved in conversion of records for future reservations. For the present, the existing system for manual processing of reservations would be continued until the cutover date. In addition, historic data from the existing system must be captured in a form compatible with the new one. This set of data provides the basis for reports on operational comparisons and for management analyses.

Planning for such a conversion can be more extensive than for a direct cutover of an entire file. This is because provisions must be made to operate two distinct systems and maintain two separate files under control of the same set of people.

File conversions represent a logical place to begin thinking about overall conversion planning. The logic stems from the fact that systems process data stored in files. Without files, there are no systems. To realize success in a system conversion, you must have the needed files in place as a prerequisite to everything that follows. Given sound plans for file conversions, plans for hardware and software changes can be formulated as implementations for the housing and manipulation of the new files.

HARDWARE UPGRADE

Conversions that involve hardware only (without changes in software) are an inevitability of CIS operations. Such changes can involve the upgrading or changeover of central processors or the addition or swapping of peripherals—usually to increase capacity or to support a new application. Another factor that can lead to conversions involving hardware only is the reliability of service. One often-stated intent of new architectures has been to reduce maintenance costs by building diagnostics and improved components into equipment. The planning implications for hardware changeovers can involve:

- Recompilation (to take advantage of added capabilities)
- Operating system modification (to accommodate new system parameters)
- Equipment changeover phasing (to accommodate application processing).

All three of these factors may be present in any given changeover. To illustrate, return to the systems design and conversion problem of Esther

Producto, introduced and described in Chapter 9. Assume that management at National Research Associates has authorized a conversion that involves replacement of the existing mainframe with a larger, compatible system. The changeover also involves installation of new, higher-capacity disk drives. The tape drives used for logging and backup will not be changed.

On the surface, the compatibility of mainframes might make this look like a relatively simple conversion. However, there are implications in all three of the planning areas identified above.

Recompilation

On many systems, recompilation of application programs provides the means for taking advantage of the new capacities. For example, the disk files of the new system have more tracks, and increased recording density per track, than those for the old system. These new parameters must be incorporated into the application programs to realize one of the major benefits of the cutover.

This is a classic case requiring a full-scale file conversion at a time when the system is out of service—over a weekend, for example. This is also an excellent example of a situation in which a one-time file conversion program would represent a best-available solution. The conversion, based on current technologies, would operate along these lines:

- A one-time program would be written to convert the existing disk files to formats that take advantage of the new storage devices.

- The existing files would be written to and stored on tape.

- Modified and recompiled application programs configured to the specifications of the new disk files would be loaded into the system.

- The tape-stored files would be written to the new disk devices under control of the modified software.

Operating System Modification

The operating system establishes the interface between application programs and computer hardware. To do this, of course, the operating system must contain exact specifications of the equipment to be driven. In the NRA case, the operating system would have to be modified to accommodate both the new mainframe and the higher-capacity disk drives.

In the NRA situation, suppose the new mainframe incorporates a vastly increased primary memory—from 1 megabyte to 4 megabytes. Without an operating system upgrade, the new computer would continue to operate as though it had the old, smaller memory. With a change to the appropriate system parameters, the operating system automatically will adjust to be able to accommodate more users concurrently and/or to provide larger partitions for each user.

Clearly, the larger capacities and faster access times of the new disk drives also require modification of the operating system parameters before they can deliver the advantages for which they were purchased. Particular care may be needed to adjust the operating system to the capacities and features of disk drives. The need for adjustments to accommodate recording density is obvious. In addition, the hardware/firmware features of the drives themselves may require operating system adjustments.

For example, all operating systems using large disk files have some provision for alternate track selection. This feature is applied each time the system fails in a disk writing operation. A retry sequence is executed under which the writing operation is repeated a given number of times, such as three. If the write function fails on the third try, the operating system writes the data to an alternate track and records the failed track as inoperative. Read operations for the affected track are rerouted accordingly. Each individual make or type of disk drive may require some variation in its alternate track processing sequence. For example, newer drives may make six attempts before giving up on a bad track.

Installation standards also may come into play. When a disk has a given number of bad tracks, perhaps four or six, it is replaced. This parameter may require separate adjustment, since larger capacity disks may have more alternate tracks available. These provisions must be accommodated in the operating system functions and condition reporting messages. The relatively minor nature of these changes serves to illustrate the detailing necessary in equipment conversions.

Equipment Changeover Phasing

The NRA situation is typical in that the continuity of use for files acts as a determiner of the scheduling of equipment changes. Different considerations apply for the active, on-line files and for the files archived on magnetic tape.

As described above, the conversion of the disk files can take place over a weekend or other interim period. Timing for these conversions is a major planning factor in itself. Over a normal weekend, for example, there probably will be routine file maintenance and/or batch processing requirements. Major conversions typically are scheduled to take advantage of extended periods of equipment availability. Three- and four-day holiday weekends become favorite targets for equipment conversions.

Equipment conversions often present special requirements for space and power. In the text processing application at NRA, for example, it would be necessary to provide floor space and power for two sets of disk drives and two central processors. Dual configuration operations would take place at least over the conversion period. Then, once the new hardware and software elements were up and running, the old equipment could be powered down and removed.

In other situations, a "push-pull" approach may be appropriate. This type of planning can provide for straightforward replacements of individual hardware units, up to and including a central processor. In a CPU conversion, for example, the old system can be disconnected on a Friday night, the new one plugged in, and tests performed over a weekend. The new processor then would be up and running with existing software on Monday morning. If software conversions were required, they would be scheduled for another weekend. Remember: Conversions are applied to one system element at a time.

In the NRA situation, an important planning provision was to maintain the old, existing tape drives. This is not directly a conversion plan but is an element of planning often needed to facilitate conversions and to make ongoing operation of new equipment practical for an extended transition period. Assume that the old tape subsystem at NRA had a density of 1,600 bpi. As part of the same transition, new tape drives with higher recording densities (6,250 bpi for example) could be installed. However, a conversion of tape formats would have increased the complexity of the transition: It would have been necessary to have drives of two different densities in a single system—or to use more expensive, dual-density drives—to accommodate both existing and newly recorded archival files. A simpler and more cost effective method, then, was to retain the 1,600 bpi drives. Simplicity comes from avoiding a cutover, cost saving from the fact that the 1,600 bpi units carry lower rentals. Further, retention of the 1,600 bpi units eliminates the significant expense of converting historic files to a new storage format.

HARDWARE VENDOR CHANGE

This category of conversion does not happen frequently in commercial organizations because of the extensive work involved in total conversion of hardware and software (architectural) transitions. The typical business or industrial organization has more invested in application software than in hardware and associated system software. Therefore, most organizations that use computers for business applications tend to resist architectural changes.

The computer industry recognized and dealt with the displacement problems of architectural changes during the 1960s. During this era, computers made the transition from discrete, semiconductor components to integrated circuits. At the same time, design of computer architecture was revolutionized.

Computers introduced prior to 1960 had been designed for designated purposes—scientific or business. The generation of machines introduced in the 1960s marked the birth of general-purpose computers that could be software-adapted for virtually any use. These changes were sufficiently radical to push using organizations into a major reprogramming of assembly-language programs that had not yet been converted to third-generation languages, as well as extensive file conversions for all programs.

In response to widespread user outcries against the reprogramming costs involved, manufacturers adopted methodologies known generally as "upward migration" or "system migration" that avoided reprogramming problems. That is, beginning with the computer generation dominated by the IBM System/360 and its contemporaries, each new model of computer was closely compatible with its predecessors within the architectural heritage established during the major conversion of the 1960s. As each manufacturer introduced new, higher-capacity computers, great care was taken to provide for relatively painless carryover of existing application programs, including full compatibility of compilers.

Today, an architectural change occurs only when a user switches from the mainframe of one manufacturer to another. As indicated, the costs that are involved make such decisions rare in commercial organizations. However, a large portion of computer-using organizations are in the public sector and, thus, are subject to competitive bidding for each equipment transition. It is not uncommon to encounter a conversion that calls for new architecture and requires changes involving hardware, system software, and application programs as well.

This type of conversion, in effect, is a throwback to the era of the 1950s and 1960s, in which any systems change was a total change. An architectural conversion can involve these special planning dimensions:

- Parallel operation during conversion becomes a must if care is to be taken to change and test one aspect of a system at a time. The standard practice is to move one application at a time.

- The need for parallel operation, in turn, means that the using organization must provide duplicate facilities so that the old and new systems can operate concurrently.

- When an architectural change takes place, the backup and restart capabilities of the system must be re-established from scratch. There must be new contracts to provide for maintaining service in the event of an outage of the system with the new architecture. New support capabilities must be identified in collaboration with the manufacturer and with other users. In addition, old contracts for backup and recovery should be maintained for some extended interim period, in case an unforeseen problem arises that did not appear at the time of conversion.

- All application programs, even if they remain in the same programming language, must be recompiled and tested from scratch. That is, each module and every system of programs must be tested as though the application was brand new. Every converted application must be established from scratch. This is a major reason why extensive parallel operation is required.

SOFTWARE MODIFICATION

Just as software exists at multiple levels, so does the planning for a software conversion involve multiple levels of concern and preparation. Separate measures are needed to deal with changes and requirements at the following levels:

- Operating systems

- Batch to on-line conversions

- Interactive systems.

Operating Systems

The more an organization expects from its computer system, the more likely it is to go through a changeover in operating systems. In particular, operating system conversions are needed to support advanced versions of central processors or high-performance peripherals that are introduced by the manufacturer. In many instances, hardware changes mandate operating system conversions.

Another reason for a conversion involving an operating system is to enhance system performance. Opportunities of this type have proliferated as computer scientists have evolved software with increasingly comprehensive capabilities. Typical conversions involve changes from DOS (Disk Operating System) to OS (Operating System) or from either of these to VM (Virtual Machine). Some users also have made the more extensive conversion necessary for implementation of UNIX.

From a planning standpoint, the main requirement lies in providing for any necessary modifications that affect the interaction of the operating system and application programs. Different operating systems generally require modification in the control language that establishes operating parameters for execution of application programs. This means, then, that some modifications of initializing commands may be required for every application that runs in an affected installation.

Batch to On-Line Conversions

This category of conversions deals with the data capture function and implies a changeover from off-line to on-line keyboarding. Basic requirements for balancing of totals established before and after input keyboarding exist in both types of operations. The major differences are that entry is through on-line, rather than off-line, devices and that, in most instances, different personnel handle the work. In the majority of cases, a conversion involving a batch-to-on-line transition will mean also that the input function moves out of a central computer facility and is distributed into a user operation.

In terms of conversion planning, distribution of input responsibility poses the greatest challenges. In addition to the conversions of hardware and software discussed above, there is also a challenge of establishing identification and access patterns for users, of creating procedures for balancing of batch totals, and of training users to become computer-proficient.

All of these changes, of course, may involve an environmental change if the organization is not equipped with data communication capabilities. Remote data entry, of course, implies some form of communication linkage between the user site and the computer. If this is the case, considerable study and lead times may be necessary to request and review proposals from communications vendors and to allow lead time for the installation and testing of communication facilities.

Interactive Systems

Implementation of interactive capabilities may call for plans that encompass all of the requirements cited above in connection with on-line input. That is, if the organization does not already have on-line capabilities, provision must be made for setting up necessary links or networks.

In addition to all of the implications of on-line service, a conversion to interactive processing imposes major planning requirements in the areas of access control, distribution of user identification (passwords) for access purposes, and extensive user training. All of these requirements, of course, are compounded by conversions involving hardware (particularly expanded disk storage), communications facilities, software, and interactive application programs. A conversion involving interactive service may involve a series, or sequence, of conversion activities to be implemented one at a time.

System testing also takes on special dimensions when interactive service is initiated. Testing involves a complex chain of events. First, the hardware configuration, including communication interfaces, must be established and assembled. Technical testing establishes that the configuration will carry signals—not much more. Then, application programs must be tested in modules and for the system as a whole. After all of this testing is done, a final challenge lies in determining whether the system will handle the volume for which it is designed. One typical method of doing this is to assemble the entire system, including communication gear and terminals, and drive as many applications as possible through the configuration to determine whether the system can survive overloading and recovery according to the design specifications.

Case Discussion/Assignment

Restudy the case scenario and review the case assignment at the end of Chapter 8. Assume that work has gone forward on the selection and installation of a large mainframe to serve the merged NRA organization. As part of the planning for this transition, it is necessary to transport application programs from the existing NC system to run on the new computer. Prepare a plan for the program conversion, assuming that the new compiler will be 97 percent compatible with the compiler used at NC.

Discussion Topics

1. Explain what is meant by the statement: The first and foremost rule of conversions is to change only one thing at a time.

2. What is a parallel conversion of data files and what special requirements must be considered by planners of parallel conversions?

3. In a full system conversion, why is it logical to convert files first?

4. Describe the planning requirements for converting operating systems.

5. How is an audit trail used to maintain the integrity of file conversions?

12

OVERSIGHT MANAGEMENT

Abstract

In most organizations, expenditures for computers, information systems, and software usually are large enough to warrant the attention and approval of capital budget mechanisms. For this reason, oversight is a critical requirement and is provided for by capital budgeting processes. Although ultimate approval and decision-making responsibilities may lie at executive levels, oversight responsibilities are allocated to all organizational levels. The responsibilities and implications of oversight are many and complex. Just as life-cycle approaches help to establish workable sequences of events in systems development projects, oversight also lends itself to a structured approach. Under this approach, incremental evaluations of results, decision making, and resource commitments are made possible. Tools for oversight management take many forms—but common factors can be identified. Basically, charts, reports, and diagrams are used to present data on activities, performance, and testing. These data are compared with design and budget specifications to identify conditions that require attention. Throughout the process, oversight managers should be aware that change is inevitable, manageable, and often desirable—and should direct their activities accordingly.

250

THE ROLE OF OVERSIGHT

Oversight, in a linguistic sense, means to look over, to see what's happening. In a business sense, oversight is the continual monitoring that managers apply to business functions for which they are responsible. In effect, the observations of an oversight process compare progress or ongoing operations with expectations. If expectations and realities match, no action is needed. If there is serious deviation, something must change. Either expectations or operations (budgets, schedules, or both) have to be altered.

Oversight is a critical requirement for any function, project, or development that comes under an organization's capital budgeting mechanisms. In virtually every organization, expenditures for computers, the systems that use computers, and the acquired software packages that drive them are large enough so that the oversight provisions of the capital budget process come into play.

The responsibilities and implications of oversight are many and complex. Just as a life-cycle approach helps to establish a workable sequence of events for the development of the system, so also does the responsibility of oversight lend itself to a gradual, step-by-step monitoring that makes possible incremental evaluations of results, decision making, and commitment of resources.

The relationships between oversight and systems development projects are illustrated in Figure 12-1. This diagram shows oversight both as an intermittent activity, represented by the diamonds between project phases, and a continuity, represented by the oblong boxes that run the length of the project. The purpose of this diagram is to show a continuity of interaction between project activities and project monitoring. Conventional flow diagrams often fail to stress the fact that oversight is ever present. Managers are free to interact with project activities at any point, just as CIS professionals or users involved in a project are free to report to and seek guidance from managers. This interactive availability is demonstrated by the fact that two-way arrows are used to connect phases with the oversight system, while the formal decisions reached during phase reviews are passed along on a one-way basis.

Another characteristic of oversight management centers around the composition and divided responsibilities of the group that exercises oversight responsibilities. There is a tendency to think of project oversight as a high-level executive function only. In reality, executives manage projects by exception, committing funds or asking questions on the basis of reports that

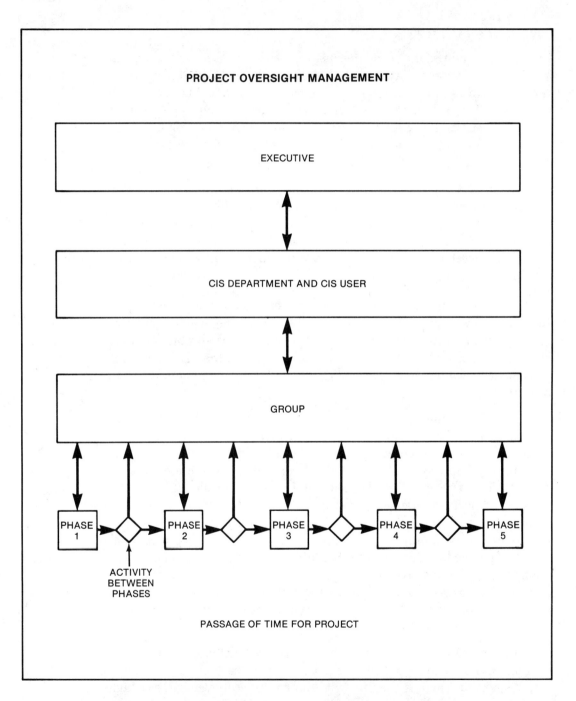

Figure 12-1. *This view of the systems development life cycle identifies decision points and stresses the viewpoint and role of oversight management.*

indicate results do not match expectations in some specific area. Ongoing responsibility for project monitoring is vested at all levels of an organization.

For example, a lead programmer in the CIS function might question a design suggestion or recommend consideration of another version of a software package or language compiler. In the same manner, the training director might question the appropriateness of equipment or procedures for the user population. User supervisors or managers also might check in with suggestions or objections at any point. In each case, the feedback/response loop focuses upon and ends at the level of the oversight structure that is most appropriate for reaction to any given situation.

Top management does not have to be targeted for receipt of every report or responsible for every decision. As indicated by the examples above, specialists within the oversight group should handle analysis and decision making within their own areas of expertise and authority. The very idea of oversight is to have mechanisms in place to react to what is happening, when it happens. This approach to oversight has been characterized as "constructive worrying."

OVERSIGHT RESPONSIBILITIES

One of the important requirements of oversight, in any field, is objectivity. Therefore, a separation must exist between those who build systems and those who evaluate the quality and workability of systems. Given this separation, members of the oversight group for any given project assume responsibilities like those described below:

- Oversight involves project tracking. Elements followed on a continuing basis include schedules, budgets, and capabilities of those designing or implementing a system at any given time.

- Project documentation must be reviewed and evaluated by objective evaluators. The review process should be applied to all formal documents developed in the course of a project, including manuals and equipment or software specifications. Evaluation should be done by technically or managerially qualified individuals with no stake in the project. The purpose of these reviews is to identify important content omissions or items that are not workable within the context of the new system.

- Each new CIS system is charged with solving a specific problem. The overseers are responsible for determining that the problem being attacked is the one identified for solution. There are many classic stories about technically exquisite systems that solved a problem other than the one originally targeted. Also, business problems have ways of taking on new shapes or directions. The oversight team must monitor the project to be sure that the users' problem does not undergo major change while the project is in work. If the problem changes, the solution, by definition, will not work. Therefore, the oversight group must be ready either to change the direction of a project or to abort the project if the problem no longer exists.

- In addition to sensitivity over changes in the problem itself, the oversight group also must be aware of external or environmental conditions that can affect a system. For example, a system might be developed to comply with a regulation that is canceled. In other instances, a new hardware announcement may obsolete a portion of a planned system. Many systems plans changed in the face of decreasing communications costs that followed the deregulation in the telecommunications industry.

- Perhaps the most difficult of the responsibilities and challenges faced by overseers lies in staying clear of the day-to-day decisions and operations of the system project team. Members of the oversight group must remember their job is to provide feedback and guidance. They are not supervisors and definitely are not systems developers.

OVERSIGHT MANAGEMENT TOOLS

Feedback and response on project activities require specific sets of communication end products. Some of these involve reports generated from within the project. Others are evaluation tools applied by the oversight group. Together, these tools provide capabilities to develop a composite view that provides a basis for evaluation and decision making. These tools include:

- Snapshot reports
- Dependency charts
- Dynamic adjustment of the mix of project skills
- Structured project logs
- Independent reviews
- Comparisons with similar projects
- Project glossaries
- Process diagrams
- Economic analysis

- Status reporting
- Acceptance testing
- Project leader's notebook.

Snapshot Reports

Periodically, often weekly, the project leader provides a *snapshot report* to the oversight manager. This report typically is a form letter reproduced on a copier. The project leader indicates status information in spaces left blank for this purpose. Examples of entries, as shown in Figure 12-2, include the size of the project staff, summaries of interviews or other data gathering activities, and notations about whether progress is keeping up with the plan or falling behind.

Dependency Charts

Figure 12-3 shows a contrast between a *dependency chart* and a process chart. Note the similarity between dependency charts and project planning network diagrams such as CPM (Critical Path Method) or PERT (Project Evaluation and Review Technique). A dependency chart shows both sequences of occurrence and relationships among the tasks and activities of a project—over the allotted time span. On large projects, dependency charts can take up 10 or more feet of wall space.

Dependency charts can be developed under control of special system software such as the EZPERT package offered by Systonetics, Inc., Fullerton, CA. An alternate method is to piece charts together manually on large rolls of paper. One of the authors has found it useful to set up a large bulletin board. Events to be included are noted on index cards that are pinned in place and moved until a suitable path of relationships is established. The actual connections are created through use of colored string. If the facility is available, the bulletin board can become a dynamic, adjustable dependency chart, with pathing indicated according to strings of varying colors.

Some manufacturers of schedule boards provide magnetic displays with plastic-covered magnets that can be arranged to form dependency charts.

Regardless of technique, the purpose is the same: A dependency chart illustrates the working sequence that a project must follow to complete development of a system. In reviewing snapshot or other reports, oversight team members can track progress by identifying the tasks performed and their positions in the overview provided by the dependency chart.

MEMORANDUM

DATE: June 6, 19xx

TO: Project Steering Committee

FROM: P. J. Bowles

COPY: B. R. McAlister, E. Producto

RE: SOFTWARE MAINTENANCE STUDY GROUP
        Weekly Status Report No. _5_

Please excuse this format; to get status information to you
each Friday without excess work, I have filled in the blanks
on this standard message.

1. The Study Group consists of _18_ members plus
   secretary.

2. During this week we have interviewed: _6_ branch
   offices, _4_ change teams, _2_ support centers, _3_
   computer-based support systems. Re-interviews (are)
   (are not) a problem.

3. The charting and process documentation is (keeping up
   with the interview) (running late) (losing ground).

4. There are _37_ ideas/suggestions in the file, up from
   _33_ last week.

5. There are _63_ documents in the Library, up from _59_
   last week. The backlog of unreviewed documents stands at
   _21_.

6. Firm interview schedules are in hand for _3_ weeks in
   the future. We (are) (are not) having problems with
   cooperation, support, or study personnel.

7. _No_ key memos/reports are attached to this status
   report.

8. Highlights/problems from this week are:
   Routine week, no problems.

Figure 12-2. *Project progress can be communicated on "snapshot reports" like the one
shown here. This is a form memo with spaces for filling in status information.*

CONTRASTING DEPENDENCY CHARTS AND PROCESS CHARTS
e.g., PERT versus Information Flow

DEPENDENCY CHARTS	PROCESS CHARTS
1. Logic of development sequence.	1. Manufacturing build and assembly sequence.
2. Depict deliverables and tasks that feed (are fed by) other tasks.	2. Show all steps required to produce a product in production.
3. Include administrative tasks.	3. Only related steps.
4. Usually only one level.	4. Multi-level required for most complex/large processes.
5. Rigorous time base.	5. Depicts one complete cycle (quasi time based).
6. Supports resource analysis and makes interfaces visible. Goal is get the wherewithal in the proper place at the proper time.	6. Supports facilities/skill/process sequence analysis. Goal is improvement to cyclic process.
7. Schematic.	7. Exhaustive.
8. One-time.	8. Ongoing.
9. Detail unknown and unknowable, much uncertainty.	9. Full detail knowable if proper investment is made.

Figure 12-3. *This table compares features of dependency charts and process charts in the oversight of systems development projects.*

Dynamic Adjustment of the Mix of Project Skills

Membership of a project team typically is dynamic. That is, project team membership changes as a system takes shape. A number of user group management members usually will be present during the early, analysis and general design, phases. Then, as work becomes more technical, programmers and database specialists may join the team. As implementation begins, users rejoin the group to prepare operations and training manuals and to participate in testing.

Data on the makeup of the project team are included in the regular snapshot reports issued by the project leader. Report content should highlight any shortages of or late arrivals by key people. The project leader should evaluate the consequences of any staffing shortfalls in terms of their impact upon the overall schedule. Should a pattern of lateness or shortages be identified, significant rescheduling might be required.

Structured Project Logs

A *structured project log,* in effect, is a special kind of filing system used to accumulate reference materials that will guide subsequent maintenance of the system. A structured log takes the form of a stringently, logically indexed notebook. Structured logs are produced under guidelines which include:

- A highly detailed table of contents should be created in advance of the project as a guide and planning tool and should be formatted for easy scanning.

- A checklist within each section should identify the items and content to be added as part of each phase and every activity.

- Separate sections should be provided that instruct project team members and later maintenance personnel in the use of the project workbook.

Independent Reviews

An objective reviewer should read and critique all external documentation generated by a project. This individual must have the background required to understand the material. Ideally, the reviewer should be a member of the end-user organization, a person who eventually will share responsibility for operation and use of the completed system.

Reviews should emulate the procedure followed in structured walk-throughs or desk checking of systems and/or programs. That is, the reviewer reads the documentation as a scenario to be played out in his or her group or department in the future. The idea is to look for and identify gross oversights or missing links within the functional designs or processing sequences that are presented. In addition, excessive numbers of minor inaccuracies, oversights, omissions, or misstatements can be interpreted as a sure sign that the work behind the document is substandard. This description of the review function also serves to identify an important characteristic: The reviewer concentrates upon content and comprehensibility of the materials, not on syntax and grammar.

Solid managerial judgment is required to know when to sound an alarm over inadequate or inaccurate content of project documentation. Examples can include a lack of performance or response-time targets, failure to discuss all of the conditions of restart in an operations manual, or training materials that are inappropriate for their intended audiences.

Comparisons With Similar Projects

Planning always can benefit from the guidance of past experiences. Therefore, it is a good practice to compare a current project with completed developmental efforts that are similar enough to support comparison. The challenge lies in defining and identifying earlier projects that truly are "similar."

Project attributes to be considered can include size, cost, time schedule, relevant experience of the technical leadership, numbers of vendors involved, numbers of user organizations involved, size of the database, size of the communication network, numbers of development items being reduced to common practice for the first time, and other factors. Comparability has to be the key in the selection of models. For example, it would not be practical to compare a project that developed an on-line system with one that is developing a batch system.

By-products of comparisons are plans that benefit from applicability of past experience. For example, given a similar processing structure, past experience can provide guidance on how many lines of code to expect in a given program, how many people will be needed to generate the code, and how long the activity should take at alternate staff levels.

Project Glossaries

A classic problem of system project management has been the language barrier. Computer people are famous for speaking in a jargon all their own and for developing new terminology faster than old terms can be comprehended.

It is essential that users and computer professionals have a clear-cut set of standard terms that have the same meaning for all participants in any project.

The way to achieve universal meaning is for project team members to identify terms that are confusing to them. Supporting practices then should be in place to incorporate all such terms within a project glossary and to record clear definitions for each term. As projects move forward, a glossary becomes an important tool. For example, a glossary can be used to build data dictionaries for situations in which agreed-upon designations become names for data elements. In addition, a glossary is a valuable source of support data for the writing of manuals and training materials that will be understood clearly by all persons with a need to know.

The project glossary should be reproduced and made available to all key members of the project team and all managers involved in project oversight. Keeping the project glossary current will help managers to understand the commitments of resources they are authorizing and will avoid situations in which exquisitely designed systems solve problems other than those stated at the outset.

Process Diagrams

Process diagrams originated in the automotive industry, where they are used to show all of the materials flows and manufacturing actions necessary to complete a manufacturing cycle. For a computer system, a process diagram shows the flow of data both into and out of the system, the computation processes that occur within computer-executed and manual functions, inputs, outputs, actions taken by departments that contribute to or use the system, and interrelationships among all involved factors. A process diagram for a computer-inclusive system is illustrated in Figure 12-4.

Process diagrams of this type can be particularly valuable for orientation and decision making by managers with project oversight responsibilities. With all organizational entities and functions identified in sequence, any manager with an overall knowledge of his or her business is able to develop, rapidly, a full understanding of what is happening and where. Diagrams of this type also are valuable for comparing the features and functions of existing and proposed new systems.

Economic Analysis

A development project is justified by savings or values projected for delivery. In the interim between authorization and completion of a project, costs are incurred and cost-related decisions must be made on a daily basis. Examples include decisions such as authorization of overtime or temporary assignment of additional people in an attempt to bring a system product in on time when work has fallen behind. Other decisions can involve the allocation of computer time for additional testing to overcome situations in which unexpected numbers of bugs must be eliminated.

Each decision of this type has its clear-cut trade-offs. Formal modeling techniques and associated software packages are available and may be useful for situations involving major commitments or decisions rendered complex through the compounding of numerous minor expenditure adjustments.

Status Reporting

Given that all deliverables for a systems project are identified and scheduled in advance, a major management oversight methodology is simply to require periodic reporting on levels of progress and/or completion. Challenges faced by project overseers center around avoiding optimism and vagueness in report content.

Members of a project oversight group hold both purse strings and personal evaluation power that can affect the careers of project team members. Nobody wants to look bad in his or her reports to a project oversight group or steering committee. There is a natural tendency to give the impression that all aspects of a development program are under control. People tend to want to avoid and/or bury negative information.

To get a true picture of what is happening, overseers should set standards and ask questions that are aimed at obtaining relevant information. To illustrate, one type of undesirable report centers upon percentage of completion for a task or activity.

A programming supervisor, for example, might come before an oversight committee with an indication that a job is 75 percent or perhaps two-thirds complete. This kind of information has no meaning in terms of completing and implementing a system. Presented with this kind of feedback, an overseer should inquire, as an example, how many modules there are within a system of programs being developed and how many have been coded and tested satisfactorily. This is meaningful, measurable information. Also, this kind of information can provide a basis of useful comparison from one reporting period to another. For instance, if the number of completed and tested modules does not increase appreciably between reporting periods, this could lead to questions about where problems are being encountered.

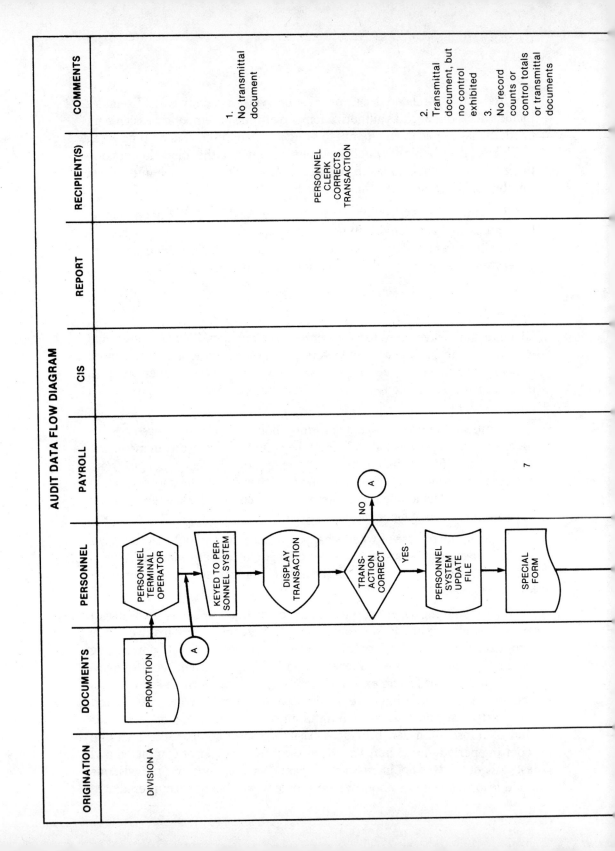

AUDIT DATA FLOW DIAGRAM

ORIGINATION	DOCUMENTS	PERSONNEL	PAYROLL	CIS	REPORT	RECIPIENT(S)	COMMENTS
DIVISION A	PROMOTION	PERSONNEL TERMINAL OPERATOR → KEYED TO PERSONNEL SYSTEM → DISPLAY TRANSACTION → TRANSACTION CORRECT (NO→A / YES→) → PERSONNEL SYSTEM UPDATE FILE → SPECIAL FORM				PERSONNEL CLERK CORRECTS TRANSACTION	1. No transmittal document 2. Transmittal document, but no control exhibited 3. No record counts or control totals or transmittal documents

7

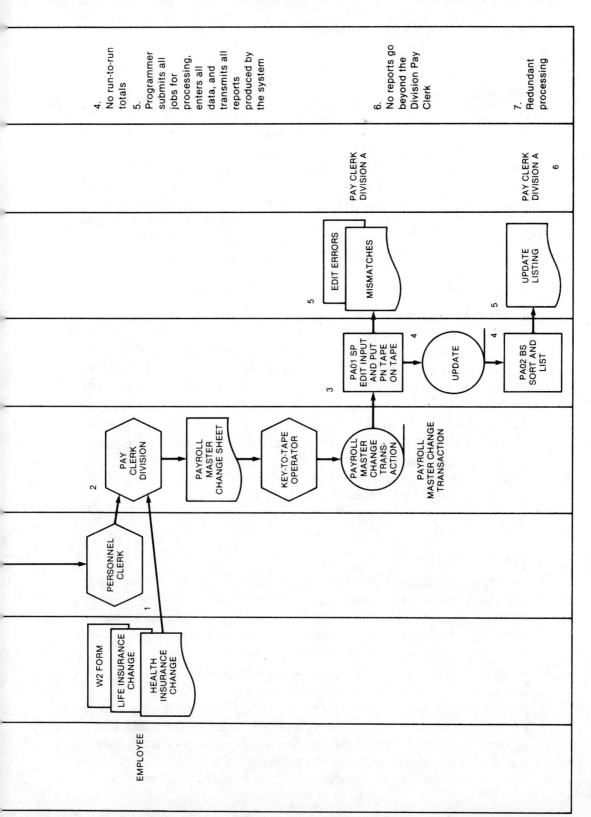

Figure 12-4. *This is an example of a process diagram for a complete information system.*

Acceptance Testing

Ultimately, a system is only as reliable as the ingenuity of the people who design the pre-installation acceptance tests. A completed system generally is deemed acceptable when it performs up to established specifications and the applied acceptance tests are exhaustive in presenting the conditions and requirements of the operational system. Given these criteria, an important management policy in oversight of systems development should be that users establish acceptance tests and are closely involved in the application and evaluation of those tests. Formal acceptance of an operational system clearly should be a user responsibility.

Project Leader's Notebook

In addition to general project documentation, the project leader should retain a running record that is, in effect, a diary of the directions and decisions that shape a project. Included should be accounts of the alternatives considered in shaping each decision or directive, and the reasons for selection.

Although the project leader's notebook can be regarded as a personal record, its entries should be sufficiently clear and complete for review by objective parties, such as members of the oversight team. Also, since project leadership often changes at some midpoint, the notebook should be clear enough to document policies and philosophies for the person who may be assigned to supervise the project's completion.

CHANGE CONTROL

The nightmare of computer systems development is that a project is 99 percent complete—forever. Change requests are part and parcel of *every* systems development project. Managers with oversight responsibility should be aware of the problems that can result from system changes and should have policies and practices in place to deal with change requests.

It is worth stressing that change is not bad in itself. To the contrary, change and flexibility are integral requirements for computer systems. The problem, rather, is to recognize that a project team is a special organization that requires a blend of high-level, high-priced people. Project teams should accomplish certain, specified results. Then they should be disbanded, leaving ongoing operation and maintenance responsibilities to in-place mechanisms and organizations for dealing with those expected requirements.

Persons who serve on development projects may, at a later time, become involved with maintenance of the same systems. In particular, users will initiate maintenance requests and must approve changes. These responsibilities parallel those associated with development projects. Also, systems analysts or programmers who work on a given development project may be called upon to modify designs or programs at a later time. However, a clear-cut differentiation must exist between project work and ongoing job responsibilities of those who might perform special duties during a project.

Within these guidelines, broad categories of types of changes can be established for prioritizing change requests: Changes can be classified as *necessary* and *nice.*

Necessary changes, obviously, are those that must be made at given times or under specific circumstances. One type of necessary change results from legal or regulatory requirements. For example, the formula applied to develop tax statements may be changed; or a new tax may be levied. If so, programs must be altered accordingly and under directed schedules.

Another type of mandated change can result from management decisions. For example, acquisition of a new division or introduction of a new product line may require some types of system modifications that must be incorporated within a system under development even though these features were not included in the original project plan.

The other type of mandated alteration to a system can be classified broadly as occurrences of "oops!" situations. That is, despite the best professional efforts of all parties, a necessary feature or element of a system is overlooked during planning and development. At the point of discovery, there is consternation. People wonder how such an obvious blunder could have slipped through. Analogies can be found in the post office designed without mail drops or the skyscraper designed with no provision for elevators. These things do happen. Something clearly has to be done. Even though changes to developing systems should be avoided, these changes must be made.

Oversight managers should recognize that there may be a need to authorize unexpected and/or unscheduled changes to systems under development. However, approvals should not imply the authorization of blank checks. Each change should be understood fully in terms of consequences, degree of necessity, and budgetary value. It is conceivable that a change could be costly enough to justify scrubbing a project. At the very least, each change, even those that may seem trivial, should be understood, justified, and authorized specifically. Budgeting practices for changes should be the same as for basic project authorizations.

The litmus test for authorization of changes, as indicated earlier, lies in determining whether a necessity or a desire is involved. Those changes that would be nice to have should be recorded in the project's "wish book" for later (perhaps immediately following conversion) implementation under maintenance procedures. This is not to say that desirable (as distinct from necessary) changes are not important. They are important. But they have their place and should have specific procedures that apply to their implementation.

As a final rule, all changes, no matter when or how they are made, must be incorporated into system documentation. There can be temptations to let things slide. For example, maintenance may involve a simple modification to an existing program. The person handling the request for modification wants to be responsive. So the program segment is modified and tested thoroughly. On user approval, the new program is put into use. System documentation falls prey to good intentions. If this type of "service" is rendered often enough the documentation for an operational system can become useless. A standard that can be applied to avoid such occurrences is to require that all changes be documented first, before programs or procedures are modified.

Case Discussion/Assignment

Review the case situation introduced in Chapter 8 involving the selection of hardware for the NRA computer center. Assume you are a member of the management committee with oversight for this project. Prepare a list of 10 questions about capabilities, costs, schedules, facilities, personnel, or other topics that you would ask Esther Producto and her staff to answer at the conclusion of the first phase of this project. Assume that a feasibility study has been completed and a request is being made to carry forward implementation of the hardware conversion program.

Discussion Topics

1. What is a dependency chart and how is a dependency chart used by oversight managers?

2. What benefits are realized by planners in comparing past and present project activities?

3. When historical reviews are made by planners, the nature and scope of the past projects should be similar to present activities. What types of similarities should planners look for?

4. What is the purpose of project glossaries?

5. An initial step in the decision-making process is to identify the specific problem or situation to be solved. Under what kinds of conditions do oversight managers redefine the objectives of a project? Give examples.

A

TASK AUTHORIZATION PROCEDURE MEMO

MEMORANDUM

DATE: _____

  TO: Project Leaders, Managers, Account Managers,
        Directors, Officers

FROM: Esther Producto

  RE: Task Authorization Procedure

This memorandum describes the procedure for using Task
Authorizations (TAs) and will be used to initiate tasks throughout
NRA. The only exceptions are very short-term tasks that are
performed by Technical Services.

This procedure is effective upon receipt of this memorandum. All
new work must be initiated using the TA procedure. Please read
this memorandum carefully.

A. REQUIREMENTS

The requirements to be satisfied by this procedure are:

Visibility   Management needs visibility into the many tasks
                 that are ongoing. Too often we find that our
                 resources are being used for tasks about which
                 we are unaware.

Control   Through this procedure, we can control
                 priorities and enforce good cost accounting
                 practices for all departments.

Billing   This procedure will allow project managers to
                 specify accounts to be charged and, in the case
                 of maintenance tasks, provide the necessary
                 backup information for billing.

Companywide   This procedure is applicable to every department
               within the organization. Every task performed
               for another department will be associated with a
               Task Authorization.

B. ASSUMPTIONS

   1. The current billing system is unchanged.

   2. The overhead to support this procedure should be kept to a
      minimum.

   3. All work for clients that requires personnel time will be
      covered by Task Authorizations.

   4. All work for another NRA department will be covered by Task
      Authorizations. All short-term tasks for Technical Services
      are exempt from this procedure. We will continue to use the
      Technical Services Work Order procedure for the usual short-
      term tasks that Technical Services performs. However, major
      tasks of some duration, such as implementing a new system
      into production, should be reported to Technical Services
      via the Task Authorization procedure.

C. THE TASK AUTHORIZATION PROCEDURE

   1. Initiating a Task Authorization. Generally, the initiator is
      the account manager, although the initiator can be the
      client, a department manager (or director), or an NRA
      officer.

      The initiator calls the control person and asks for a TA
      number. Control logs the initiator, the title, and addressee
      for the TA. Control then issues the TA number. The TA number
      is the next number in sequence from the log maintained by
      control.

      The initiator completes the TA, giving as much information
      as possible about the task or tasks being specified. The
      information required can be in the form of a referenced
      document, such as a functional or system specification. If
      more than one task is requested, all related tasks must be
      charged to the same account number.

      An information flow diagram of the Task Authorization
      Procedure is attached to this memo along with a copy of the
      Task Authorization form.

If the TA requires user/client authorization, the project manager obtains the appropriate signature and gives the user/client a copy of the TA form. The project manager then keeps a copy of the TA for his/her files and sends the original TA to control.

2. Control. Upon receipt of a TA, control creates an entry for the on-line file containing summary and status information about all TAs, keeps a copy of the TA for the control files, and sends the original TA to the appropriate director or department manager.

   During the lifetime of the TA, control may receive updates concerning the schedule and/or priority of the TA. These updates will be in the form of supplements to the TA. Upon receipt of a supplement, control will update the on-line status file, keep a copy of the change document, and send the original TA to the account manager or to the director, depending on the direction of the flow.

3. Director. When the director or department manager receives a TA, he/she will review it to make sure that it contains enough information to allow the staff to do the task(s) requested. A director may choose to have someone else perform the acceptance review, or he/she may establish a minimum level of effort so that he/she reviews only TAs that exceed that clip value. The director also verifies that the account number provided is appropriate to be charged. If the TA is acceptable, the director signs in the place provided and sends it to the group manager or to the supervisor responsible for scheduling the work.

   If the TA is not acceptable, the director has the responsibility of informing the initiator immediately about the reasons why the TA is not acceptable. If the problem is simple (incorrect account number), the correction may be made by informing control of the change. If the problem is not solvable quickly and easily, the director notes his/her objections on the TA, keeps a copy, and returns the TA to control. Control will note "not accepted" in the on-line status file and return the TA to the initiator. Under this latter condition, the initiator must prepare a new TA to replace the unacceptable one.

4. Group Manager. The group manager or supervisor responsible for scheduling the work reviews the TA and schedules the work in conjunction with the project leader. The group manager then requests a supplemental TA number (an alphabetic suffix) from control and issues a supplemental TA

showing the planned schedule. The supplemental TA travels in the reverse direction of the flow of the original so that the initiator (account manager) receives a copy after the TA has passed through the director and control.

The group manager keeps a copy of the TA and sends the original TA to the project leader.

5. Project Leader. The project leader or supervisor who is responsible for completing the task(s) requested uses the TA as his/her authority to do the work and to charge personnel time and other resources to the account number provided.

6. Work Complete. When the work is complete, the project leader signs and dates the TA and sends it to the group manager. The group manager signs and dates the TA, sends it to control, and signs and dates the copy he/she retained originally and sends that copy to the director.

Control completes the entry in the online status file, notes the completion on the copy that had been retained (control file), and sends the completed TA to the account manager.

The account manager is responsible for ensuring that the task(s) now complete are billed correctly and that the user/client is notified of completion. When the account manager has taken the action necessary to bill the customer, he/she informs control that the TA has been billed. Control flags the TA record on the on-line status file as "billed."

The TA will appear on the current status report one more time and then will become a history record.

7. Priorities. Three levels of priorities may be assigned to a TA. Usually, priority is assigned by the initiator, but can be assigned by the director or group manager, depending on the overall impact of the TA. If the initiator assigned a priority, anyone wishing to change the priority must issue a supplemental TA. This will serve to notify all parties of a change in priority.

The three levels of priority are:

Low. This is the same as no priority. The TA will be handled in turn, on a first-in, first-out basis, unless there is some good reason for scheduling it in conjunction with some other TA, such as one requiring change to the same program.

High. This is interpreted as meaning a task is more important than all low priority TAs pending for the user/client or project. It will be scheduled as soon as possible.

Immediate. This TA requires immediate attention! In all probability it will have been walked through the information flow process to get it into the hands of the project leader as soon as possible. This priority should be reserved only for those times when an emergency truly exists.

When there is a question as to which user/client's work gets priority over another, the director and the concerned account manager are responsible for setting the priorities. If they cannot agree, the Executive Vice President will be asked to determine priorities.

8. Supplemental Task Authorizations. The purpose of a supplemental TA is to inform the parties of a change in priority, change in schedule, change in estimate, or a change in required date. The information flow is the same as the original TA, except that if the initiator is the department doing the work, the direction of the information flow is reversed from the original TA. Control will assign suffixes in alphabetic order to indicate supplemental TAs.

9. Estimate. If an account manager requires an estimate to obtain the user/client's approval for a change to a system, he/she should request the estimate with a TA. A TA asking for an estimate automatically will be handled as a high priority TA by the receiving department.

TASK AUTHORIZATION					
DATE ISSUED:	DATE REQUIRED:	TASK AUTHORIZATION NO.:			
CLIENT:	ACCOUNT NO.:	PRIORITY: I H L			
TO:		ACCEPTED:			
FROM:		APPROVED:			
BILLING INSTRUCTIONS:					

TITLE:	HOURS		DELIVERY DATE	
DESCRIPTION OF TASK(S):	EST.	ACT.	EST.	ACT.

NATIONAL RESEARCH ASSOCIATES

Figure A-1. *This is a Task Authorization form that identifies a project and outlines work to be done.*

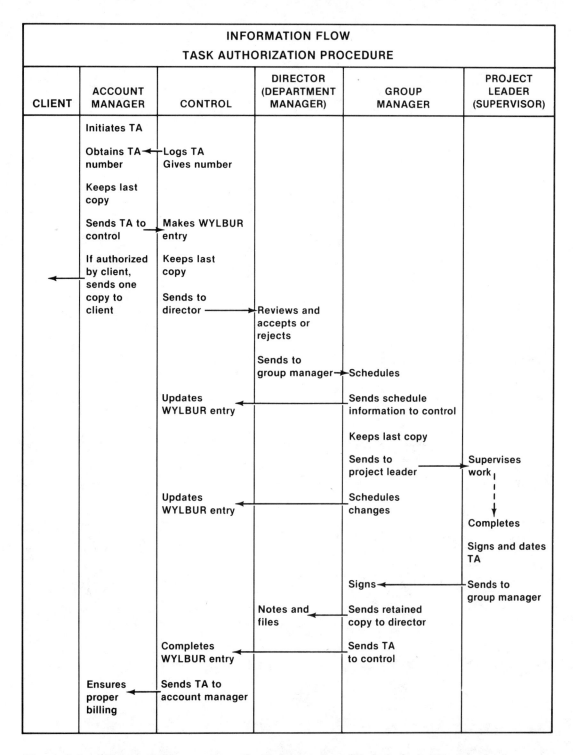

CLIENT	ACCOUNT MANAGER	CONTROL	DIRECTOR (DEPARTMENT MANAGER)	GROUP MANAGER	PROJECT LEADER (SUPERVISOR)
	Initiates TA				
	Obtains TA number	Logs TA Gives number			
	Keeps last copy				
	Sends TA to control	Makes WYLBUR entry			
	If authorized by client, sends one copy to client	Keeps last copy			
		Sends to director	Reviews and accepts or rejects		
			Sends to group manager	Schedules	
		Updates WYLBUR entry		Sends schedule information to control	
				Keeps last copy	
				Sends to project leader	Supervises work
		Updates WYLBUR entry		Schedules changes	Completes
					Signs and dates TA
				Signs	Sends to group manager
			Notes and files	Sends retained copy to director	
		Completes WYLBUR entry		Sends TA to control	
	Ensures proper billing	Sends TA to account manager			

Figure A-2. *This process diagram covers the implementation of Task Authorization procedures.*

B

SUPPLEMENTARY CASE PROJECT

The case of National Research Associates and its CIS planning requirements is traced through most of the chapters of this book. Some of the chapter-ending case references cite an RFP (request for proposal) to be developed for a new communications/data switching facility. That RFP is reproduced as Appendix C in this text. This Appendix provides a series of supplementary assignments and/or potential class or term projects that can be completed in conjunction with the RFP document in Appendix C.

Each of the assignments or sets of instructions below can be completed through use of information contained in the text and/or the RFP document.

1. Identify the resources that would have had to be used within the project that produced the RFP in Appendix C. Describe the contribution of each of these resources. Also outline the interaction among these resources by describing the structure and sequence of phases for a project that produced this RFP as its output.

2. Note that the purchase of a complete communication system, including telephones, has been assigned to Esther Producto, Manager of Information Resources at NRA. Explain the management reasoning that would lead to this assignment, as distinct from placing responsibility in an independent telecommunications group.

3. Develop a training plan for the executives who will use the new system.

4. Develop a training plan for the secretaries who will use the new system.

5. Develop a training plan for the security personnel who will use the new system.

6. NRA has a wide range of security concerns and responsibilities associated with its use of communication facilities. These concerns cover access to NRA people, inbound calls, outbound calls, and access to data resources. From the RFP alone, identify as many security concerns as you can and describe how the provisions of the RFP attempt to enhance system security.

7. Identify and describe at least three major features of the telephone system that are to be software driven. For each, explain why software control is the desirable approach to implementing the capabilities.

8. Identify and describe at least three features of the new communication system that are expansion oriented.

C

REQUEST
FOR PROPOSAL

REQUEST FOR PROPOSAL

for

A TELEPHONE SYSTEM

for

The Miami Office

of

National Research Associates

9926 Any Street

Miami, FL 34249-2138

August 22, 19XX

OVERVIEW

National Research Associates is a relatively new not-for-profit corporation performing policy analysis for agencies of the U.S. Government and other organizations. National Research Associates employs a staff of about 900. The main office is in Miami, Florida, and a remote site is in Baltimore, Maryland, where about 90 people are employed. The existing system in the Miami office is a GTE Stroger electromechanical switch, model PABX 320.

George Bornloser is the Vice President, Finance and Administration. He will not be involved directly until the vendor proposals have been evaluated. The procurement is the responsibility of Esther Producto, IRM manager. She should be your primary contact. Ms Producto will be assisted by several persons. Stan Lineman, manager, Telecommunications Services, will provide site tours and answer (or get answers to) any questions you may pose.

NRA seeks to be a leader in on-line office automation. In 1977, one of the parent divisions of NRA designed, constructed, and installed a digital switch to allow any terminal to be connected to any host computer, so all computer services would be available to all terminals. This switch, known locally as the Automatic Port Selector (APS) is similar in function to commercially available contention data switches. Today the 1,000 lines of APS systems (there are several installed at NRA) interface terminals to 9 computers (440 ports).

The present APS systems are working well and we have no intention of transferring that terminal load to the new telephone switch immediately. However, we are interested in integrated voice and data and will be retiring the APS equipment at some time in the future. Therefore, this RFP requests that "full voice and demonstration data" be installed initially, with a possible expansion to full data sometime in the future.

We also have a procurement under way to replace the telephone switch in the NRA field office in Baltimore (160 lines, no data). Do not be confused by these parallel activities.

A note about this RFP. In our files of background material, we found a draft RFP prepared by a vendor. We modified and shaped this RFP to suit our purposes. Some of the words from the original draft remain. These should not be construed as any endorsement or preference for the original vendor. Further, if your system provides the equivalent function in a slightly different way, rest assured we will find that acceptable.

We appreciate your interest in providing a new telephone system for the NRA Miami Office. We will hold a bidders conference on September 6, 19XX, at 2:30

p.m. Please plan to attend. At this session we will try to answer all your questions. We do not plan to publish the question and answer dialog, so please have a representative attend.

All responses are due October 4, 19XX.

The original proposal must be mailed in duplicate to:

> Esther Producto, IRM Manager
> National Research Associates
> P.O. Box 1234
> Miami, Fl 34249-2138

TABLE OF CONTENTS

V. STATION FEATURES

A. Required Station Features Descriptions

B. Required Station Features Check List

VI. DATA FEATURES

A. Required Data Features Descriptions

B. Required Office Automation Features Descriptions

C. Optional Office Automation Features Descriptions

D. Required Custom Diagnosis Features Descriptions

E. Required Data Features Check List

F. Required Office Automation Features Check List

G Optional Office Automation Features Check List

H. Required Custom Diagnosis Check List

VII. SYSTEM ADMINISTRATION AND CALL DETAIL RECORDING

A. System Administration Features Descriptions

B. System Administration Features Check List

C. Station Message Detail Recording Features Descriptions

D. Station Message Detail Recording Features Check List

E. Station Message Detail Recording Features Questions

VIII. EMERGENCY CONFIGURATION

A. Power Outage Descriptions

B. Fail Safe Descriptions

C. System Documentation Descriptions

D. Emergency Configuration Check List

IX. INSTALLATION AND TRAINING

A. Installation

B. Special Cabling Requirements

C. Installation Plan

D. Training

E. Administrative Training

F. Floor Plans

G. Installation Questions

X. MAINTENANCE AND WARRANTY

A. Maintenance and Warranty

B. Maintenance and Warranty Questions

C. Special Engineering Services

XI. PRICING

A. System Pricing Information

I. TERMS AND CONDITIONS

A. General

1. You are hereby requested to submit your lump sum price proposal for furnishing, fabricating, delivery to the job site, unloading, storing, installing, testing, and setting into operation all of the hereinafter described TELEPHONE SYSTEM.

2. NRA reserves the right to reject any or all bids submitted and shall make awards in any way we deem advisable in our own best interest.

3. System proposals should be based upon the requirements and specifications detailed herein. Failure to meet all of the enclosed specifications does not necessarily preclude further consideration. However, ALL EXCEPTIONS MUST BE NOTED CLEARLY.

4. The term "Required Features" refers to those features that must be provided as part of the basic system configuration. Further, the "Required Features" are to be included in the proposed basic system price.

5. Items identified as "Optional Features" will be considered as additional enhancements that may or may not be ultimately installed, based on economic justification. "Optional Features" are to be priced separately, over and above the basic system price.

6. To aid NRA in the evaluation process, the bidder should use either the outline and numbering scheme in this Request for Proposal, or provide a cross reference list from this outline to your proposal.

7. NRA prefers all new equipment. If Bidder is proposing used equipment, it must be so noted. Warranty and maintenance provisions must be the same as if the equipment were new.

B. Scope of Work

1. The Bidder shall furnish all supervision, labor, materials, equipment, tools, supplies, incidentals, and services necessary for the proper installation of the proposed system. The Bidder shall complete the work in a professional manner, and shall pay all fees and secure all necessary permits.

2. The work must be done in accordance with the plans and general specifications of this RFP.

3. The specific instructions contained herein shall apply and shall describe further and/or modify the work as described by the enclosed specifications.

4. The scope of the work specifically shall include furnishing an operational system that satisfies the requirements of this RFP.

5. Proposals shall be accompanied by a Bidder profile. This serves to identify the history of the bidding company with respect to its ability to accomplish the proposed system objectives. This information, including audited financial statements, should provide pertinent data regarding client list, names of client contact (as well as the number), and type and line size of the systems installed.

6. Your proposal should indicate whether installation and/or maintenance functions are performed through subcontractors or directly by the bidding company.

C. Factors Affecting Contract Award

1. The Bidder's past performance, overall organization, equipment reliability, and a proven ability to perform and complete contracts will be vital elements—together with the content of their bids—in the award of the contract. Bidder should be prepared to include any or all statements contained in the proposal in the final contract for equipment and services.

D. Time of Completion

1. The Bidder shall provide a detailed time schedule for the proposed system to reflect the shortest reasonable interval to order, receive, and install the entire system. Bidder will install the proposed system on schedule, as proposed, with a maximum grace period of three weeks and will be penalized one thousand dollars ($1,000) per working day of delay beyond the grace period.

2. Our target schedule is:

a. RFP Release	August 23, 19XX
b. Bidders Conference	September 6, 19XX
c. Proposals Due	October 4, 19XX
d. Contract Award	November 22, 19XX
e. Cutover	May 24, 19YY

E. General Specifications

1. Contract performance shall include the furnishing of all labor, materials, equipment, and services necessary, or reasonably incidental to, the

installation of one complete and operating communications system. It shall be the responsibility of the Bidder to furnish a working system that meets all the requirements stated in this bid request. The new system must be installed completely and tested prior to the removal of the existing system. The Bidder will be responsible for the coordination of the removal and return of the present system to the local utility. The removal must be completed within six weeks of the date of acceptance of the new system. Final payment will be withheld until the removal of the old system is completed.

2. The bidder shall handle all contacts with the local telephone company, and also will be responsible for the Tie-Line interface with the NRA Baltimore office and with other common carriers (i.e., SBS).

3. Before submitting your bid, take into consideration the amount and character of work to be done and of the difficulties involved in its proper execution. Include in your bid all costs you deem proper and sufficient to cover all contingencies essential to the installation of the proposed system.

4. In making your site survey, note carefully the space available in the proposed switch room and the telephone closets. If insufficient space is available for the old and the new equipment to operate side by side, be sure your proposal addresses any temporary arrangements that may be required.

5. All environmental requirements, such as heat dissipation, ventilation, temperature and humidity operating ranges, air conditioning, and master electrical ground must be stated by the Bidder. These essentials will be provided by NRA in accordance with specifications in the accepted bid.

6. Electrical power connections required for all communications equipment to be installed will be provided by NRA and should not be included in costs. Any non-standard outlets required by the Bidder shall be identified in the bid. Bidder also shall include a list of the type of electrical connections required.

7. NRA requires that installation include conditioning of electrical power provided by the electric utility. This should include the capability to withstand lightning strikes, brownout, and total power outage. A minimum two-hour battery backup is required.

8. If subcontractors are to be used for any part of this contract, the Bidder must supply a list of names of the subcontractors and the jobs they will perform.

9. Switch operation must include a standard EMI/EMF filter so that the operation of local computer and communications equipment and of local electronic equipment is not affected in any way.

II. EQUIPMENT SPECIFICATIONS

"Equipped" items identify the equipment that is required by NRA at cutover. "Wired" installation is to be completed by the Bidder; it is the capacity of the proposed system at cutover without adding cabinets or major hardware other than circuit boards (i.e., line cards, trunk cards). "Capacity" also is to be completed by the Bidder; it is the maximum capacity of the proposed system if it were to be expanded to its limit.

A. Common Equipment Specifications

	Equipped	Wired	Capacity
1. Extensions	1,600		
2. Direct Outward Dial Trunks	37		
3. Off-Premises Extensions	8		
4. Direct Inward Dial Trunks	50		
5. PBX Inward Dial Trunks	30		
6. Tie-Lines on Rotary with 6 wire E&M interface with STC COM II MUX capable of pulse dialing to Baltimore	8		
7. Out SBS (WATS) on rotary	13		
8. Power Failure Transfer Trunks	25		
9. Attendant Consoles	6		

B. Station Equipment Specifications

	Installed	Pre-Wired
1. Single-Line Telephones *	1,140	
2. Secretary-Type Telephones *	130	
3. Executive-Type Telephones *	80	
4. Attendant Headsets	12	

* All with Message Waiting Lights

C. Definitions

The following definitions are applicable to engineering and pricing of the system configuration.

1. **"Secretary-Type Telephones"** means a digital telephone with a LCD display that will show the origination and the destination of the incoming call. There must be at least 20 buttons that can be used for multiple line appearances, and 20 buttons that can be defined at the instrument for special functions such as call forwarding (total: 40 buttons).

2. **"Executive-Type Telephones"** means a digital telephone with at least 10 buttons that can be used for multiple line appearances, 20 buttons that can be defined at the instrument for special functions such as call forwarding (total: 30 buttons), and an integral microphone/speaker for group discussions.

D. System Requirements

The telephone switching system described herein shall be a common-control, stored-program electronic PABX with solid-state circuitry.

The switching system shall use computer-based common control consisting of a central processor and memory to provide call processing, features, administration, and testing functions. Control of the switching system shall be by software programs stored in RAM and loaded from an external storage device.

1. **Modularity.** The proposed system will be flexible in design so that modular expansion in traffic, capacity, cabinets, lines, trunks, and other associated hardware and software features can be accomplished easily without interruption of service to NRA.

2. **Traffic handling.** The switching system furnished must be non-blocking and have the necessary memory, real-time processing capability, and peripheral hardware to provide ultimate traffic handling capacity of 1,200 data terminals (non-blocking) and simultaneously 2,000 voice lines (9 ccs per station at P.01 grade of service). Note, the system initially installed will have only 8 data terminals for demonstration data and 8 data extensions.

3. **Network Interface Requirements.** The system must be capable of interfacing with the Bell System network for full services as: direct-inward-dial trunks; two-way local trunks; outgoing trunks; inbound and outbound WATS; Foreign Exchange trunks on either a two-wire or four-wire basis, including loop start or ground start signaling; access to other common carriers, including satellite circuits, pulse to tone, tone to pulse, and interface to Equal

Access. Six-wire interface with E & M signaling for Tie-Line trunks must be supported.

4. **Off-Premises Extensions.** At the present time, there are six off-premises extensions in Miami. Periodically, we lease a local facility for a project and install extensions in it. The proposed system must be able to interface with these tariffed circuits as provided by the local regulated carrier.

5. **Trunk Interfacing.** All trunk interfaces must comply with the Federal Communications Commission's Rules and Regulations—Part 68, dealing with certified equipment.

6. **Single-Line Telephones.** It is NRA's desire that all voice transmissions be digitized at the handset and that the analog signal be reconstituted, if required, at the interface with the Telco trunks. Please quote the station equipment two ways: one with digital single-line instruments, the second with analog single-line instruments.

7. **Analog Rotary Requirement.** In any event, there will remain the 15 analog instruments now installed in a special area. These phones are and will remain analog instruments. They are connected to a Candela Controller that acts as an intelligent call director. To the new switch, this unit must merely look like eight internal lines on a rotary. The interface will be DTMF. In the future, there may be other projects that require similar service. A Candela, or other equivalent, may be installed for each of these several projects.

8. **Redundant Critical Electronics.** Redundant Critical Electronics are required. The proposed system must be configured with sufficient redundant equipment so no single failure will render more than a small fraction of the system inoperable.

9. **Call Screening.** Management has directed that all incoming (from the public telephone network) calls be screened. Therefore, we desire to handle incoming calls in the following way:

a. For those employees whose calls are routed through a personal secretary, an incoming call dialed to a specific extension will ring on the secretary's desk with a dual indication (both audible and visible) that this is an incoming call from outside the building. Extensions covered by a secretary must be transferrable as a group to another secretary or to the message desk in the telephone office. Later, when the secretary returns, the group transfer can be reversed. Further, if any messages had accumulated during a secretary's absence, these should be retrievable.

b. For individuals who do not have a personal secretary, an incoming call dialed to a specific extension will ring to a professional telephone operator at an "advanced message desk." Here, a display instrument will identify the call as an incoming call from outside the building and display the extension number of the called party.

The operator will speak to the caller and verify the identity of the party wanted. If all is in order, the operator will extend the screened call to the party called. If the called party does not pick up by the third ring, the call will be forwarded automatically to the message desk, which will offer to take a message. If a message is left, the operator will illuminate a "message waiting" light on the called party's telephone handset.

Upon return, the called party will see the indicator light and can call the message desk to retrieve any accumulated messages.

c. All telephone instruments on private lines will be connected directly to an incoming line in a logical equivalent to current practice, i.e., the individual's phone will ring to the incoming calls and no intercepts will occur. If the individual wishes to forward his/her calls temporarily to another number, this will be possible.

d. The main NRA number is the only one that will be listed in telephone directories, the Telco's telephone directory service file, on the covers of NRA's publications, and elsewhere. All calls to this number will be treated as institutional calls and answered by a professional telephone operator. This operator will interrogate the calling party, determine the identity of the person desired, look up that person's extension (using a CRT to access an automated directory), and make the connection. If the desired party does not answer in three rings, the call will be routed to the message desk, or other predetermined alternate.

e. For off-shift, weekend, and holiday operations, a specially trained guard will answer a display phone. All institutional calls, all message desk calls, and all calls normally screened by private secretaries will be routed to the guard station. The display will classify the call and identify the called party if that person's name is known to the system. After screening incoming calls, the guard will transfer them to an appropriate inside telephone (if the called party is thought to be in the building) or take messages if the called party does not answer in three rings.

E. System Requirement Questions

1. a. What is the manufacturer's name, model number, and/or the name of the proposed system?

b. When was the first of this series installed in a customer facility?

2. a. Does the switching matrix require balancing for traffic when line and trunk cards are installed?

   b. If the traffic pattern changes, is rebalancing required?

3. How much memory is included in the proposed system and what is the ultimate memory capacity of the model proposed?

III. SYSTEM FEATURES

A. Required System Features Descriptions

1. **Class of Service:** The Class of Service (COS) feature is used to control which trunk group and categories of features can be used by a particular extension.

2. **Direct Inward Dialing:** This type of service allows a party in the public telephone network to dial an extension number and ring a station or a group of stations within the system directly, without internal operator intervention.

3. **Direct Outward Dialing:** This feature enables a station user to dial an external call over outside trunks without direct attendant assistance.

4. **Flexible Station Numbering:** This feature makes possible a flexible assignment of extension numbers within the system.

5. **Multiple Distinctive Ringing:** This feature provides a capability for two distinctly different types of station ringing to enable a user to distinguish between an internal or external call, including a trunk-queued call back.

6. **Single-Digit Access for Services:** This feature enables a station user to place an outside call without assistance by dialing a single digit prefix.

7. **Data Privacy:** This feature enables an extension user to protect a data call from any intrusion. This feature is invoked by an access code. For the duration of the private call, the extension is protected from receipt of the call waiting tones, attendant or executive busy override.

8. **Fixed Call Forwarding:** The system must be configured so that all incoming calls will ring at the called station for a predetermined number of rings and, if not answered, forward the call automatically to a preselected extension, hunt group, distribution group, or attendant console. This will be done under either busy, no answer, or both conditions, as controlled by the Class of Service tables for individual lines. This feature also should be programmed to be activated differently on internal and external incoming calls.

9. **Abbreviated Dialing Between Groups of Stations:** This feature allows stations to be arranged for intercom service, so persons in a common department or work group can call each other by dialing fewer digits than the extension number.

10. **Call Pick-Up—Group:** This feature enables station users to answer a ringing call within the particular group of extensions defined as a call pick-up

group. By dialing a special code (3 digits or symbol), any station user in the group can answer, hold or transfer an incoming call.

11. **Hunting Station:** This feature enables stations to be arranged in groups within a particular organizational function (e.g., Purchasing). The stations do not need to follow each other in consecutive numerical order. When a dialed number associated with the hunt group is busy, the system will scan the list of extension numbers and connect the call to the first available station.

12. **Night Service:** This feature enables the chief attendant to turn a switch or key, or keyboard a command when closing the switchboard. Preassigned trunks then are routed to preselected stations so that persons calling on those trunks will be routed to a specific station after hours. Incoming calls on the main number, and on all DID extensions except those designated as night lines, will be forwarded in bulk to a "secretary-type telephone" installed at the main guard post. The guard on duty can screen incoming calls and transfer them as appropriate. In the morning, the chief attendant must be able easily to restore normal service.

13. **DTMF:** This is the ability to transmit and receive, on the trunk and extension side of the PBX, the tone signaling protocol known as dual-tone-multiple-frequency. This feature supports push-button dialing by all telephones within the system.

14. **DTMF to Rotary Conversion:** This feature enables the system to receive tone signals from the station side and send either tone or rotary dial pulses on the trunk side. All trunks should be able to receive either DTMF or rotary signals from the network.

15. **Intercept Treatment:** This feature enables calls directed to an inoperative or unused extension to be forwarded to the attendant for answering. Also, if a station attempts to place a call denied by its class of service, the call will be directed to the attendant or to a recording.

16. **Multiple Trunk Groups:** This feature enables the system to provide a selection of different groups of trunks. The selection of trunks within a group may be sequential or random. Each group of trunks may be accessed by a distinct access code.

17. **Automatic Network Dialing:** This feature permits ease of dialing between several locations connected by tandem Tie-Lines. The network is accessed by entering one symbol or a two digit code.

18. **Least Cost Routing:** This is a program-controlled feature that automatically selects the most economical route for an outgoing call. The user dials the same access code (usually 9) for an external call regardless of the call destination. The call is placed on the least costly circuit according to

the customer-specified information stored in the routing tables of the system. This feature must work with Other Common Carriers and Equal Access. Priority handling of this feature should be controlled by Class of Service. The Least Cost Routing feature must provide a configurable time-of-day routing capability to assure that the least expensive facilities are used.

19. **Common Carrier Trunking:** The proposed system's memory must be configured to support multi-carrier services and be capable of adding, deleting, and changing digits in conjunction with the Least Cost Routing feature.

20. **Multiple Consoles:** This refers to the capability of the system to have more than one attendant console.

21. **Automatic Program Load:** This feature refers to the capability of the system to reload the system's software program automatically. Loading usually is accomplished with a cartridge tape recorder or disk drive unit. This feature is used after a commercial power failure or at times when the system's self-diagnostic feature has initiated a system restart. The system must maintain a record of each restart and the reason for that restart.

22. **Universal Station Cabling:** This is the capability of the system to provide universal station cabling so the single-line telephones, six-button telephones, 10-button telephones, and electronic telephones can be moved or relocated to new locations on existing cable by means of a software entry (database change).

23. **Self-Diagnostics:** This feature enables the system to perform self-testing of the software and hardware. Errors that are detected must be made appropriately available and printed or stored in memory.

24. **Local Maintenance Capability:** With this feature, various maintenance functions can be performed via an on-site terminal connected to a 25 pin RS232-C data interface and cable, operating at speeds up to 9.6 BPS asynchronous.

25. **Remote Site Services:** The proposed system must be capable of providing service to remote locations. From time to time, temporary office space is rented near NRA headquarters. It is desirable that these sites be served off the main NRA switch and that any personnel transferred from the main site to a temporary site be able to take their phone (extension) numbers and their terminal addresses with them.

26. **Paging Access:** The existing NRA paging system must interface with the new switch so telephone attendants, guards, or special electronic equipment can access the paging system via the telephone system.

27. **SMDR Port:** an interface allowing data regarding internal and external traffic flow, which has accumulated since the last bulk transfer, to be transmitted to a recording/processing device.

28. **Multiple Digital Networks:** The proposed system must support multiple digital networks, including Telenet, CSNet, Milnet, Uninet, Tymnet, and Arpanet.

29. **Four Digit Dialing:** The proposed switch must support a unified numbering plan so that a person in the Baltimore office can dial a four-digit extension in Miami and Miami can dial a four-digit extension in Baltimore.

30. **Call Queuing (Trunk) Call Back:** This feature enables a user who attempts an outgoing call that cannot be completed due to a busy trunk group to enter a code that instructs the system to call back the user when the trunk is available. After this feature is activated, the user may hang up his or her phone and wait for the system to call back. The system must provide a distinctive trunk queuing call back ring. Priority handling of this feature should be controlled by Class of Service.

31. **Remote Access to PBX Services,** a/k/a **Direct Inward System Access (DISA):** This feature allows an employee from outside the system to access system features and trunks by dialing a special DISA telephone number. The call may be made from any pushbutton (DTMF) telephone through an incoming central office trunk assigned to the DISA feature. The system provides dial tone when the trunk is seized and must require a unique valid authorization code from each specific user to activate this feature. The normal Class of Service controls must be applied and the Station Message Detail Record entries must be identified uniquely.

32. **Area Code/Office Code Toll Restriction:** This feature provides basic functions of Area Code Toll Restriction. With the addition of office code toll restriction, the software will also analyze the second three digits (office exchange code) and divert the call if those digits do not identify an exchange number permitted by the dialing station's Class of Service.

33. **Shared Tenant Services:** Sometime in the future, NRA may occupy a building whose floor space is greater than that required for NRA alone. Under these conditions, we would like to have one telephone system installed and one universal wiring plan, but have multiple sets of trunks feed the common CBX and, through a sophisticated control dictionary, provide a single set of operators with the information necessary to handle calls for two or more independent corporations, collect accounting information so the cost of call handling can be allocated equitably, and allow the various tenants to have different patterns of privileges and restrictions on individual telephones as dictated by their corporate profiles.

B. Required System Features Checklist

Respond by "yes," "no," or "not available" as to whether the feature is standard in the proposed system as defined in the preceding description section.

	Standard Feature of System	Price If Optional
1. Classes of Service		
2. Direct Inward Dialing		
3. Direct Outward Dialing		
4. Flexible Station Numbering		
5. Multiple Distinctive Ringing		
6. Single-Digit Access for Services		
7. Data Privacy		
8. Fixed Call Forwarding		
9. Abbreviated Dialing Between Groups of Stations		
10. Call Pick-Up—Group		
11. Hunting Station		
12. Night Service		
13. DTMF		
14. DTMF to Rotary Conversion		
15. Intercept Treatment		
16. Multiple Trunk Groups		
17. Automatic Network Dialing		
18. Least Cost Routing		
19. Common Carrier Trunking		
20. Multiple Consoles		
21. Automatic Program Load		
22. Universal Station Cabling		
23. Self-Diagnostics		
24. Local Maintenance Capability		

Respond by "yes," "no," or "not available" as to whether the feature is standard in the proposed system as defined in the preceding description section.

	Standard Feature of System	Price If Optional
25. Remote Site Services		
26. Paging Access		
27. SMDR Port		
28. Multiple Digital Networks		
29. Four Digit Dialing		
30. Call Queuing (trunk) Call Back		
31. Remote Access to PBX Services		
32. Area Code/Office Code Toll Restriction		
33. Shared Tenant Services		

C. Optional System Features Descriptions

1. **Remote Site Multiplexer:** In the near future, it is presumed that some sort of a remote multiplexer, properly configured for the mix of voice and data lines (9,600 baud), would be required at each remote site and a complementary cabinet would be required near the main switch. Proposals should include the cost of two optional configurations:

   a. Fifty telephones and 35 terminals at the remote site.

   b. One hundred telephones and 70 terminals at the remote site.

2. **Prerecorded Announcements:** This feature provides the capability of playing out prerecorded announcements. The recordings will be made locally and implemented in addition to supporting switch functions.

3. **Security Monitor:** The electronic security monitor now installed in Miami must interface with the switch (via a gateway), and send a digital message that is to be transformed into an audio message, and then route the resulting audio message to the public address system, one or more extensions and off-site locations, preferably without the use of external auto dialers and recording equipment.

4. **Billing Codes:** At the present time the NRA accounting system treats all telephone expense as overhead. At some time in the future, we may wish to direct-bill the costs for some projects or to partition the organization into two

or more accounting units and bill the costs accrued for each accounting unit to that unit. The proposed SMDR system must support the following:

a. Associate a permanent accounting code with each station and place that accounting code on each SMDR record involving that station.

b. Insist that each toll call be accompanied by a valid accounting code before the call is accepted by the switch.

5. **Accounting System Software:** The system must provide batch programs (preferably COBOL running on an IBM 370 under MVS) to process the SMDR tapes and prepare accounting reports.

6. **Cross Calling:** If the same vendor wins contracts for Miami and Baltimore, we want a unified numbering plan and advanced features that require coordination between the two switches, i.e., Call Forwarding, Message Waiting, etc. If the two switches are not of a compatible design, the proposed system for Miami must be at least capable of implementing cross-calling without custom engineering.

D. Optional System Features Checklist

Respond by "yes," "no," or "not available" as to whether the feature is standard in the proposed system as defined in the preceding description section.	Standard Feature of System	Price If Optional
1. Remote Site Multiplexer a: 50/35 b: 100/70		
2. Prerecorded Announcements		
3. Security Monitor		
4. Billing Codes		
5. Accounting System Software		
6. Cross Calling		

E. System Features Questions

1. Describe how the Least Cost Routing tables are reconfigured in the event we elect to add a carrier or cease doing business with an existing carrier.

2. Is it possible to make a connection to an all-digital network using T-1 carriers?

3. Describe how we would configure and reconfigure the digital services as we add and subtract networks.

4. a. In the event of a transfer to the standby computer, are calls in progress lost?

   b. What information is recorded in the proposed system at the time of transfer to the standby computer?

5. What is the start-up procedure of the proposed system in the event of battery backup exhaustion?

6. How are 12-digit international calls handled?

IV. ATTENDANT FEATURES

A. Required Attendant Console Features Definitions

1. **Alphanumeric Display:** Displays utilizing alphabetical and numerical indications are required to allow the attendant to process calls and to handle callers in a fast and efficient way. A typical display provides the following information:

   a. Identification of the source of an incoming call or a recalled call.

   b. Class of service of a calling extension or trunk group.

   c. Called number or calling extension/trunk number.

   d. Name of calling party

   e. History/status of the call to this point.

2. **Automatic Recall:** This feature automatically alerts the attendant by visible and audible signals when a call has not been answered within a predetermined amount of time (usually 15-20 seconds), or a certain number of rings. The attendant is able to recapture the call, provide a status report to the calling party and then reconnect the call. This assures that no calls are lost within the system.

3. **Busy Extension Verification:** This feature provides the attendant with a visual display that indicates whether an extension is busy, idle, or out of order.

4. **Busy Trunk Verification:** This feature enables the attendant to access each trunk of the system individually to verify busy/idle condition.

5. **Called Station Status Display:** This display provides the attendant with information about the current condition of the called extension. The information displayed is Ringing, Camped On, Busy, Holding, Forward Condition, Out of Service, Not Assigned.

6. **Class Of Service Display:** This visual display provides the attendant with the Class of Service assigned to the internal party calling the attendant or intercepted by the attendant.

7. **Identification of an Incoming Call:** This feature provides information to the attendant about the source of an incoming call. The information provided is incoming tie trunk call, incoming central office (CO) trunk call, incoming WATS call, and incoming Foreign Exchange (FX) call.

8. **Identification of Recall:** This feature provides information to the attendant about the source of the call being recalled. The information

provided is a call transferred to the attendant, a serial call returned to the attendant, a held call returned to the attendant, a camped-on call returned to the attendant, and a ringing call returned to the attendant.

9. **Trunk Group Busy Indicators:** This feature provides the attendant with a visual display indicating a busy condition of each trunk group (i.e., Outward C.O., Outward WATS, etc.).

10. **Trunk to Trunk Connections:** This feature enables the attendant to connect an incoming trunk of any type to an outgoing trunk so that the outside caller may be given access to a needed circuit, such as WATS, FX or Tie-Line, etc.

11. **Through Dialing:** This feature allows a station restricted from a facility (or trunks) to gain access to that facility through the attendant. The attendant has the flexibility of either selecting the trunk, dialing the call, and joining the trunk to the station user or selecting the trunk and joining the station user to the trunk so that the station user can dial the call.

12. **Hold:** This feature enables the attendant to place incoming calls (internal and external) on hold at the console, until the attendant can process them.

13. **Camp-On to Busy Station With Indication:** This feature enables the attendant to place a call on hold at a busy extension by camping the call onto the extension. The busy extension will receive an audible tone indicating that another call is waiting.

14. **Call Splitting (Two-Way):** This feature enables the attendant to alternate between the calling and called parties associated with a particular loop select button. This permits the attendant to consult privately with either party.

15. **Conference Capability:** This feature allows the attendant to establish a conference for one to six parties. The parties may be either internal or external. To do this, the attendant dials the desired internal extension or outside number. When the desired party is reached, the call is transferred to the requesting party's extension and the new party is voice-announced by the operator.

16. **Speed Calling:** This feature permits the attendant to dial external numbers by use of abbreviated codes which correspond to a system directory of frequently dialed numbers. These numbers can be accessed by dialing a two- or three-digit code. Once accessed, the system will dial the full number, including the access code for the trunk. The numbers stored by the system must be at least sixteen digits. Programmed pause between number sets is required.

17. **Switched Loop Operation:** This feature permits a variable number of calls to be held in queue until they are answered by the attendant. Calls in queue will be directed to the attendant on a "first in, first out" basis.

18. **Two-Jack Operation (Headset/Handset):** This feature provides the capability to utilize either a handset or a headset with the attendant console.

19. **Volume Control:** This feature provides the attendant with the ability to control the volume of the incoming call signal.

20. **Silent Monitoring:** This feature makes it possible to connect a handset or headset to the attendant console so that the attendant can be monitored for training purposes. The calling party should not hear any audible indication that the call is being monitored.

21. **Alarm Indication:** This feature provides a visible and audible indication of a system malfunction. An indication of the nature of the malfunction is required (i.e., major or minor).

22. **Lamp Check:** This feature enables the attendant to perform a verification that all of the alphanumeric displays and lighting displays on the console are operating properly.

23. **Attendant Paging Access:** This feature enables the attendant to dial an access code or depress a feature button to activate an external paging system.

24. **Serial Call:** This feature enables the attendant to place a series of calls for the same incoming calling party. Upon being answered initially by the attendant, the incoming calling party informs the attendant that he/she desires to talk with more than one person. The attendant can extend the call and activate the serial call feature, which automatically will return the calling party to the attendant after each call is completed.

25. **Automated Directory:** Operator access via a CRT to the current directory.

B. Required Attendant Features Checklist.

Respond by "yes," "no," or "not available" as to whether the feature is standard in the proposed system as defined in the preceding description section.

	Standard Feature of System	Price If Optional

1. Alphanumeric Display

2. Automatic Recall

Respond by "yes," "no," or "not available" as to whether the feature is standard in the proposed system as defined in the preceding description section.	Standard Feature of System	Price if Optional
3. Busy Extension Verification		
4. Busy Trunk Verification		
5. Called Station Status Display		
6. Class of Service Display		
7. Identification of an Incoming Call		
8. Identification of Recall		
9. Trunk Group Busy Indicators		
10. Trunk to Trunk Connections		
11. Through Dialing		
12. Hold		
13. Camp-On to Busy Station With Indication		
14. Call Splitting (Two-Way)		
15. Conference Capability		
16. Speed Calling		
17. Switched Loop Operation		
18. Two-Jack Operation (Headset/Handset)		
19. Volume Control		
20. Silent Monitoring		
21. Alarm Indication		
22. Lamp Check		
23. Attendant Paging Access		
24. Serial Call		
25. Automated Directory		

C. Attendant Console Features Questions

1. Describe the console's ability to handle calls simultaneously (i.e., maximum number of calls held, ringing in, and being processed at the same time).

2. What occurs after the maximum call-handling capacity of the attendant console is reached?

V. STATION FEATURES

A. Required Station Features Descriptions

1. **Station to Station Dialing:** This feature enables any station connected to the system to call any other station in the system by dialing the extension number. No attendant assistance is needed.

2. **Direct Outward Dialing:** This feature enables a station user to dial an external call directly over outside trunks without attendant assistance (provided this is allowed by the COS entry for that station).

3. **Tone Dialing:** This feature enables a user to place a call by dialing the number via a pushbutton telephone.

4. **Call Transfer:** This feature enables a user connected to another party to transfer that party to another extension by dialing a code followed by the number of the extension that is to receive the call. The initiator of the transfer may stay on the line to announce the transfer. In this case, the initiator of the transfer and the third party are connected. The original party remains on hold, split from the conversation, until the initiator hangs up.

5. **Call Forwarding—Variable:** The station user can define his/her telephone service so that it will forward an incoming call immediately to a selected extension, hunt group, or attendant console. This is done for both busy or for no-answer conditions on individual lines. An audible signal on the originating station will remind the station user when individual calls are forwarded. This definition is done by dialing a short code and then the forwarded-to number at the originating extension (to activate or deactivate). When the forwarded-to extension is busy, the incoming caller must receive a busy signal. This feature overrides Fixed Call Forwarding.

6. **Call Hold:** This feature allows a user to place the other party of a conversation in a hold status by dialing an access code and then hanging up the receiver. Key telephones are not required for this feature.

7. **Call Waiting Indication:** This feature is activated when a call is directed to a busy extension, under certain circumstances. If a call is parked on a busy extension, or camped onto a busy extension, the user of the busy extension will hear an audible tone through the receiver in the handset. The other party in the conversation does not hear this tone.

8. **Call Pick-Up—Directed:** This feature allows an extension to answer ringing calls or acquire calls held for another extension by dialing a code and the ringing extension's number.

9. **Call Pick-Up—Group:** This feature allows an extension within a group of related telephones to acquire a ringing call within the group by dialing an abbreviated code.

10. **Call Park:** This feature enables a user to transfer a party to an idle extension and to place the party on hold for that extension. This is accomplished by dialing an access code, followed by the desired extension number.

11. **Hunting—Group:** The hunting feature allows stations to be arranged in groups within the system. The stations in a particular group do not need to follow each other in consecutive numerical order. Calls directed to this group will attempt to ring the first station of the group (definable) and will search through the sequence of extension numbers included in the group (definable) until answered.

12. **Conference:** This feature allows one party of a conversation to add additional internal and/or external parties to the call. The initiator of the conference dials the party to be added and joins the called party to the existing conversation by dialing a code.

13. **Private Line Capability:** This feature makes it possible for a dedicated trunk to be directed permanently to a specific extension number. The user of this extension can make an outgoing call on this trunk without dialing a special access code associated with the trunk.

14. **Release:** This feature enables a station that is left off the hook for an excessive period of time to receive a howler tone and be released from its connection to the switching portion of the system.

15. **Random Number Assignment:** Station numbers should be associated only by software with the line numbers. Then, users moving to other locations within the same dial system may take their telephone numbers with them without rewiring.

16. **Privacy:** This feature enables an extension user to protect a voice call from any intrusion. This feature is controlled via the Class of Service tables.

17. **Last Number Dial—Repeat:** This feature allows a station user to store a number just dialed that is expected to be called again. The number is stored by dialing a "save" access code when a busy tone is heard. To redial the number, the user goes off the hook and dials an abbreviated code.

18. **Do Not Disturb:** This feature allows a station user to prohibit ringing on his/her station, by dialing a code from that station.

19. **Access to Paging:** This feature permits station users with the proper Class of Service to dial an access code and activate an external paging system. (This is predicated on the Attendant Paging Access feature being present.)

20. **Message Waiting Lamps:** Indicator lights advise the owner of a phone that a message has been taken during his/her absence.

B. Required Station Features Checklist

Respond by "yes," "no," or "not available" as to whether the feature is standard in the proposed system as defined in the preceding description section.	Standard Feature of System	Price If Optional
1. Station to Station Dialing		
2. Direct Outward Dialing		
3. Tone Dialing		
4. Call Transfer		
5. Call Forwarding—Variable		
6. Call Hold		
7. Call Waiting Indication		
8. Call Pick-Up—Directed		
9. Call Pick-Up—Group		
10. Call Park		
11. Hunting—Group		
12. Conference		
13. Private Line Capability		
14. Release		
15. Random Number Assignment		
16. Privacy		
17. Last Number Dial—Repeat		
18. Do Not Disturb		
19. Access to Paging		
20. Message Waiting Lamps		

VI. DATA FEATURES

A. Required Data Features Descriptions

1. **Data Class of Service:** The privileges awarded to each data terminal shall be controlled by a data Class of Service table.

2. **Call Initiation:** It should be possible to initiate calls from either a keyboard or a telephone handset.

3. **Simultaneous Phone and Terminal Use:** From a single desk, both the phone and the terminal must be available for use simultaneously.

4. **Data Signaling Speeds:** The standard variety of signaling speeds is required, including DC contact closures, 300 baud, up through and including 56 KB synchronous.

5. **Data Signaling:** For all the speeds listed in the previous paragraph (except DC and 56 KB), both synchronous and asynchronous signaling must be supported.

6. **Protocol Converters:** The switch must have provision for on-board protocol converters. As protocol requirements change, it must be possible for vendor field personnel to reconfigure the stack of converters available to the switch so the right combinations are available, in the right quantities. The conversion dialogs we wish to have at installation are:

   ASCII - RS232 to IBM 3270. The proposed system must support a standard commercial protocol converter package that can be used by plugging it into slots in a switch cabinet and defining the capabilities of the newly added converter in the software control tables. The SMDR data must identify the use and the number of sessions rejected due to protocol converter unavailability.

7. **Terminal Types and Host Computers:** Today we have the following terminal types and host/software combinations installed:

Terminal# Types#W	Host/Software#W
ASCII (RS232)	IBM 3033/MVS,TSO,WYLBUR
IBM 3279	DEC 11/780/785/UNIX BSD 4.2
SUN MICROSYSTEMS	SUN MICROSYSTEMS/UNIX BSD 4.2
IBM PC	
APPLE MACINTOSH	

8. **High Speed Network:** From the table provided above, it is clear that NRA now has three types of host equipment presently installed. If we move this load onto the new switch and continue with this class of service, we may

eventually have 1,200 terminals connected to the switch accessing 30 different host services. We anticipate many of these circuits would run at 56 KB. For discussion purposes we call this "single network service." In addition, we foresee more advanced terminals that would require 1-10 MB bandwidth. At the present time, we see this high-speed service architected as a second network of coax or fiber or possibly switched over the telephone network, if shielded twisted pair were used as cable (with proper terminations) and if the switch could allocate bandwidth adaptively to provide signaling speeds in megabyte ranges when required. In your proposal please discuss:

a. How will speeds to 56 KB be provided?

b. How can speeds up to 10 MB be accommodated?

c. If a single-cable plant can be used for all data service, should some less-exotic cable plant be installed in the present facility?

d. If a separate system is recommended for the megabyte data, how can the gateways be architected so the two switches can communicate?

NOTE: In your proposal, make clear what is proposed and costed in the initial contract, what is in the future, and whether the future costs are projected or firm.

9. **Terminal Wiring:** As indicated in the table above, several terminals were obtained from IBM and natively require coaxial cable. The proposed system must have features that will allow transmission over the telephone wire network so an extra network of coax is not required.

10. **Terminal Session Initiation:** When a terminal wishes to initiate a session, two sequences are acceptable. In the first case, every different computer service (text processing, electronic mail, scientific calculation, etc.) will be given a separate telephone number. To initiate a terminal session, the person at the terminal dials or keyboards the number for the desired service. If the called service is allowed in the Class of Service table entry associated with the calling terminal, the connection will be made and the terminal will be in direct contact with the log-on software in the requested service. In the other case, no telephone numbers will be published and a single button or keyboard sequence will place the terminal in dialog with the switch itself. The switch will present a menu of the services that are allowable to the terminal. The person at the terminal will select the desired service from the menu. Once this has occurred, the switch will make the connection between the terminal and the requested service, and then the terminal will be in contact with the log-on software for that service.

11. **Password Validation:** It will not be necessary for the switch to be aware of (or validate) passwords or personal identifiers prior to connecting the

terminal with the requested service. The switch may presume that if a person gains access to a terminal, he/she is authorized to use that terminal at least to begin the log-on dialog with the requested service.

12. **Data Session Reporting:** The SMDR data must log fully all data sessions by recording the originating number, the called number/desired service, the time of day, the length of the session, and the protocol conversion facilities used (if any).

13. **Data at Installation:** As initially installed, the system must be configured to provide only enough data capability to demonstrate a full range of functions. This will require service for eight terminals, all of which will be co-located with a telephone, speed ranges from 300 baud to 56 KB, and one each of the protocol converters enumerated in paragraph 6 above.

14. **Data Expansion:** After one or more expansion steps, the switch must support 1,200 terminals, 30 host computers, with 800 terminals active simultaneously, and 100 of the active terminals requiring protocol conversion of some variety.

15. **Transmission Speeds:** For load purposes, the proposed system must be compatible with the following speeds used by the 800 terminals:

Transmission Speed (Kbps)	Number of Terminals Active Simultaneously
1.2	20
2.4	30
9.6	630
19.2	100
56.0	20

16. **Executive Work Stations:** Some vendors have announced executive work stations that consist of a personal computer and an electronic telephone. This combination provides both voice and data service, a personal directory of frequently called numbers, and the ability to connect to both voice mail and electronic (digital message) services. We desire three of these advanced work stations to be installed with the initial system for evaluation purposes. The work station's personal computer feature must be either IBM PC compatible or under the control of the Unix BSD 4.2 operating system.

17. **Modem Pooling:** Some of the terminals will have to access remote computers via the public network. A pool of standard modems must be provided to support this access. The switch must allow for field reconfiguration of a stack of modems so that modems of the proper speed and intelligence can be installed physically and entered into the software

configuration table. The SMDR data must identify the use and number of sessions rejected due to modem unavailability.

18. **Dial-In Speeds:** Pending all digital (T-1) signaling, the proposed system must support the following Dial-In speeds(bps): 300; 1,200; 2,400.

19. **Data Circuit Configuration:** If the Class of Service table allows a given terminal to make outbound data calls, it must be possible for the person at the terminal to indicate the modem requirements at the time the call is initiated. The switch must then configure the outbound circuit with the requested modem.

    NOTE: Even if a second megabyte network is installed as discussed in paragraph 8 above, the switch should be sized to this projected load.

20. **Digital Circuit Compatibility:** In the future, it is anticipated that digital end-to-end circuits will be installed so the switch should have the capability to allow incoming/outgoing calls to the public network via T-1 lines.

21. **Data Security:** To provide security for incoming data calls, the switch should have a dial-back capability or the ability to interface with a dial-back device such as the LeeMah. If the dial-back capability is integrated into the unit, the control tables and the traffic logs must be integrated rather than separate.

22. **Compatible Statistical Multiplexors:** Transparent data services are not required as long as the Headquarters is at 9926 Any Street and uses the APS equipment. However, when the Headquarters is moved to the new site, all of the data services will go through the Miami switch to access the host computers installed in Florida. At that time the desired configuration will be a multiplexor in Baltimore transmitting to Miami using a synchronous protocol and using the integral mux/demux features of the Miami switch. Alternately the configuration would consist of compatible statistical multiplexors in Baltimore and Miami, with the output of the Miami multiplexor being data inputs to the switch. Thus, except for possible limitations on signaling speed, a person operating a terminal in Baltimore would behave exactly as if he or she were in Miami. Please describe your proposed configuration in detail.

23. **Standard Features:** Presumably the operational features found on any modern standalone data switch are standard in the integrated voice/data switch being proposed. In your proposal, supply full feature enumeration covering at least the following: autobaud, queuing, split speed, isochronous transmission protocol, plus software controls providing status, reset, disable/enable, etc.

B. Required Office Automation Features Descriptions

1. **Message Waiting Lamp:** All telephones installed must be provided with a message-waiting light.

2. **Message Lamp Control:** The switch must control the message-waiting light by turning it off and on--on command. It must be possible to request that the light be extinguished from the handset that has the light illuminated, from a central message desk, or from one of the attendant's consoles.

3. **Office Automation Programs:** You must provide the ability for packaged or customized programs that can run either in a low-priority partition of the switch's control computer or in a separate, attached computer to provide various office automation functions.

4. **Office Automation Light Access:** It must be possible for an office automation feature to request that the switch illuminate a message-waiting light on an individual telephone and later to request that that light be extinguished.

5. **Multiple Message-Waiting Lamps:** The lamps must provide separate message-waiting lights for each office automation feature, e.g. electronic mail and voice mail messages.

6. **LAN Gateways:** The switch must support, through custom engineering if necessary, gateways to one or more Local Area Networks (LANs).

7. **LAN Gateway Capability:** Through use of the gateway, it must be possible for an adjacent automation system to request connection to a telephone or a terminal with or without protocol conversion, and vice versa. It must be possible for an adjacent system to communicate with the office automation packages discussed in paragraph 3 above. It also must be possible to use the gateway to illuminate or extinguish a message-waiting light. All calls across the gateway must be recorded on the SMDR, along with a user ID number provided by the outboard processor.

8. **External Computer Interfacing:** It must be possible for an external computer system to interface across a gateway and to appear to the switch such as the administrative console.

9. **Directory Update:** If we choose to do directory updates on an external computer, we will then take the batch of directory changes, format them properly, and transmit them across a gateway interface to update the internal control directory in the switch.

10. **Attendant CRT:** Similarly, it must be possible for an external computer to appear as an attendant CRT and to send a request for directory information across a gateway so that the phone number (or other directory data) associated with an individual's name can be obtained.

C. Optional Office Automation Features Description

Office Automation Applications: Electronic (digital message) mail and voice mail are two of today's popular office automation functions. Please quote their costs separately, as options, together with all of the hardware necessary for their operation.

NOTE: For each office automation package quoted, state the traffic capacities and storage volumes, along with the method used for sizing these resources.

D. Required Custom Diagnosis Features Descriptions

1. **Diagnostics:** The proposed system must have built-in diagnostics. In the standard configuration, these must allow use of the diagnostic mode so that a given line card, circuit, and terminal combination can be exercised. It is presumed further that the change of status masks and the exercise program would be obtained from an on-line maintenance program library. Thus, if an electronic telephone malfunctioned or was suspected of a malfunction, it could be turned over for maintenance automatically or under operator control. The system would fetch the right programs automatically from the maintenance library, send messages to the suspected unit, and verify the responses from that unit so that a maintenance person could be dispatched with the proper tools, equipment, and spares if a malfunction were detected.

2. **Maintenance Library:** The maintenance libraries must be extendable in the field by customer personnel (after suitable safeguards, of course) so any special office automation (terminal) equipment we might choose to attach can be exercised and diagnosed with the switch's standard facilities.

3. **Electronic Voice Capability:** The switch must have an electronic voice which is used for directory service or audio messages to users.

4. **Electronic Voice Function:** The voice must be accessible by custom maintenance programs capable of talking a user through a complicated diagnostic procedure. In addition to being able to access the vocoder from a maintenance program, it must be possible to add some words to the stored voice vocabulary.

E. Required Data Features Check List

Respond by "yes," "no," or "not available" as to whether the feature is standard in the proposed system as defined in the preceding description section.	Standard Feature of System	Price If Optional

1. Data Class of Service

2. Call Initiation

Respond by "yes," "no," or "not available" as to whether the feature is standard in the proposed system as defined in the preceding description section.	Standard Feature of System	Price if Optional

3. Simultaneous Phone and Terminal Use

4. Data Signaling Speeds

5. Data Signaling

6. Protocol Converters

7. Terminal Types and Host Computers

8. High Speed Network

9. Terminal Wiring

10. Terminal Session Initiation

11. Password Validation

12. Data Session Reporting

13. Data at Installation

14. Data Expansion

15. Transmission Speeds

16. Executive Work Stations

17. Modem Pooling

18. Dial-In Speeds

19. Data Circuit Configuration

20. Digital Circuit Compatibility

21. Data Security

22. Compatible Statistical Multiplexors

23. Standard Features

F. Required Office Automation Features Check List

Respond by "yes," "no," or "not available" as to whether the feature is standard in the proposed system as defined in the preceding description section.	Standard Feature of System	Price if Optional

1. Message-Waiting Lamp

Respond by "yes," "no," or "not available" as to whether the feature is standard in the proposed system as defined in the preceding description section.	Standard Feature of System	Price if Optional

2. Message Lamp Control

3. Office Automation Programs

4. Office Automation Light Access

5. Multiple Message-Waiting Lamps

6. LAN Gateways

7. LAN Gateway Capability

8. External Computer Interfacing

9. Directory Update

10. Attendant CRT

G. Optional Office Automation Feature Check List

Respond by "yes," "no," or "not available" as to whether the feature is standard in the proposed system as defined in the preceding description section.	Standard Feature of System	Price if Optional

Office Automation Applications
a. Message Mail

b. Voice Mail

c. Other, specify:

_____

H. Required Custom Diagnosis Check List

Respond by "yes," "no," or "not available" as to whether the feature is standard in the proposed system as defined in the preceding description section.	Standard Feature of System	Price if Optional

1. Diagnostics

2. Maintenance Library

3. Electronic Voice Capability

4. Electronic Voice Function

VII. SYSTEM ADMINISTRATION AND CALL DETAIL RECORDING

A. Required System Administration Features Descriptions

1. **Moves, Adds, and Changes:** NRA wishes to administer the system itself. We must be able to perform moves, adds, and changes with telephone administrative personnel who have been trained properly, and by calling upon on-site technicians to change any back panel wiring that may be required. The system control tables and the electronic operators' directory and the printed directory should be provided in an integrated fashion, requiring that the changed administrative information be keyboarded only once.

2. **Wire Inventory:** After the system is installed, a wiring database and a program to maintain it are required and must be delivered as a part of the contract. Thus, we will know what cable pairs are in use and which ones are available for other services. In addition, if any cable pairs are removed from service due to noise, damage, or other problems, they should be flagged in the database so they are not accidently reused. It is preferred that there be an administrative processing link from the moves, adds, and changes process (see previous paragraph) so that adds or changes involving wiring are passed across and reflected automatically in the wiring database.

   A model procedure is required (automated for an IBM 370 or PC) to maintain a perpetual wire and cable inventory (trunks, risers, terminators, station lines, etc.). This inventory must track each item through its various states: in-use, spare, questionable, unusable. Further, sets of wires that are in use must be linked so each complete electrical path is recorded.

3. **Equipment Inventory:** When the system is finally installed, an equipment database is required that describes all of the installed equipment and all of the on-site spares. A computer program (IBM 370 MVS and COBOL) must be provided to maintain this inventory. The inventory database must be updated from a transaction data file created by the switch when changes in equipment assignments are made a part of a move, add, or change.

   A model procedure is required (automated for an IBM 370 or PC) to maintain a perpetual equipment inventory (handsets, cables, pluggable units, etc.). This inventory must track each item through its various states; in-use, repairable, serviceable, salvaged.

4. **Reconciliation of Bills:** A computer program (COBOL, IBM 370, and MVS) must be provided to read the SMDR tape as one input, read the tapes from the serving utility and the OCCs as additional inputs, process all of these data, and issue three sets of reports. These are first, the reconciled charges from the carriers so the undisputed charges can be paid; second, the disputed charges from each of the carriers, i.e., those carrier charges that have no counterpart on our SMDR tape; and third, a complete recapitulation of all reconciled charges by NRA Account Code, just as if direct billing were going to take place.

5. **Traffic Measurement Capability:** This feature will collect information on activities of the system. This information should be collected for activities relating to trunks, consoles, hunt groups, and common equipment. Important information, such as queuing the use of data services, all internal calls, as well as peg counts for trunk groups, should be noted. The output must be in a form suitable for input to an IBM 370 or compatible computer, either via RS232 communications or via magnetic media. Sample procedures reports and software (for an IBM 370 or PC) are required. If malfunction alarms and attendant corrective actions are not machine readable, manual procedures, sample logs, and interpretation instructions also are required. (See also SMDR references above.)

6. **Traffic Statistics:** Full statistics must be captured, as described in the previous paragraph, so traffic analyses can be generated to allow lines to be configured and balanced as the new site is opened and as the staff and computers are transferred to the new site.

B. Required System Administration Features Check List

Respond by "yes," "no," or "not available" as to whether the feature is standard in the proposed system as defined in the preceding description section.	Standard Feature of System	Price If Optional
1. Moves, Adds, and Changes		
2. Wire Inventory		
3. Equipment Inventory		
4. Reconciliation of Bills		
5. Traffic Measurement Capability		
6. Traffic Statistics		

C. Station Message Detail Recording Feature Descriptions

1. **Station Message Detail Recording--Outward:** Station message detail recording is a feature that outputs data on external calls in a form suitable for input to an IBM 370 or compatible computer, either via RS232 communications or via magnetic media. The system should provide the following information about outward calls:

   a. Date of call

   b. Starting time of call

   c. The called extension number

   d. The access code dialed

   e. The called number

   f. The priority invoked, if any

   g. The duration of the call--hours, minutes, seconds

   h. The facility used to route the call (trunk number).

2. **Station Message Detail Recording--Inward:** This feature refers to the capability of the system to collect and output data about incoming calls to the system. The storage devices are the same as those used for outward station message detail recording. The system should provide the following information about incoming calls:

   a. Date of the call

   b. Starting time of the call

   c. Duration of the call

   d. Incoming trunk number

   e. Called extension number

   f. Call disposition/handling history/internal routing.

3. **Station Message Detail Recording—Internal:** All internal activity including station-to-station voice calls, terminal-to-host data calls, and all attendant actions shall be logged on the SMDR device. The system should supply:

   a. Date of the call

   b. Starting time of the call

   c. Originating instrument/station number

d. Called instrument/station number/service number

e. Codes for attendant activity (as appropriate)

f. Duration of the call.

4. **Feature Usage Statistics:** This refers to the ability of the system to store various kinds of information in memory about station usage, feature usage, and error occurrence. The information provided by this feature should make possible location of user problem areas, which require additional user training.

5. **Program for SMDR Interpretation:** A series of computer programs, designed to run on IBM 370 equipment under MVS, must be provided to perform traffic analyses on the SMDR records.

D. Station Message Detail Recording Features Descriptions Check List

Respond by "yes," "no," or "not available" as to whether the feature is standard in the proposed system as defined in the preceding description section.	Standard Feature of System	Price If Optional
1. Station Message Detail Recording—Outward		
2. Station Message Detail Recording—Inward		
3. Station Message Detail Recording—Internal		
4. Feature Usage Statistics		
5. Program for SMDR Interpretation		

E. Station Message Detail Recording Features Questions

1. Describe the procedure for reconciling SMDR detail history (in the accounting sense) with the monthly telephone bill. Is computer software available to perform this reconciliation?

2. Is the Station Message Detail Recording feature an integral part of the system or a separately attached device? If it is attached separately, who manufactures the computer and who performed the programming?

3. If the Station Message Detail Recording subsystem is not made by the manufacturer of the proposed system, what are the maintenance arrangements?

4. Will your company certify that the estimates of charges for long distance calls used in Least Cost Routing and recorded in the Station Message Detail Reports to be within 3 percent of the common carrier charges at the time of cutover?

5. Will your company keep the call routing parameters used in routing and in call detail processing current after the initial installation and reflect promptly call and circuit rate charges?

6. What carriers are covered by your rate table maintenance service?

7. Is there an additional charge for this or is it included in the maintenance fee?

8. Are trunk and carrier designation reported on the SMDR records for all incoming and outgoing calls?

9. a. What type of customer account code capability is available with the Station Message Detail Reporting feature?

   b. What is the maximum number of digits per account code?

   c. What is the maximum number of account codes?

10. Will the Station Message Detail Reporting feature record calls made by use of the Remote Access to PBX Services feature?

VIII.   EMERGENCY CONFIGURATIONS

A. Power Outage Descriptions

1. **Disable Data Circuits:** As noted elsewhere in this specification, the switch should be installed with enough batteries to power the system for two hours following a failure of commercial power. Under these conditions, the switch must be engineered to disable the data circuits automatically. (All the computers will be inoperative without commercial power.)

2. **Power Failure Phones:** When the batteries are exhausted, the switch must power itself down gracefully and leave 25 prespecified telephones mechanically connected to individual trunks to the central office. Thus, if the switch is completely disabled, these 25 telephones will behave just as though they were 25 individual independent private lines to the central office. (We will prespecify the locations for these phones so the guards, the nurse, and the executives all have outside lines, in addition to having at least one line in every physical area that is isolated or compartmented from the rest of the building.)

3. **Power Failure Phone Operation:** When the system is operating in the degraded mode and neither commercial power nor battery power is available, the basic functions equivalent to a Bell 2500 series telephone must continue to operate, i.e., dial, talk, ring; but no displays, and no special lights, or other features.

B. Fail Safe Descriptions

1. **Partial System Disaster:** In the event a disaster strikes one remote site or one wing of the main building, leaving the remainder of the offices intact and habitable, the telephone system shall survive and provide normal service to the habitable offices. Thus, if a fire damaged a 500-pair cable, any circuit not associated with the damaged cable should be operative (i.e., line cards should not blow, buses should not overload, circuit breakers should not trip, and power supplies should not fail, except perhaps those associated with the damaged circuits).

2. **Internal Service:** Similarly, if an earthquake or other community-wide disaster damaged the trunks to the utility or the OCCs, the switch shall continue to operate and provide in-plant communications as long as there is power.

3. **Commercial Power Failure:** If commercial power fails, the system shall continue to operate until the specified limit of the batteries has been

reached; i.e., if commercial power fails and room cooling ceases, the system must shed data load and/or cabinets supporting displays and other special features so the equipment does not overheat while battery power remains. If the system is not so engineered, battery-powered emergency fans should be included in the proposed configuration.

C. System Documentation Descriptions

1. **Attendant Instructions for Major Failure:** When the operators' manuals for the system are prepared, a chapter must address emergency reconfiguration and recovery. Thus, if it is necessary to shed load during times of commercial power outage or to disconnect shorted central office trunks manually after an earthquake, these instructions must be provided. In addition, instructions must be provided so we can operate for an extended period on less than normal current draws (as in a brownout) and so we can exist with basic telephone service even though the special features and all data are disabled.

2. **Operational Documentation:** After a period of degraded operation, it will be necessary to reconfigure the system and regain all normal services and make certain occurrence entries in the SMDR and maintenance logs. All of this should be covered in the operational documentation.

D. Emergency Configurations Descriptions Check List

Respond by "yes," "no," or "not available" as to whether the feature is standard in the proposed system as defined in the preceding descriptions sections.

	Standard Feature of System	Price If Optional

A. Power Outage

1. Disable Data Circuits

2. Power Failure Phones

3. Power Failure Phone Operation

B. Fail Safe

1. Partial System Disaster

2. Internal Service

3. Commercial Power Failure

Respond by "yes," "no," or "not available" as to whether the feature is standard in the proposed system as defined in the preceding descriptions sections.

	Standard Feature of System	Price If Optional

C. System Documentation

1. Attendant Instructions for a Major Failure

2. Operational Documentation

IX. INSTALLATION AND TRAINING

A. Installation

1. The Installation Section should be priced as a separate section and shall include the following:

   a. Identify all necessary materials including all cable, Main Distribution Frame (MDF), Secondary Distribution Frame(s) (SDF), blocks, terminals, frames, racks, and associated hardware to install the equipment listed in Sections II, VI, VII, and VIII.

   b. Labor

      (1) Specify labor necessary to install equipment listed in Sections II, VI, VII, and VIII.

      (2) Specify labor necessary to engineer, test, prepare customer configuration data and cutover the system as described in Sections II, VI, VII, and VIII.

2. The selected vendor shall install the system utilizing generally accepted telephone industry installation practices.

3. The selected vendor agrees to comply with all city, county, and state codes in regard to the installation of materials and labor, as outlined in this specification.

4. The selected vendor will be responsible for the complete engineering of the switching system, network, station apparatus, and installation.

5. The vendor will coordinate with other contractors as is necessary, at its own expense, for any supporting trade work that may be required. All such work will be supervised by vendor. Vendor must obtain lien releases from all subcontractors.

6. NRA will survey each area to determine the proper station hardware arrangement, including necessary preparation of customer data input for the Class of Service tables.

7. The complete Miami facility probably will have to be recabled. The site tour will cover the proposed switch room, the interbuilding cable runs in the basement halls, the telephone closets, the collection of ducts (all full), and open wall cabling that now exist. Creative installation planning will be required to install new cable, to have the resulting installation presentable, and not to disturb the existing cabling for other communication systems

325

(there are several) that will remain in operation and be unaffected by the new PABX installation.

To reduce the cost of cabling, surface-mounted wire mold will be acceptable in all offices but executive offices, where invisible wiring is required. Further, the new hall ceilings should allow connecting wiring to be concealed easily and neatly. After the wiring is completed, NRA painters will paint the wire mold to blend with the walls of the offices. Each proposal must be explicit on how the various aspects of the recabling will be addressed. If more than one cabling plan is presented, describe the pros, cons, and costs of each one separately.

8. If conduit is required, NRA will be responsible for the installation and material costs of the conduit. This must be noted in your bid.

9. The main distribution frame (MDF) will be engineered to meet the "wired" switch configuration and should be designed to make expansion as economical as possible.

10. All feeder cable shall be engineered to meet the equipped configuration and provide for 25 percent growth.

11. The selected vendor will be responsible for all cable from the MDF to each telephone instrument and/or associated miscellaneous hardware.

12. The MDF, all SDF(s), and terminal locations shall be marked properly to identify all network facilities, terminals, and hardware functions. These codes shall be entered into the wiring database.

13. All equipment installed shall be held in place firmly by fastenings and/or supports that are adequate to sustain their loads with an ample safety factor.

14. The vendor shall keep a competent installation supervisor on the job site during the entire installation.

15. Prior to cutover, the vendor shall test all network facilities, switching system, station, cabling, and miscellaneous apparatus to insure that all system functions and features are operational in keeping with the final design.

16. One complete set of as-built engineering drawings will be furnished to NRA prior to cutover. These must detail the entire cable plant, including exact locations for each terminal, distribution frame, and cable assignment. NRA also desires a copy of the location data in computer readable format suitable for an IBM 370 and a computer program to maintain the data.

17. Acceptance of the system will occur upon successful completion of Acceptance Test. Acceptance Test procedures are to be agreed upon mutually after configuration and performance specifications are finalized.

18. The selected vendor will conduct user training at the NRA facility for attendant and station users.

B. Special Cabling Requirements

1. For security purposes, the Miami facility is divided into office spaces with three levels of security. Fifty percent of the Miami facility is an open (unclassified) area. This area encompasses all of the physical support facilities, including the telephone switch room and the main computer room. After clearance by a lobby guard, any authorized person (including installers) can work unescorted in this area.

2. About 50 percent of the Miami facility will require installers to work on nights, weekends and/or under escort. When work is done in this area, it should be planned so the disruption to the NRA work force is minimized. (Can cables and drops be pulled down a hall on one or two consecutive days so there would be no further activity until the instruments were installed?)

3. NRA has a small number of other areas that are controlled tightly. When work is performed in these areas, it must be performed by personnel who have DOD Secret clearances. Furthermore, it may be necessary to have this work performed at night or over the weekends in several intensive sessions monitored by escorts and/or the NRA guard force. Fortunately, the total number of telephones and the total volume of cabling in these areas is small. One of these areas has a Candela Micro Switch installed; no internal phone or cabling changes are anticipated in this area. The interface to this device is standard DTMF/analog signaling.

4. NOTE: When the site tour is taken, be sure that cable runs are planned so no unnecessary cables enter, leave, or run through either of the two kinds of restricted access areas. All recabling done inside either type of restricted area shall be shielded twisted pair.

C. Installation Plan

Describe in detail, the installation schedule of events after receipt of an order until cutover of the system. Provide a PERT chart for a similar installation project, if one is available.

D. Training

Describe the type of pre-cutover training and ongoing training to be provided for attendants and station users. Specify the following:

a. Agenda for training

b. Length of time for training classes

c. Types of handout literature to be used

d. If video instruction is available

e. Charges, if any for training.

E. Administrative Training

1. Two persons must be trained in the procedures for performing moves, additions, and changes.

2. Two persons must be trained in the procedures for analyzing traffic and other operational statistics.

3. Two persons must be trained in the procedures for maintaining the perpetual equipment inventory.

4. Two persons must be trained in the procedures for maintaining the perpetual wire and cable inventory.

5. The training offered for one of our technicians to perform preliminary diagnostics/maintenance before your maintenance technician arrives should be included in the price.

   a. Where is this training given?

   c. How long does it take?

   d. Can additional personnel receive this training if the skilled person terminates after receiving the training?

   e. If video or computer-assisted instruction is offered, include pedagogical validation of its sufficiency.

F. Floor Plans

1. A set of floor plans will be available to each vendor at the time the site tour is taken.

G. Installation Questions

1. Describe the space, electrical and environmental requirements for the proposed switching equipment.

   a. Power: volts _____, amperes _____, KW _____.

   b. Heat dissipation: _____BTU/hr.

   c. Recommended temperature range: _____to _____.

   d. Recommended humidity range: _____to _____.

   e. Maximum operating temperature _____ and humidity _____ if the air conditioning is off.

   f. Weight of proposed system: _____.

   g. Foot print of proposed system: _____.

   h. Clear area required for service: _____.

   i. Is switch room cabling in overhead trays? _____.

   j. Wall space for punch blocks: _____.

   k. Space for desk, chair, spares cabinet: _____.

   l. Space for equipment and batteries for backup power: _____.

   m. Other requirements: describe.

2. What is the maximum distance an attendant console can be installed from the PBX switching equipment?

X. MAINTENANCE AND WARRANTY

A. Maintenance and Warranty

1. During and after the warranty, NRA requires a maximum of two-hour response time for major system failures, and one business day for minor system and station-related failures. Provide a definition of a major and minor system failure. Service for the system must be available 24 hours a day, seven days a week or, alternately, nine hours per day, five days per week.

2. Include a copy of the post-warranty maintenance contract. Include a standard clause regarding your maintenance cost escalation policy. The replacement of worn, aging, or abused instruments must be covered in the above.

3. A Remote Maintenance Capability feature that permits various maintenance functions to be performed by dialing over a standard incoming trunk from a remote location to the system should be included. This feature must be enabled/disabled by a NRA employee and the system must provide some method of password protection when this feature is enabled.

B. Maintenance and Warranty Questions

1. Describe, with as much detail as possible, your company's standard practice for providing maintenance and service for a system of this kind. Be sure to identify the following:

   a. Any tasks to be performed by NRA (Attendant, Administrator, and/or Technician)

   b. Any tasks to be performed by maintenance personnel

   c. All tasks to be performed by bidder

   d. All tasks to be performed by manufacturer; e.g., maintenance of software.

2. What software/hardware changes can a trained NRA technician perform without voiding the warranty?

3. What preventive maintenance work will be performed on this system and at what frequency?

4. Describe your company's policy regarding:

   a. Escalation up the maintenance hierarchy in the event a stubborn problem occurs

   b. Any provisions/guarantees for controlling maintenance costs following the warranty year through and including the tenth year after installation

c. The cost to expand the system to the wired for configuration in the next 10 years

d. The cost to add full data in the next 10 years, and any exchange/credit we may get for analog components we release.

5. Describe, in detail, your company's plan for repair or replacement of the system in event of a catastrophic failure of the system. (i.e., fire, flood, tornado, etc.)

C. Special Engineering Services

1. From time to time, as part of its office automation research, NRA may need changes to the standard switch hardware or software to support special devices. Are procedures in place to allow us to:

a. Document our request?

b. Obtain an estimate of the costs and schedules involved in making changes?

c. Sign a development contract for the custom features we desire if we desire to proceed?

2. If procedures for special engineering services are not standard in-house, are there special engineering services available outside?

XI. PRICING

A. System Pricing Information

	Digital	Analog
1. Equipment (Sections II, VI, VII, VIII)		

a. Single-line instruments and line cards
    Digital 1140 _____ model_____
    Analog 1140 ___ model ____
	_____	_____

b. Secretary type instruments Digital 130 _____ model ____	_____	
c. Executive type instruments Digital 80 _____ model ____	_____	
d. Attendant Consoles 6_____		_____
e. Attendant headsets 12_____	_____	
f. Central switch, software, and batteries	_____	
Total Equipment	_____	_____
2. Installation Labor	_____	_____
3. Cable Plant Labor	_____	
4. Cable Plant Materials	_____	
5. Freight and Drayage	_____	
6. Insurance During Transit and Installation	_____	
7. Subtotal	_____	
8. Sales Tax	_____	
9. Total Purchase Price*	_____	

INDEX

Page numbers in *italics* refer to figures in the text.

A

V

U

W